I0124676

Sex Scandals, Gender, and Power in Contemporary American Politics

Sex Scandals, Gender, and Power in Contemporary American Politics

Hinda Mandell

Gender Matters in U.S. Politics
Juliet A. Williams, Series Editor

BLOOMSBURY ACADEMIC
NEW YORK • LONDON • OXFORD • NEW DELHI • SYDNEY

BLOOMSBURY ACADEMIC
Bloomsbury Publishing Inc
1385 Broadway, New York, NY 10018, USA
50 Bedford Square, London, WC1B 3DP, UK
29 Earlsfort Terrace, Dublin 2, Ireland

BLOOMSBURY, BLOOMSBURY ACADEMIC and the Diana logo
are trademarks of Bloomsbury Publishing Plc

First published in the United States of America by ABC-CLIO 2017
Paperback edition published by Bloomsbury Academic 2024

Copyright © Hinda Mandell, 2017

For legal purposes the Acknowledgments on p. xi constitute
an extension of this copyright page.

Cover photo: Capitol Building, Washington, DC. (zrfphoto/iStockphoto)
Cover design by Silverander Communications

All rights reserved. No part of this publication may be reproduced or
transmitted in any form or by any means, electronic or mechanical,
including photocopying, recording, or any information storage or retrieval
system, without prior permission in writing from the publishers.

Bloomsbury Publishing Inc does not have any control over, or responsibility for,
any third-party websites referred to or in this book. All internet addresses given
in this book were correct at the time of going to press. The author and publisher
regret any inconvenience caused if addresses have changed or sites have
ceased to exist, but can accept no responsibility for any such changes.

Library of Congress Cataloging-in-Publication Data
Names: Mandell, Hinda, author.
Title: Sex scandals, gender, and power in contemporary American politics /
Hinda Mandell.
Description: Santa Barbara, California : Praeger, an Imprint of ABC-CLIO,
LLC, [2017] | Series: Gender matters in U.S. politics |
Includes bibliographical references and index.
Identifiers: LCCN 2016054600 (print) | LCCN 2017011142 (ebook) |
ISBN 9781440843273 (hardcopy : alk. paper) | ISBN 9781440843280 (ebook)
Subjects: LCSH: Political corruption—United States. | Politicians—Sexual
behavior—United States. | Sex scandals—United States. |
Sex scandals—Press coverage—United States.
Classification: LCC JK2249 .M355 2017 (print) |
LCC JK2249 (ebook) | DDC 320.973081—dc23
LC record available at https://lccn.loc.gov/2016054600

ISBN: HB: 978-1-4408-4327-3
PB: 979-8-7651-3001-8
ePDF: 978-1-4408-4328-0
eBook: 979-8-2161-4390-1

Series: Gender Matters in U.S. Politics

To find out more about our authors and books visit www.bloomsbury.com
and sign up for our newsletters.

To my family, always.
To mom and dad, forever.

Contents

Contents

Series Foreword

From the nearly century-long campaign for women's suffrage to ongoing contestation over reproductive rights to 2012 presidential candidate Mitt Romney's meme-worthy claim of having "binders full of women," politics has been a central staging ground in the United States for debates about gender. The 2016 presidential campaign was no exception. For the first time in the nation's history, a woman received a major party nomination to head the ticket as candidate for president. As it happens, the Republican Party nominee also served as a lightning rod for discussions of gender issues, particularly in the days following revelations of his vulgar boasting about the sexual assault of women. The eventual outcome of the 2016 presidential election took many experts by surprise, revealing that many observers had badly misjudged how women would cast their votes. In the end, the 2016 campaign season confirmed not just the ongoing centrality of gender in U.S. politics but that we still have a long way to go in understanding *how* gender matters—to each of us as individuals and as members of a shared polity.

The *Gender Matters in U.S. Politics* series pushes the boundaries of existing research on gender and politics. Traditionally, political scientists have engaged the subject of gender primarily by looking at differences in the way men and women behave—as voters, candidates, leaders, policymakers, activists, and citizens. Today, there is growing recognition—within the field of political science and beyond—of the critical need to think more broadly and more deeply about gender. Across the social sciences, researchers now recognize that gender is not only an individual attribute but a "socially constructed stratification system" that plays a central role in determining an individual's place in the social order."[1] At the same time, scholars are bringing a more intersectional perspective to the study of gender in recognition of the influence of race, sexuality, and other axes of social difference on gender identity and gender politics.[2] These new ways of conceptualizing gender have far-reaching implications for political scientists with interests in topics ranging from electoral behavior to social movement mobilization to media and politics.

The books in this series address a wide array of topics—from conservative women pundits to political cartoons—to demonstrate the far-reaching, and sometimes quite unexpected, ways that gender is mobilized in contemporary political discourse. Some authors bring new insight to the study of gender in familiar settings, such as grassroots political campaigning. Others take a closer look at gender politics in less-well studied contexts, such as media coverage of political sex scandals—thereby reminding us that that politics doesn't stay neatly within the boundaries of official institutions. And while some books in this series highlight the persistence of gender inequalities, others draw attention to the distinctive ways women's political roles have changed in the wake of second-wave political activism and legal reforms as well as technological advances that have given new forms of voice and visibility to historically marginalized groups. Finally, while the terms "women and politics" and "gender and politics" have in the past sometimes been used synonymously, the authors in this series emphasize that gender impacts the lives of women *and* men.

The books presented in this series are intended to inform, engage, and inspire its readers to think in new ways about issues of deep importance to all of us. In making clearly written, empirically grounded, and thoughtfully argued research available to interested audiences, this series aims to spark conversation and produce new understanding.

—Juliet A. Williams
Department of Gender Studies, UCLA

Acknowledgments

Quite simply, this book would not have come to fruition without Jessica Gribble, my editor at Praeger, who has ushered this project from inception to publication. One day, in October 2014, I received an email out of the blue from Jessica Gribble, who saw a paper abstract I wrote with Dr. Alison Dagnes of Shippensburg University, and she wanted to talk about potential book ideas. While that paper abstract, for the Northeastern Political Science Association conference, had nothing to do with scandal (it explored motherhood and the 2014 midterm campaigns in the United States), it was an entrée to a relationship to Jessica for which I'm grateful. Thank you for your feedback, guidance, and direction throughout this process. I'm lucky to have found myself in your path.

I would also like to extend my gratitude to Ali Dagnes, whose previous scholarship and books on political scandal have impacted my work, and for her willingness to work with me on that "moms and midterms" project in the first place.

To Dr. Juliet A. Williams, professor of Gender Studies and Associate Dean of the Division of Social Sciences at UCLA, who is also a series editor for Praeger's Gender Matters in U.S. Politics, of which this book is a part, I say this: the book you edited in 2004 with Dr. Paul Apostolidis, *Public Affairs: Politics in the Age of Sex Scandals*, has grounded my work since I began studying scandal in 2008. Thank you for your path-breaking research.

Speaking of which, this book would not have been possible without the coaching, feedback, and education I received from Dr. Carol Liebler, my dissertation advisor and professor of Communications at the S.I. Newhouse School of Public Communications.

To the media, I acknowledge the speed at which you break news, which is humbling for a person writing a long-form book that is built on current events. Alas, I can't be held responsible for breaking news that renders my facts out of date. This is especially true when it comes to news relating to the former politician Anthony Weiner, whose sexting scandals—four at last count—transpire so frequently that it's hard to keep up.

To Dr. Gina Masullo Chen, assistant professor in the School of Journalism at The University of Texas at Austin, thank you for your statistical prowess, which formed the basis of chapter 2, and for being the best collaborator a person could ask for in our other research projects together.

To Paula Rodriguez and Nanna Rasmussen, graduate students in the Communication & Media Technologies program at RIT, thank you for lightening my load and the help you provided in the research phase of the book.

I'd like to thank the anonymous reviewers and the editorial team of *Women's Studies in Communication*, whose comments on chapter 5 led to a more robust piece of research and to whom I am grateful for their close readings of the text.

Financial support from RIT, particularly within the College of Liberal Arts, made this research if not possible—at least feasible. I am supremely grateful for grant funding that covered costs relating to transcriptions, gift cards for interview subjects, copy editing, purchasing of photo rights, and course releases. I'd like to credit RIT's Paul A. and Francena L. Miller Research Fellowship, which granted me time to do this work. Gratitude is owed to my former chair, Dr. Patrick Scanlon of the RIT's School of Communication, and Dr. Jamie Winebrake, dean of the College of Liberal Arts at RIT, for your support of my work.

Thank you to the 22 interview participants, whose insights, opinions, and life experiences formed the basis of chapter 8. To Drs. Kelly Martin, Tamar Carroll, and Katie Terezakis, who began as colleagues but quickly emerged as dear comrades and friends, thank you for providing a continuous stream of stress relief, outrageous humor, and camaraderie. To Dr. Vera Fridman, who is my core.

To my family, nuclear, immediate, and extended, thank you for the encouragement and always-positive outlook that continues to buoy me. To Jacob and Becky, the best siblings a gal could ask for. To my husband, thank you for growing my heart. To Mirabelle and Eddie, our everything and next generation. And to my parents, who have left an inimitable imprint on my life: Mom, the poet and writer Karen Mandell, who always has an opinion about everything and is right even when I refuse to see it. And to Dad, the innovator Fred Mandell, who's been a wise old man probably since age 38, when I was born.

CHAPTER 1

Political Sex Scandals: How and Why Gender Matters[*]

When a freshman state legislator named Angela Wozniak from upstate New York admitted in 2016 that she had a sexual relationship with her legislative director (a man who was not her husband), a headline from the local *Buffalo (NY) News* boomed, "Wozniak Shattered the Wrong Glass Ceiling."[1] That's because when it comes to sex scandals, there's little accolade for women who act like men. And Wozniak was following a script typically reserved for a gender not her own.

By the tender age of 28, Wozniak—a Republican, married lawmaker from suburban Buffalo, New York, and mother to a toddler—was serving as a first-term legislator in the New York State Assembly in 2015, and surreptitiously (for the moment) *schtupping* a male member of her staff. Her political downfall came when the Assembly Ethics and Guidance Committee publicly released findings that the lawmaker retaliated against her two-for-the-price-of-one staffer/lover when he broke off their sexual relationship.[2] Wozniak was officially censured: The ethics committee banned her from hiring interns and ordered an independent investigator to survey the climate of her legislative offices twice a year. The day after the committee's tsk-tsk hit the press, Wozniak released a boilerplate video of apology, as emotionally vapid as a financial transaction at the grocery store: "I showed very poor judgment in having a relationship with a staffer, and for that I would like to apologize to my family and to my constituents," she said.[3] Soon after, the one-term legislator announced she wasn't seeking reelection.

Wozniak's biting political failure was amplified by this: She rode into political office on the coattails of ethics reform when her immediate

---

[*] This chapter is based on my article, "Scandal-less: Why Are Female Politicians Immune to Sex Scandals?," *Bitch* 64 (Fall 2014): 50–57.

predecessor from that Buffalo-area district, Dennis Gabryszak, a Democrat, resigned in disgrace from the assembly after sending lewd video to his female staffers. Wozniak was supposed to herald a new era of political forthrightness (or at least sexual propriety). On her first day as an assemblywoman in Albany, an office video released by the New York State Assembly Republicans showed this fresh-faced elected official—the future of the party—who said she was focusing on "cleaning up Albany."[4] Well, maybe she tried before succumbing to the allures of something dirtier.

This example shows that women—or least this one woman in particular, and perhaps a handful of her romping female brethren—can act just as brashly, aggressively, and boorishly as men. But don't let this example lead you to believe that parity exists between the sexes when it comes to political sex scandals. This is one area where women can be proud to lag behind men.

This book examines the American institution of the political sex scandal in order to explore how scandal turns politics into a spectator sport, contributes to the mistrust of government, causes citizens to question politicians' competence, and diminishes politicians' ability to do good by and for the people who elected them. Media coverage of political sex scandals commonly devolves into frenzied sleaze fests that hold hostage the attention of the American public and play into gendered narratives. My goal within these pages is to demonstrate that scandals are a representation of society's broader gender dynamics (and gender subversions), conveying messages that range from subtle to obvious about power and morality. While political sex scandals involve public officials elected to do the people's work, we now live in an age where their most seemingly private behavior can have wide-ranging public consequences. And these consequences impart messages about gender roles.

Consider the political-wife dynamic as an example. In this book I devote three chapters to exploring media reaction and public response to the often clichéd-yet-still-fascinating trope of the political wife who stands in staunch support of a husband-politician who put his parts (and phones) where he shouldn't have. But what corollary examples do we have of political husbands who stand by their woman, the wife-politician? In order to tally up a list that features loyal husbands of philandering wives, we first need a list of philandering women who are politicians or are political aides.[5] I compiled such a list and initially proposed a chapter in this book on media coverage of these husbands titled "'Stand by Your Wife?' When Scandal Cuckolds a Husband." A selection of political-husbands who made the list in recent years include: Doug Hampton, whose wife had an affair with Nevada senator John Ensign in 2009; Bill Lockyer, the

California state treasurer, whose wife—a former county supervisor—was caught in a meth and sex-tape scandal in 2012; Scott Broadwell, whose wife had an affair with CIA Director David Petraeus in 2012; Heath Peacock, whose wife was caught in an illicit embrace with Louisiana congressman Vance McAllister in 2014; and Jeremy Arnold, whose then wife dropped out of a New York State Senate race after announcing she had an affair. (She later returned to the race but lost in the primaries.) My goal was to analyze the social story lines that emerged in news coverage when a politically connected woman cheats on her husband. Yet my problem, I would soon learn, is that media coverage of these husbands was so sparse in their descriptions that I didn't have much to work with.

For instance, when news first broke in 2012 that the CIA director David Petraeus had an affair with his married biographer, Paula Broadwell, the *New York Observer* described Scott Broadwell in this emotionally vacant way: "Ms. Broadwell's book site also identifies her as being married to Scott Broadwell, an interventional radiologist with whom she has two children."[6] A similar dry style and matter-of-fact tone could be found in the example of Doug Hampton, whose wife had an affair with Nevada senator John Ensign. For instance, the *Washington Post* wrote in 2009 that "according to the statement Ensign's office issued yesterday, Doug Hampton's lawyer approached Ensign's lawyer last month about a financial settlement."[7] And when the *Contra Costa (CA) Times* newspaper reported in 2012 that the husband of the scandal-tarnished Nadia Lockyer wanted a divorce, following her dramatic spiral into drug addiction and an extramarital affair, it did so in a boring, straightforward way: "California Treasurer Bill Lockyer has filed for divorce from former Alameda County Supervisor Nadia Lockyer, who had an affair and has struggled with a drug abuse problem in recent months."[8] (The couple has since reconciled.)

In stark contrast to this toned-down coverage of political husbands, we have hysterical, speculative, emotional, and descriptive coverage of political wives, which this book will make abundantly clear. A simple reason for the disparity is the common occurrence of a press conference as a mechanism to control the scandal feeding frenzy, where the wife takes "her place" next to her husband at the podium. That situation lends itself to hyperdescriptions of the wife's face and body and allows for easy pondering of what their marital future may hold. In contrast, in the examples listed here of political husbands whose wives were caught in scandal, there were no major, nationally televised press conferences where the husband's presence was expected (or demanded). This example of the scandalized political husband is but one instance of how gender plays a role in our expectations of unfolding scandal narratives.

While sometimes dismissed as scintillating events, political sex scandals are more than superficial stories. But even as superficial stories they hold value as cultural relics for analysis. As engrossing narratives scandal stories are easy to understand and fun to follow along. But their juiciness shouldn't preclude us from excavating these stories for the following reasons: First, a politician's or candidate's scandalous activity (alleged or actual) can involve illegal behavior. Second, political sex scandals can prompt the resignation of the offending politician, thereby impacting the political field.[9] Third, these scandals occupy the time and mental space of governing leadership when an ethics investigation is launched. Fourth, these events further diminish the reputation of government and stoke its mistrust among an already deeply cynical and politically disinterested public.[10] And last, as witnessed in the 2016 election, sex scandals can also impact the presidential race—even when the offending politician (I'm looking at you, Anthony Weiner) isn't the one running for the highest office.[11]

Before diving deeper into the gendered landscape of contemporary political sex scandals—don't forget to plug your nose!—it's first worth (a) visiting the concept of scandal as a social institution and (b) defining key terms.

POLITICAL SEX SCANDAL AS A SOCIAL INSTITUTION

An easy way to identify a social institution is to spot an activity or behavior (such as having sex) that has become routine by people who fulfill specific roles (such as politicians).[12] The scandal script helps clarify the contours of this social institution. When approaching scandals one at a time, the individual differences between each scandal (a swift resignation here, a press conference asserting innocence there) may prevent us from making connections between scandals. But when we view scandal as an institution in the aggregate—with set characters and patterns of behavior, even if there are differences within these patterns of behavior—we witness the repetition of processes in unfolding scandals, or what sociologist Joshua Gamson calls "a common script."[13] This includes an "accusation or revelation, broadcast, denial and/or confession, and, frequently, a comeback or attempted comeback."[14] For political sex scandals, this script is composed of routine roles for those including the politician, the spouse (typically a wife), the family, the public, the individuals with whom the politician was having a sexual encounter, members of the political party, and the opposition. It is clear that it's not just the sheer volume of news coverage devoted to political sex scandals—which accounts for up to 25 percent of all news coverage when a major scandal unfolds[15]—that imbues social meaning to these frenzies. Rather, it's the expected routine making of events when we learn of a politician's sexually philandering extracurricular activities, as sociologist Gamson noted. The events themselves have become routine, even if this particular routine is rather juicy.

Now that I've made the argument that political sex scandals represent a social institution, and all social institutions are worthy of study, allow me to backtrack and spend some time with the key words that compose the first part of the book's title: "Sex scandals," "gender," and "power." And then once we do that we'll take that nosedive exploring potential reasons behind the gender gap in political sex scandals.

SCANDAL

One way to think about the occurrence of scandal is to consider that "corruption is a constant and scandal is a variable."[16] Therefore, there's a perpetual occurrence of transgression (i.e., politicians regularly do bad things behind closed doors). However, the publicity of such activity ebbs and flows. Violations that do not generate media publicity remain unknown to the public (and therefore politicians continue to do illicit things to which the American public remains blissfully unaware). John B. Thompson, a political scientist who has written extensively on political scandal, attributes five qualities to these events. First, scandals involve the breach of "values, norms, and moral codes."[17] Second, scandals involve secrecy. Third, people disapprove of this covert behavior. Fourth, people publicly express their disapproval of these social-norm violations once they find out. Finally, politicians, and those involved in their illicit behavior, risk a damaged (or destroyed) reputation.

The media play a key role in this five-ingredient recipe for scandal. It's clear that public revelation is necessary for an event to explode into a scandal.[18] The media's job as a transmitter of culture—which also revels in its naughty play-by-play mechanisms during unfolding scandals—is to publicize and pursue scandal stories and their various plotlines. If the public is not aware of the morally treacherous event in question, then a scandal cannot transpire. It is also important to note that the breach of a sexual norm does not have to actually take place in order for there to be a scandal—it only has to be alleged.

GENDER

Gender sits at the heart of this book on scandal. Researchers differentiate between gender, which is an achieved performance, and sex, a biological marker.[19] Gender differences between men and women are normalized by rooting them in biology. "They are rendered normal, natural features of people and provide the tacit rationale for differing fates of women and men within the social order."[20] Gender scholars differentiate between biological sex—being born with male and female "parts"—and gender, or traits ascribed to females and males that are rooted in a fixed naturalness and justified accordingly.[21] "Thus gender differences, or the sociocultural shaping of 'essential female and male natures,' achieve the status of objective facts."[22] Gender, therefore, is not a biological, natural destiny, but a social performance that is repeated, engrained, and regulated by society. There is a "self-regulating process" that happens in gender performance in an effort to self-monitor one's gender construction with the naturalized norms of one's biological sex.[23]

People are "biologically guided" by the fact that they are born with certain physical traits and anatomies. Their biology, according to popular argument, guides people's physical appearance, manners, professions, sexual natures, and their very being. Yet it is gender, not biology, that actually guides behavior, and it is gender performance that builds on the perception that men and women possess inherently different and opposing traits. Male and female "attributes" are culturally embedded and repeated in social activities, behaviors, and performance. As I'll make clear throughout this book, including later in this chapter, gender dynamics unfold throughout political-sex-scandal narratives as well.

POWER

Let us now turn to power—that elusive force which is difficult to define,[24] but—like pornography—you know it when you encounter it. The 1959 foundational text, *Studies in Social Power*, offers numerous technical definitions of power—many including mathematical formulas—that are far too inaccessible for this writer's brain. But it also provides other definitions that are more relatable, each of which tries to tackle the contours of power. For instance—and with acknowledgment of the outdated, gendered writing—"an individual may have power over another as a result of being able to influence him a) by direct physical power over his body, b) by rewards and punishment, or c) by influence of public opinion."[25] Or consider this definition: "Power may be defined as the capacity of the individual, or group of individuals, to modify the conduct of other individuals or groups in the manner which he desires."[26] And there is also the elegantly phrased "power may be defined as the production of intended effects."[27]

There are also different theoretical approaches to studying power. For example, in a structural approach, scholars assert a theoretical framework in which certain people and organizations have power and others are rendered powerless.[28] In the poststructuralist approach, power is not possessed. Rather, "it is continually circulating and allows more possibility for the role of individual agency."[29] The French philosopher Michel Foucault argued that "power is neither given, nor exchanged, nor recovered, but rather exercised, and that it only exists in action."[30] For this book, I take mostly the latter approach to studying power specifically because we see how precarious the power perch is when a politician is caught in scandal. Suddenly, in a span of time that can unfold in minutes, a politician is stripped of his or her influence, and it's the public who now holds power over this person's professional fate—in the form of public opinion, which can be eviscerating. When the power tables are turned, and the once formidable politician is now dependent on the whims of the public to maintain his or her seat, we see that the definitions of power in the 1959 book, *Studies in Social Power*, still make sense. But now it's members of the public and media institutions who can influence the politician to resign or apologize or terminate a run for public office. Through this dynamic we see that power, indeed, is no fixed commodity. And it's not that it's fleeting, either; it's just vulnerable to each politician's sexual kryptonite.

Now that we've defined political sex scandals as a social institution and defined key terms, let's return to the noted gender gap in their occurrences.

THE OLD BOYS' CLUB OF POLITICAL SEX SCANDALS

There is one obvious fact that you will see unfold again and again throughout the pages of this book, and that's the plethora of male politicians, and the dearth of female politicians, caught up in sex scandals.

Let's explore this reality. Scholars, armchair experts, everyday civilians, and those in politics offer a range of potential explanations for the gender gap in political sex scandals. The theories are often more rooted in opinion than hardy analysis. Some point to biology (arguing that men like to sow their seeds) or psychology (pontificating that men are more likely to boast oversized egos) or even statistics (prognosticating that since there are more men than women in politics, there are simply going to be more scandals with men). But the fact is that there are so few female-instigated political sex scandals that—if we pursue the statistical argument for a minute—we'd expect to find around 20 percent of scandals out of Congress belonging to women, since that's the rough number of seats women hold.[31] But you tell me: When was the last time a woman in Congress was caught in a sex scandal of national notoriety? At the time of writing we're still holding our breath on that one. But it's not a scorecard of men

POLITICIANS PONDER WHETHER TO HAVE A SEX SCANDAL:

SENATOR
XY

SENATOR
XX

GAME!

TOTALLY LAME.

A tallying of contemporary scandals reveals a quantitative difference in the frequency of sex scandals involving male vs. female politicians. (Courtesy of Hinda Mandell)

batting 100 and women batting zero. According to my scandal compilation, which is the basis of chapter 2, I've spotted nine instances—since 2004—when a woman politician was at the center of a sex scandal. When we attempt to account for the difference in volume of male versus female scandal, it's useful to start with a historical perspective. In 1789 George Washington was elected president of the United States. Women didn't gain the right to vote until 1920. That's a stretch of 131 years where men held elected office without even women having the right, on a federal level, to enter the voting booth. The year 2017 marks one century since the first woman, Jeannette Rankin from Montana, assumed office in Congress. (Montana voted in 1914 to allow non-Native women to vote.[32]) Since then, a total of 313 women have served in the Senate or House of Representatives, according to history.house.gov.[33] In other words, if we were to take all of the women who've ever served in Congress, they'd fill only 58.5 percent of seats in the *current* congressional class. If that's not sobering enough, consider the 2014 report from the Institute for Women's Policy Research, which predicted that we won't have gender parity in Congress until 2121. A baby born today would have to live until the age of 104 to see a congressional class that has equal parts men and women.[34] So the women who serve within the highest levels of political office continue to do so in a man's world. And this world is naughty.

Tallying up the list of male politicians who've put nookie before civic duty, conducted sexual affairs during office hours, and let power go to both big and little heads is a daunting task, and the sexual indiscretions of men in American politics would fill at least one presidential library and is tantamount to a Herculean task. But a preliminary and incomplete totting of elite, pervy politicians in a post–Bill Clinton cigar/blue-dress era would have to include former New Jersey governor James McGreevey, who proclaimed, "I am a gay American," after being caught in an affair with a hired aide; former Florida congressman Mark Foley, who sexted with congressional pages; former Idaho senator Larry "Wide Stance" Craig, who attempted to solicit sex with a man in a Minneapolis airport bathroom; Louisiana senator David Vitter, whose name (along with his predilection for diaper play) was found in the little black book of the D.C. Madam; former New York governor Eliot Spitzer, who enjoyed romps with high-end escorts; Spitzer's successor David Paterson, who admitted that he and his wife had multiple affairs; John Edwards, the presidential candidate who got carried away with his campaign videographer; former South Carolina governor Mark Sanford—now a congressman from that same state—whom we'll all recall used the excuse of "hiking the Appalachian Trail" to explain away a sexy-time absence; former Nevada senator John Ensign, who did the deed with a staffer who happened to be his wife's best friend from high school; former New York congressman Chris Lee, who e-mailed shirtless photos of himself—from his congressional account, no less—to women he met via Craigslist; former New York congressman Anthony Weiner, who had a thing for tweeting crotch-specific selfies; former California governor Arnold Schwarzenegger, who fathered a son with his longtime housekeeper; and Louisiana congressman Vance McAllister, a father of five who was caught making out with a female staffer whom he fired as soon as news of the scandal broke.

It might not be exhaustive, but it's certainly exhausting. And that's not even touching the scandals that have been part of American presidencies since the founding of our nation, which we'll touch on next chapter. From Thomas Jefferson and Sally Hemmings to the Kennedy brothers and Marilyn Monroe; from illegitimate children to ill-placed cigars, the presidential sex scandal is its own category that prompts BuzzFeed lists and TV specials. Yet to date there's never been prolonged news coverage at the national level of a "Congresswoman Antonia Weiner" sending sexy tweets of her nether regions. No media spotlight on a "Governor Eliana Spitzer," going wild with escorts (while still wearing her black trouser socks) in a five-star hotel in the nation's capital. There's certainly no news of a "Congresswoman Vanessa McAllister," swapping spit with her staffer, only to immediately fire him and declare that she's still going to run for reelection, or of a mysterious black book bursting with the erotic preferences of the Capitol's women.

But male politicians and sex scandals are like white on rice. The *Washington Post* reported in 2014 that of 39 major sex scandals that have occurred since 1974—all involving male politicians—17 involved Democrats and 22 involved Republicans.[35] Republicans cheated on their wives more than Democrats, while Democrats were more likely than Republicans to be involved in scandals involving workplace harassment or assignations. Many of these findings were replicated in my own research, which I will explore next chapter.

Still, the formula hasn't changed, and the recipe for the American political sex scandal is quite basic: simply put, men in power typically avail themselves of people at their disposal. Founding fathers, including Alexander Hamilton and Thomas Jefferson, can attest to what it's like to live under the white-hot gaze of the sex-scandal spotlight; indeed, the fledgling newspaper industry of the 18th and early 19th centuries, which was then divided by political party lines, thrived on publishing rumors about candidates and elected officials, offering real-life story lines as raunchy as any historical bodice-ripper. Historian and editor John H. Summers writes in the *Journal of American History* that the goal was to root out immorality in private so that the government would be virtuous and free from tyranny in public.[36]

Yet the gleeful news coverage of politicians' sextracurricular activities came to an abrupt halt in the early 20th century, as the field of journalism attempted to coat itself with a glossy patina of professionalism (translation: journalists started to get buddy-buddy with political elites and didn't want to jeopardize access to a cozy relationship). With timing as everything, Presidents Wilson, FDR and Kennedy, among others, could frolic in freedom, without worrying about reading the details in the morning's newspaper. And frolic they did—after all, you can't become a scandal if no one wants to write about it.

By the end of the 20th century, the pendulum of political sex scandals swung back again, and both the public and the media industry were ready to consume and produce sex-scandal news coverage. Watergate, in the early 1970s, showed journalists that politicians couldn't and shouldn't be trusted or protected. In 1991, Anita Hill exposed the egregious behavior of her supervisor, the Supreme Court nominee Clarence Thomas, in televised hearings. And later that decade the advanced media and cable-news system, along with the Internet's growth spurt into sex-confident young adulthood, set the stage for a frenzy surrounding a presidential intern, a cigar, and a DNA-encrusted blue dress. President Clinton's Oval Office fling with an intern became famous the world over, even though his activities couldn't have differed much from those of his presidential predecessors.

Clinton's Republican foes eagerly denounced the president and championed calls for his impeachment. Yet it didn't take long (thanks to the generous monetary encouragement of *Hustler* magazine-publisher-turned-hypocrisy-hunter Larry Flynt) for news to break in 1998 and 1999 that these same Republican political enemies, including House Speaker Newt Gingrich, Rep. Henry Hyde of Illinois, Rep. Bob Barr of Georgia, Rep. Bob Livingston of Louisiana, and Rep. Dan Burton of Indiana, harbored their own sexy-time secrets.

Yet through it all female politicians have sat on the sex-scandal sidelines—until the past few years, although you'll have to wait until the next chapter in this book for my prognostication about women and scandal, and why more women (well, less than 10) are getting caught in scandal. In a book about gender and scandal, it's worth searching for an explanation about this scandal disparity. Are female politicians better at keeping it zipped or simply better at keeping the unzipping out of the media's unyielding scandal spotlight? It can't just be that female politicians are too "Pollyanna-ish" for illicit activities. It's tempting to think, rather, that political sex scandals are just as gendered as politics itself has long been.

"[Politicians] go through a rather grueling process in order to get elected, and once in office people kiss [their] ass constantly," said Dr. Alison Dagnes, professor of political science at Shippensburg University. "For men it gives them validation that they can pretty much do what they want and that they are the hottest guy in the room. It amplifies in men a sense that they are as important as everyone says they are. But for women, I think, it's validation of all of the hard work they've done."

A communications director for a veteran congresswoman—who requested anonymity due to the sensitivity of the subject—has witnessed male politicians do what they want when it comes to private affairs, a trait that he says is absent in female politicians, at least from what he's observed of them.

"You can't control them. You can't," he said speaking of certain congress*men*. "They'll slip the leash." He added: "Usually in a big [political] operation there might be one person whose job it is to—as they said in the Clinton years—prevent the 'bimbo eruptions.'"

Indeed, though media coverage of political sex scandals has changed over the years, male politicians themselves haven't appeared to evolve. Call it the inheritance of male blinders: such figures enjoy their place in a centuries-old culture of boys'-club promiscuity; their entitlement is rewarded, and as a result they haven't tempered their behavior. Now, new technologies leave them vulnerable to scandal in ways that seem obvious to us but unfathomable to them. (Hello smartphones, and their alluring trappings, as well as social media networks with their convoluted privacy settings!) After all, scandal loves emerging technologies as tools that help proliferate all manner of misdeeds. For instance, I've identified seven instances since 2011 where politicians sent illicit photographic selfies of their underclothed bodies, which went viral (and this certainly doesn't count for the plethora of politicians who "limit" their illicit exchanges to text messaging alone, sans nude photo exchanges).[37] While Oxford Dictionaries selected "selfie" as the word of the year in 2013, politicians clearly got a jumpstart on making use of this then-new phenomenon for their own sexual appetites beginning in 2011. And people say politicos are out of touch! In these seven examples of selfie-sexting politicians, we see four examples where politicians resigned as a result of their naked photos going public and three examples where politicians opted for an apology and remained in office. We have four Republicans and three Democrats.[38] But what we don't see—at least not yet at the time of writing—are women politicians sending nude photos of themselves to potential paramours, suitors, and those caught unaware in political (selfie) cross fire.

That's not to say that rumors and accusations don't occasionally sully the reputations of female politicians. When Nikki Haley ran for South Carolina governor in 2010, a political blogger came forward with an account of an "inappropriate physical relationship" with Haley;[39] shortly afterward, another man—a paid political consultant from her opponent's campaign—said he had a one-night stand with the gubernatorial candidate in 2008. No evidence ever emerged from those allegations, and Haley vehemently denied their veracity. Her opponent's campaign then fired that chatty consultant, not wanting to be associated with what quickly appeared to be "everything that is wrong with South Carolina politics," as Haley wrote in her 2012 memoir, *Can't Is Not an Option*. As Haley recalls, "This is disgusting politics. I was—two, three months ago—Nikki who? No one was saying anything. Then we started going up in the polls, and now we have had everything thrown at us."[40]

Then there was the accusation of women-having-sex-with-women surrounding the lieutenant governor of Florida, Jennifer Carroll, in 2012. The backstory is that Carroll's former aide was fired and arrested on charges that she illegally taped and leaked political staff conversations to a newspaper. This aide then alleged that she was *really* fired because she caught Lieutenant Governor Carroll receiving oral sex from another female aide.[41] While the she-said-she-said accusations amounted to a sex scandal on simmer, the lieutenant governor resigned about a year later, following an unrelated criminal investigation into her role in an online gambling site.[42]

But overall, the dearth of sex scandals among female politicians, particularly at the national level, may simply reflect the beliefs that shape the state of politics to begin with—beliefs that often emerge well before potential candidates reach voting age. In 2012, Dr. Jennifer L. Lawless, a political scientist at American University, and her research collaborator Dr. Richard L. Fox, a political scientist at Loyola Marymount University, surveyed a national random sample of approximately 2,100 college students about running for office and working in government. The results revealed a marked difference in ideas about working for a constituency.

In their report, titled "Girls Just Wanna Not Run: The Gender Gap in Young Americans' Political Ambition,"[43] the political scientists found that "Young women are less likely than young men ever to have considered running for office, to express interest in a candidacy at some point in the future, or to consider elective office a desirable profession."[44] One in five male respondents, for instance, said they thought about running for office "many times." Yet only one in 10 female respondents agreed with that statement. The study also revealed different motivating factors in running for office, which Fox admitted looked "almost like a cliché," when reached over the phone to talk about the policy report. "Young boys are more interested in making money and having power," he said of the results. "Young women are more interested in helping people and solving problems."

Just as cliché are findings from Lawless and Fox's 2001 study, in which the team surveyed a random national sample of 3,700 women and men whom they identified as prospective political candidates, including an accomplished group of community leaders, lawyers, businesspeople, and activists.[45] The study examined the gender gap in political aspirations between men and women. Respondents were asked about their interest in running for office. The same group was resurveyed in 2008.[46] Again, a significant gender difference emerged in their responses: Men had more time for hobbies and exercise. Women had more constraints on their time. Men also had more time to devote to personal interests. By contrast, "Women have a lot less freedom in their lives," said Fox over the phone. "Literally, less time."

And though Lawless and Fox found that women whose professional background is of a sufficiently high caliber to run for political office lack free time, they also have an abundance, when compared with their male counterparts, of self-doubt.

"Women hold themselves to a hypothetical bar that no one can ever meet," said Lawless over the phone, who herself ran for Congress in a Rhode Island primary, but lost, in 2006. The old joke—that if a man lives down the street from a senator, he believes he can run for office too—seems, even in these more equitable times, to still be a single-sex proposition. Dr. Dianne Bystrom, who runs the Carrie Chapman Catt Center for Women and Politics at Iowa State University, offered her version of the joke. Men get up in the morning, look in the mirror, and say, "I can run for governor." "I think women are much more careful," said Bystrom. "They put much more thought into running for office." Lawless, the political scientist at American University, added that potential women candidates are often self-censoring.

When political strategists work with politicians and candidates, they try to gauge what type—and how much—sensitive information about their private lives may be leaked to the public.

"For [both] male or female candidates, we try to figure out what may be known and what isn't known," says Democratic strategist Celinda Lake, president of the Washington, D.C.-based Lake Research Partners. In her experience speaking to her candidates about their personal lives, though, she reports that women are more honest about telling their pollsters the sensitive details of their private lives that have the potential to harpoon campaigns. "Men," she notes, "think they can get away with [lying]—the thing that leads them to have affairs is the same thing that leads them to lie to the pollster."

Let us now consider the layout of this book as it tackles the gender dynamics within scandal.

BOOK'S BLUEPRINT

In chapter 2, I offer a breakdown of sexually scandalous behavior occurring in the political field from 1942 to 2016 in the United States. At the heart of this chapter is my own compilation of political sex scandals from which I'm able to offer analysis about the most frequently occurring types of scandals—such as sex scandals involving sexual harassment, affairs with female subordinates, affairs with prostitutes, and the list goes on. In this chapter I'll present an argument about what these scandals say about the gendered nature of power, politics, and sexual behavior in the United States over time.

In chapter 3 we dive into more lighthearted fare by analyzing political cartoons' take on scandal. This chapter pays close attention to how editorial cartoonists skewer the masculinity and sexuality of scandalized politicians from 2004 to 2014 through cultural symbols and what this says about how scandal and "wayward" sexuality discredit politicians.

In chapter 4 I turn my attention to the "other woman—or women." When Monica Lewinsky became a household name in 1998, few would assume she reveled in the crush of media attention. A decade later in 2008, we are introduced to Ashley Dupré—a prostitute and aspiring pop singer who became momentarily famous for sleeping with New York governor Eliot Spitzer. In 2013 we meet Sydney Leathers, an aspiring "personality" and entertainer who became a media starlet that year after sexting with the former New York congressman Anthony Weiner during his candidacy for mayor of New York City. In this chapter I explore how media coverage in the *New York Daily News* and the *New York Post* pits the seductive, sexily ebullient behavior of these aspiring media starlets against the sexual appetites of two New York politicians.

By chapter 5 it's time to pay heed to political wives, who represent key forces in the scandal script. These are women who just can't catch a break whether they "stand by" their scandal-blemished husband or not. This chapter pivots on media analysis of Silda Spitzer, then wife of New York governor Eliot Spitzer, who attended her husband's press conference in 2008 following news of his flings with prostitutes, and Jenny Sanford, then wife of South Carolina governor Mark Sanford. She was absent from her husband's news conference where he addressed his love affair in Argentina. The chapter reveals how scandal holds women to a double standard and how the press punishes not just the politician but also his wife for his transgressive sexuality.

In chapter 6 we return to how the occurrence of scandal impacts politicians. From 2012 to 2013 three sexual harassment scandals hit the New York State Assembly, each involving a male state lawmaker and a member of his female staff. And then in early 2015 the longstanding speaker of the assembly, Sheldon Silver, was arrested on fraud and corruption charges, further tarnishing the assembly's reputation. This chapter offers analysis based on interviews with nearly two dozen New York Assembly members about how they dealt with the scandal landscape in the assembly and how it affected their ability to do their job.

In chapter 7 I focus on how the Eliot Spitzer, Mark Sanford, and Anthony Weiner scandals impacted people, using a survey method. Analysis from 310 open-ended responses demonstrates respondents' discomfort in learning about a politician's sex life. Yet once that knowledge enters the public domain respondents said politicians and their political wives can't be trusted and that sexual foibles are indicative of a corrupt character overall.

In chapter 8 I stick with an analysis of these same three scandals but this time I interview 11 "everyday" couples in New York about which type of political wife they think did the right thing: The silent wife at the press conference (Silda Spitzer, then wife of New York governor Eliot Spitzer, in 2008), the absent wife from the conference (Jenny Sanford, then wife of former South Carolina governor Mark Sanford, in 2009), or the vocal and supportive wife at the press conference (Huma Abedin, then wife of former New York congressman and New York City mayor candidate Anthony Weiner in 2013). Analysis reveals gender differences in opinions about spousal support in times of crisis and the way a political wife should respond to her scandal-tarnished husband.

And finally, I conclude the book with chapter 9, which offers summary thoughts on scandal and gender in our still-young 21st century. Here's where I'll dish my predictions for how the landscape of political sex scandals will change in upcoming years and what it might mean for gender norms, power representations, and news coverage of these sensational events.

CHAPTER 2

A Brief History of Political Sex Scandals

The cat's out of the bag. Politicians pursue sex that—if publicized—would do damage of dazzling proportions to their image and careers. But as I've already established, and as you've intuited long before picking up this book, scandalous behavior in the political field has a long history. But what does the landscape of political sex scandals actually look like? The goal of this chapter is to break down different types of sex scandal occurrences so we can understand the contours of these events. While this chapter focuses on the nature of political sex scandals since mid-20th century, it's worth connecting contemporary sex scandals to their historical counterparts.

SCANDAL AND THE REPUBLIC

In the last two decades of the 18th century, the nascent field of American journalism "regarded [politicians'] personal morality as a legitimate field of battle,"[1] much to the dismay of the emerging class of political authority, including John Adams and Benjamin Franklin and the other political blockbuster names from that era. "Nevertheless, American politics relentlessly scrutinized the personal morality of politicians for much of the next century," writes historian John H. Summers, "and sexual misbehavior became a favorite topic."[2] (This should sound familiar.) In the immediate aftermath of the American Revolutionary War, a belief pervaded in newspapers and popular politics that a politician's private (read: sexual) behavior was indicative of his public immorality. Personal virtue was prized as the antidote to tyranny for those tasked with leading a fledgling nation.

The presence of Evangelical Protestantism in public life also encouraged public servants to present an upright character bolstered by private behavior that was pure and proper. The implicitly stated and explicitly declared attestations of modern-day politicians that they are people of quality character who prize integrity, and who value family, has its roots in the late 18th century, when "politicians of both parties heeded such admonitions and presented themselves to voters as men of sexual virtue, honor, integrity, and good judgment."[3] But as the historian Summers noted, a problem emerged. What if politicians donned a guise of morality but depravity lurked beneath their good manners? (Just imagine!) Therefore, newspapers, journalists, novelists, and political operatives participated in vigorous sleuthing to "out" hypocrites and reveal their true (immoral) nature, which had previously duped an unsuspecting public. Yet we see a sharp change of course beginning with the presidency of William McKinley in 1897, and continuing with Theodore Roosevelt, William Taft, Woodrow Wilson, and onward.[4] For instance, "Cartoonists poked fun at Taft's impressive girth," writes Summers, "but no major allegations against his sexual character surfaced in the mainstream press."[5] And when it appeared that Wilson's romantic connection to a woman who was not his (second) wife might be revealed, he drafted a public statement declaring his remorse. But newspapers never blew the cover on his affair. And years later, we now know (but the public didn't know then) that Franklin Delano Roosevelt arranged for a special car escort to transport his lover to his 1932 presidential inauguration; and let's not get started on the profligate assignations that made John F. Kennedy a lothario of mythological proportions. But the press meanwhile played dumb. What accounted for this change? Summers hinges the shift from prurience to prudishness on the evolution of American journalism. Journalism as a field began to extricate itself from entrenched party politics and established its profession as independent from the party system that previously ruled newspapers. "Reticence about the immoralities of political figures first acquired concerted support in the professionalization of journalism."[6] Journalism solidified as an autonomous profession, buoyed by the creation of the American Society of Newspaper Editors—which called for journalists to engage in "fair play" of those whom they covered. In complement to this new polished version of a preexisting profession, journalists had a pulsing desire to procure and nurture access to elites; to separate themselves from the gossip-mongering legacy of muckrakers and yellow journalism; and to maintain an "objective" viewpoint in their reportage. This new set of wants and expectations cultivated a journalism field where respected work turned sharply away from salacious material. But we know that the pendulum began to swing the other way certainly by the 1970s and 1980s, where the effects of the Civil Rights movement, the Vietnam War, Watergate, and financial crises eroded the myth that official authority works in the interests of its people. It is also at this time when media systems began to fragment, and cable TV disrupted the news landscape.

CATEGORIZING SCANDAL

Political sex scandals, at both the local and elite level, occur frequently in our political and media landscape but at irregular intervals. But what do these scandals look like in the aggregate? It was clear that in order to answer this question I would have to create a massive scandal compilation. Call it the scandal mother lode spreadsheet. The purpose of this list is to categorize political sex scandals based on the sum of their parts. To the best of my knowledge, I am not aware of another research-based effort to compile a comprehensive list of political sex scandals in contemporary American politics. While political scientists Scott Basinger, Lara Brown, Douglas Harris, and Girish J. "Jeff" Gulati[7] created a comprehensive list of contemporary political, financial, sexual, and "other" scandals in Congress, their work focused on the top tier of the political stratosphere. A compilation of political sex scandals including both the local *and* elite levels of politics would prove useful to categorize scandal across time and to create a typography for the types of behavior that creates media frenzies, which crosses party lines and levels of power and which can clog the political system through the sheer force of its distracting—and captivating—capabilities. However, here's where I must insert my disclaimer: there's no way I can attest to the exhaustive and complete nature of this list. New political sex scandals pop up like an interminable game of Whac-A-Mole, and there are certainly scandals that occurred but that I was not able to locate because media coverage of them was lacking.

In order to create the mother lode spreadsheet, I categorized each scandal based on:

- its year
- the political party of the transgressor
- whether the scandal involved same-sex or opposite-sex "activity"
- whether it occurred at the elite level of politics (for those who were a Congress member, governor, lieutenant governor, president, or a candidate for each of these positions)
- or at the local level (for those who were a state representative, county-level politician, mayor, elected judge, or a candidate for each of these positions)

- whether the scandal resulted in political failure (determined if the politician or candidate resigned, halted the campaign in the wake of the scandal, or lost in a subsequent election)
- and whether the scandal involved a list of scandal-defining variables, 44 in total, including—for instance: "Did the politician have/solicit sex with/from male prostitutes?" "Did the politician have sex with female prostitutes?" "Did the politician have extramarital sexual relations with a man?" "Did the politician have extramarital sexual relations with a woman?" "Did the politician attempt to solicit sex from undercover authorities?" "Did alcohol play a role in the scandalous events?" "Did the politician break the law?" The questions were determined by selecting key elements from each scandal. (Please see appendix A for the complete list of 44 questions.)

By answering the list of 44 questions for each scandal it was possible to determine through statistical analysis[8] whether the extent of the scandal's severity (marked by a higher number of "yeses" to the 44 questions) was more likely to result in political failure. The answer is an astounding "yes." In other words, the more wacko a scandal—with a plethora of scandalous elements—there's a greater likelihood of political failure. (Lesson to politicians: if you're going to have a scandal, just keep it simple.) But more on that to follow.

Let me now clarify how a scandal made it onto the mother lode spreadsheet. Because I am interested in whether a scandal impacts political failure, the politician caught in scandal must either run for office or serve as an incumbent in order to make the list. That's why Dennis Hastert, the former U.S. House Speaker from 1999 to 2007, is not on the list, even though he was sentenced in 2016 to prison for sex abuse crimes against children. Because he was long since retired as a politician when he was charged with a crime I did not add him to the list. Second, I am interested in scandal as an event—not a rumor. Therefore, actual allegations stemming from a specific incident must have been reported in the news, at a time when a politician is active in the political field, in order for the scandal to be counted on the list.[9] Finally, I am interested in scandals that took place mid-20th century or later, since we are interested in contemporary scandals.

To start this process of scandal compilation I searched online for existing political sex scandal lists from which to begin my work. I found my starting point at Wikipedia, with its "List of Federal Political Sex Scandals in the United States"[10] and a second helpful Wikipedia list included "List of State and Local Political Sex Scandals in the United States."[11] But these were only starting points since many people on that list didn't meet my aforementioned criteria. For the scandals that did meet my criteria I then turned to Google and LexisNexis to verify their occurrence and answer the 44 questions listed in appendix A. I also spent time Googling variations of "Political Sex Scandals in the U.S." to make sure I scraped as many incidents as possible for my list. In all, the final compilation included 64 local scandals and 70 elite scandals, for a total of 134 political sex scandals. The list includes scandals through July 2016. Let's now take a look at what this list tells us about the contemporary scandal ecosphere in the United States.

WHEN ARE THESE SCANDALS TAKING PLACE?

The median year for the 134 scandals is 2007, an astounding fact since it means the following: the same number of all political sex scandals has occurred in the past decade as has occurred in the previous six-and-a-half decades. We always knew politicians to be busy folks, and now we have a clue why. This finding reveals one certainty and a few possibilities. The certainty is that there's been a surge in scandal occurrences appearing in news accounts since 2007, and that scandal reporting has become a normalized source of news coverage and public consumption. Does this mean that since 2007 politicians have been engaging in scandalous behavior more frequently than in previous decades? This question is not answerable (although perhaps a possibility). But we do know that journalists are keen on reporting on scandalous behavior, and they no longer turn away with disinterest when they catch a scoop or witness impropriety. In explaining the surge of scandals since 2007, there is the possibility that politicians prone to scandalous behavior have either disregarded the up-tick in scandal reporting and the public's demand for scandal news, are ignorant to it, or view themselves as protected from it. Yet the numbers are clear: politicians do not appear to grasp the risks and likelihood of getting caught or having their secrets ripped open.

Another possibility is that technology plays a role in the scandal surge since 2007. Is it a coincidence or something more intentional that 2007 also marks the year that Apple unveiled its game-changing device, the iPhone?[12] The year before America was deep in its "CrackBerry" phase, when the mobile company Research in Motion fueled the addiction among those in the business and political fields with the release of the "Electron" and "Pearl" editions of the BlackBerry.[13] These devices featured cameras and chat features for the first time. I can't possibly imagine how those could be misused! Did these devices contribute to the rush of scandal publicization? Again, it's not for us to fully know but I wouldn't

underestimate the impact of technology on "outing" a politician's rau-
cous behavior, especially since smartphones have a way of stroking vanity.
They are gateway tools to slick and sly behavior.

What else was happening in 2007? Facebook was taking off at rocket
speed. Founded in 2004, with one million active users by that year's end,
growth continued at a steady clip before it began to increase exponen-
tially, year over year. For instance, *Yahoo! Finance* reported that there were
5.5 million users in 2005, which boomed to 50 million in 2007.[14] And
we know the rest is history, with Facebook reporting 1.65 billion active
monthly users by mid-2016.[15]

It's noteworthy that 2007 also marks the year that the global financial
system entered "The Great Recession."[16] As the economy floundered, a
number of politicians frolicked. Can we attribute the subsequent flurry of
scandal to overwhelmed politicians? To a media system seeking to provide
"entertainment" news as a distraction to people's financial concerns? As a
way of furthering mistrust in politicians gone awry during unsettling and
turbulent times? Were politicians themselves indulging in social media
networks, new tools to easily aid in their illicit pursuits? These questions
deserve subsequent study now that we know that 2007 is the median year
for contemporary scandal.

THE MOST POPULAR YEARS FOR SCANDAL

The years 2008 and 2011 tied as the most prolific for scandal, with each
year offering 11 political sex scandals. Those two years accounted for 16.2
percent of all scandals on the list. The Great Recession was still unleash-
ing its wrath in 2008, the year that the U.S. government voted to save
the nation's banking industry with a bailout to the tune of 16.8 trillion
dollars.[17] It also marked the year that President Barack Obama, the first
African American to hold this position, was elected to office. American
troops were still deeply entrenched in the wars in Iraq and Afghanistan.
In 2011 American engagement in its wars continued, but by this time the
Great Recession was over. President Obama announced the assassination
of September 11, 2001, mastermind Osama bin Laden at his compound in
Abbottabad, Pakistan. It was the year that Arizona senator Gabrielle Gif-
fords was shot in the head by an assailant during a constituent meet-and-
greet at a local supermarket; massive antigovernment protests toppled the
presidency in Egypt; the war in Libya resulted in the death of its deposed
leader, Muammar Gaddafi; a tsunami in Japan caused the meltdown of the
Fukushima Daiichi nuclear plant (considered the worst nuclear disaster
since Chernobyl); the war in Syria raged; and a group known as Occupy

Wall Street camped out in a Manhattan park (and spawned a national movement). I share these historical events to put the occurrence of sex scandals into their context. Powerful movements and natural forces were shaking the globe in 2008 and 2011, when politicians were caught in more sex scandals than any other year. Let us take a look at the scandals that populated the end of the first decade, and the beginning of the second decade, of the 21st century.

Tables 2.1 and 2.2 reveal that during the busy scandal years of 2008 and 2011, a total of 17 of the 22 politicians resigned or decided not to further their political careers as a result of their respective scandals. An analysis of the master scandal list shows that there is a statistically significant relationship between a politician's scandal score (the number of scandalous elements contained within each event) and the likelihood of political failure. So the higher the scandal score the greater the likelihood of political failure, with a one-unit increase on the scale resulting in a 13.6 percent greater likelihood of political failure.

Table 2.1 Political Sex Scandals That Occurred in 2008, the Year That Tied with 2011 for the Most Number of Sex Scandals

Politician	Party	Scandal Summary	Consequence
Marc Dann	D	The attorney general of Ohio had an affair with a member of his staff. There were also allegations and a financial settlement relating to sexual harassment.	Resigned
John Edwards	D	The presidential candidate had an affair with a videographer on his campaign. He fathered a child with her in 2008 but didn't admit paternity until 2010.	Ended his campaign early in 2008
Jim Gibbons	R	During divorce proceedings when Nevada governor, his wife accused him of numerous infidelities.	Lost reelection in 2010
Sam Hoyt	D	The New York assemblyman had an affair with an intern and sent her steamy e-mails.	He is the chairman of a New York public development corporation.

(Continued)

Table 2.1   (*Continued*)

Politician	Party	Scandal Summary	Consequence
Kwame Kilpatrick	D	The mayor of Detroit had an affair with his chief of staff, revealed through explicit text messages. Charges were filed against him for obstruction of justice.	Resigned, paid a $1 million fine, and was sentenced to four months in jail. He is currently serving a 28-year sentence in federal prison for racketeering and other crimes.
Tim Mahoney	D	The Florida congressman had an affair with a member of his staff and agreed to pay her $121,000.	Lost his reelection campaign, which took place in the immediate aftermath of the scandal.
J. James Marzilli Jr.	D	The state senator from Massachusetts was accused of sexually assaulting a woman and making lewd comments directed at another woman in a separate incident.	Resigned. Pleaded guilty to resisting arrest and disorderly conduct. Spent time in psychiatric hospital to treat bipolar disorder.
Robert McKee	R	The member of the Maryland House of Delegates pleaded guilty to possessing child pornography.	Resigned from office. Sentenced to prison for 37 months and had to register as a sex offender.
Scott Muschany	R	Charged with having sex with a 14-year-old girl who was his girlfriend's daughter.	Resigned. Charged with a felony of "deviate sexual assault." Found not guilty.
David Paterson	D	The New York lieutenant governor, who became governor following the Eliot Spitzer sex scandal, said both he and his wife had had extramarital affairs.	Served the remainder of his term, stepping in for Governor Eliot Spitzer, who had resigned.
Eliot Spitzer	D	The governor of New York had sex with prostitute.	Resigned.

Table 2.2 Political Sex Scandals That Occurred in 2011, the Year That Tied with 2008 for the Most Number of Sex Scandals

Politician	Party	Scandal Summary	Aftermath
John Carnevale	D	The state representative from Rhode Island was accused of sexual assault by a woman. He was indicted on charges of first and second degree sexual assault. Charges were later dropped because the woman died and therefore couldn't testify.	Remains in office
Phillip Hinkle	R	The Indiana state legislator met up with an 18-year-old man for a sexual encounter in a hotel room. When Hinkle turned violent that man changed his mind about participating in sexual activity.	Decided not to seek reelection
Gordon Hintz	D	The state representative from Indiana was issued a citation for visiting an illicit massage parlor under police investigation for prostitution. Not arrested.	Remains in office
Randy Hopper	R	The state representative from Wisconsin had affair with a woman he then allegedly hired to work for him. He was arrested on drunk driving charges, pleaded not guilty, and was found not guilty.	Lost in the 2011 election
Amy Koch	R	The state representative from Minnesota had an affair with a male staffer.	Resigned
Chris Lee	R	The New York congressman sent topless pictures to a woman he met on Craigslist using his official congressional e-mail.	Resigned
Louis M. Magazzu	D	The legislator at the county level sent nude photos of himself to a woman he never met.	Resigned

(Continued)

Table 2.2   (*Continued*)

Politician	Party	Scandal Summary	Aftermath
Robert Mecklenborg	R	The state representative from Ohio was arrested and charged with drunk driving. A stripper was with him in his car.	Resigned
Joe Stagni	R	The Louisiana city councilman texted photos of himself in his underwear to an administration employee.	Apologized
David Wu	D	The congressman from Oregon groped a fundraiser's daughter.	Resigned
Anthony Weiner	D	The New York congressman at first denied, but then admitted, to sending sexually explicit tweets and photographs to women. (The scandal resurfaced in 2013 when he was running for mayor of New York City, and then again in 2016 as his wife, Huma Abedin, served on Hillary Clinton's presidential campaign.)	Resigned

ELITE VERSUS LOCAL SCANDALS

Additionally, the scandals that made 2008 and 2011 the most pro-lific years for political sex scandals saw both elite *and* local politi-cians populating these lists, although there were more local politicians (14 in total for both years) than elites (8 in total). An analysis of the 134 scandals also reveals that local politicians, on average, score higher on the scandal transgression scale than their elite counterparts (see tables 2.3 and 2.4). In other words, local politicos get caught in scandals that are more transgressive and that have more scandalous elements than elites. For instance, remember the list of 44 questions that was answered for each scandal (appendix A)? Local politicians scored an average of 4.44 on that questionnaire while elites fared better with an average score of 3.23.

Table 2.3 Top 10 Scandalous Attributes for Local Politicians

Scandalous Element	Number of Incidents	Percentage of Local Scandals with This Attribute
Breaking the law	36	56.3
Charged with a crime	33	51.6
Affair with a woman	28	43.8
Evidence presented of scandal	16	25
Tie: underage person involved and jail time	14	21.9 each
Tie: affair with a man, sex with a female subordinate, caught by police, and sex abuse	12	18.8 each
Sexual harassment	11	17.2
Sexting	8	12.5
Sex acts involved coercion	7	10.9
Tie: female intern involved; politician held press conference to address scandal	6	9.4 each

Table 2.4 Top 10 Scandalous Attributes for Elite Politicians

Scandalous Element	Number of Incidents	Percentage of Elite Scandals with This Attribute
Affair with a woman	44	63
Tie: sex with female subordinate; breaking the law	15	21.4 each
Politician held press conference to address scandal	13	18.6
Sexual harassment	13	18.6
Criticized President Bill Clinton's scandal and then had their own scandal	10	14.2
Charged with a crime	8	11.4
Evidence of scandal presented in media	8	11.4
Tie: voted against gay rights issues and then caught in gay scandal; coercion involved	7	10 each
Tie: children out of wedlock; alcohol involved; underage people involved	6	8.6 each
Tie: politician denied the scandal; caught by police; intern involved	5	7.1 each

I can offer informed speculation as to why local scandals are more "deviant" than those belonging to elites. First, it's possible that local politicians haven't yet climbed the ranks of their political professions. They may be new to office; there may be less media attention focused on them. Yet elite politicians, who once worked locally themselves—one can reasonably assume—likely knew that if they had higher aspirations for national elected office then they may be less likely to take risks that would lead to scandal or better at covering their tracks. Elite politicians have also been tested and vetted and endorsed and gone through the political wringer. Local politicians, meanwhile, may be less likely to be part of the political machine and can be lone wolves with less oversight and less at stake. This may help conceptualize why local politicians score higher on the scandal transgression scale than their more renowned counterparts.

REPUBLICAN VERSUS DEMOCRAT SCANDALS

Scandal analysis also revealed distinct differences along party lines. First, I found that Republicans get caught in more scandals than Democrats. For instance, Republicans accounted for 82 incidents (62.1 percent) of all scandals, whereas Democrats accounted for 52 incidents (38.8 percent). Even though scandalous members of both parties equally engaged in "affair with a woman" and "breaking the law" (see table 2.5), their types of scandals differed along political ideologies. For instance, in 14.6 percent of Republican scandals we find that male politicians voted against gay rights issues but then got caught in a sexual relationship with another man. Meanwhile, this type of scandal was not ranked as among the most common scandals for Democrats. Yet Democrats got caught in sexual harassment scandals more than Republicans. And whereas Republicans were more likely to get caught with an underage person, Democrats were more likely to sext (see table 2.6).

How can we make sense of these differences? We can turn to the brain for potential answers. The neuroscientist Heather Berlin, of Mount Sinai Hospital in New York, said that "many if not most of the political differences between liberals and conservatives can be traced to differences in their brain function." Dr. Berlin pointed out that since conservatives endorse more restrictive sexual norms, their natural sexual desires are less likely to find as wide a range of healthy expressions, which makes conservatives more likely to "act out" on their "forbidden" desires in maladaptive ways. Also, since liberal sexual norms are less restrictive, "Liberal people tend to be less secretive about their sexuality," she said. "They have less to hide." This may explain why Democrats were more likely to engage in

Table 2.5   Top Scandal Types along Party Lines

Republicans		Democrats	
Scandal Type	Percentage	Scandal Type	Percentage
Affair with woman	52.4	Affair with woman	55.8
Tie: breaking the law; charged with crime	34.1 each	Breaking the law	44.2
Tie: sex with female subordinate; jail; underage person involved	17.1 each	Sexual harassment	30.8
Affair with a man*	15.9	Charged with a crime	26.9
Voted against gay rights issue and then caught in gay scandal	14.6	Sex with female subordinate	25
Sexual abuse	12.2	Tie: evidence presented of scandal; politician held press conference on scandal	21.2
Tie: politician held press conference to deal with scandal; criticized Clinton and then involved in own scandal	11 each	Coercion	17.3
Politician denied scandal when addressing the media	8.5	Caught by police	15.4
Sex offender status involved	7.2	Tie: sexting; underage person involved	11.5

*Note: Of the eight instances of women Republicans caught in scandal, seven involved them having an affair with a man.

sexual harassment—a behavior that can typically take place in a public work environment, since they may rationalize their actions as "playful" and being done "in good fun." Dr. Berlin also suggested that the mismatch between natural desires and restrictive social norms may help explain the instances where male Republicans vote against gay rights issue and then get caught in sex scandals with other men. In those instances, their effort to legislate against gay rights may be a way of rejecting internal sexual feelings that remain at odds with their political and religious ideology, yet are feelings they are unable to fully ignore or expunge.

Table 2.6   Top 10 Scandalous Behaviors for All Politicians

	Number of Incidents	Percentage of Scandals
Affair with women	72	53.7
Breaking the law	51	38.1
Charged with a crime	42	31.3
Sex with female subordinate	27	20.1
Tie: evidence presented; sexual harassment	24 each	17.9 each
Tie: politician held press conference; underage person involved	20 each	14.9 each
Jail	18	13.4
Caught by police	17	12.7
Male affair	15	11.2
Coercion	14	10.4

WHERE ARE THESE SCANDALS TAKING PLACE?

New York owns the distinction as the state with politicians engaging in the most sex scandals, with 20 scandals to its name. California ranks second with 13 scandals. Following that, there's a dip, with Louisiana, Massachusetts, Illinois, and Ohio boasting six scandals each. California is the most populous state in the nation, followed by Texas (which did not make the cut as one of the top five most sexually scandalous states), and then New York ranked as the third most populous state in the United States. Besides noting the populous nature of New York and California, which ranked first and second, respectively, as the states with the most sex scandals, any attempt to explain those states' proclivity for producing scandal-prone politicians would be flimsy. But let's go there anyhow. Perhaps the scandal ranking has to do with their geographic location, with New York as the finance hub of the nation—and inimitable in so many cultural ways—and California as the entertainment hub. For instance, does the distinction of serving as a politician from the "Empire State" go straight to the heads of certain politicians in New York? Does the fact that California has more congressional representatives make it more likely that its politicians will get caught in scandal? Does the highly competitive and grueling nature of politics in these states produce scheming, risk-loving, and wild-living politicians? These questions would be worth exploring in future research.

SCANDAL AND GENDER

In this list of 134 politicians caught in scandal, nine entries belong to women. These women entries, perhaps because they are in the minority, represent the most intriguing part of the scandal list. These womencentric scandals took place from 2004 to 2016, and the most notable part of this subgroup is that eight of the nine scandals involve Republican female lawmakers.

How can we understand the prevalence of female Republican scandal-doers? An attempt at informed speculation can lead us back to Dr. Berlin, the neuroscientist at Mount Sinai Hospital, who said one's political position can be motivated by private desires that politicians feel compelled to conceal. For instance, enthusiastically embracing a "family values" rhetoric, which is a popular conservative trope, might be a way of masking or pushing back against sexual desires that extend beyond the heterosexual and monogamous traits embedded so deeply in that narrative. A second attempt at informed speculation can lead us to the influence of the Tea Party and the interest from people with more radical and outspoken political ideologies seeking a foothold in the political process. If that is the case then these women may be swept into office due to the popular support enjoyed by the Tea Party but not yet emotionally or professionally mature to assume the duties of public service.

SCANDAL, AGE, AND GENDER

We can also focus on the ages of this scandal-tarnished subset of women politicians as a way to understand this subgroup. Through online searches I found the ages of each female politician at the time of scandal, with the exception of Katherine Bryson (see table 2.7). The median age of the remaining eight politicians is 39.5, a relatively young age for a politician, one can reasonably assume. Certainly, we know that male politicians twice that age can get caught in scandal. But I'm wondering the extent to which the median age plays a role in these scandal occurrences.

Another nuance emerges when looking further into this female group: of the nine scandal cases, seven occurred as the female politician was either running for office or within the first year or two of assuming office. In these cases, scandals decimated politicians' future work and potential as an elected official, since in eight of the nine scandals the female politician either resigned or did not seek reelection as a result of the scandal (see table 2.7). Therefore, these scandals have a three-point impact. First, they occur, on average, when the politician is relatively young. Second,

Table 2.7   Political Sex Scandals Involving Women Politicians

Politician	Party	Scandal Summary	Aftermath
Katherine Bryson	R	In 2004 the state representative from Utah was caught on surveillance footage with her male lover. Her husband allegedly installed the camera to catch a thief.	Did not seek reelection
Nikki Haley	R	In 2010 the South Carolina gubernatorial candidate vehemently denied having extramarital affairs, after both a blogger and political operative alleged they had been intimate with her.	Won election
Amy Koch	R	In 2011 the member of the Minnesota Senate admitted to an affair with a male Senate staffer.	Resigned senate leadership and said she would not seek reelection
Jennifer Carroll	R	In 2011 the Florida lieutenant governor was accused of engaging in oral sex (in her office) with a female aide.	Resigned in 2013 at the request of the governor
Nadia Lockyer	D	In 2012 the county supervisor was caught in a meth and sex-tape scandal with a man.	Resigned to receive treatment for her drug addiction
Gia Arnold	R	In 2014 the candidate for New York State Senate said she had an extramarital affair with a man and she was going to drop out of the race. She later returned to the race but left her husband and three children.	Lost election
Cindy Gamrat	R	In 2015 this member of the Michigan House of Representatives had an extramarital affair with a male member of the legislature.	Expelled from the Michigan legislature due to misuse of taxpayer money and her cover-up of the affair

(Continued)

Table 2.7   (*Continued*)

Politician	Party	Scandal Summary	Aftermath
Tara Mack	R	In 2015 this member of the Minnesota House of Representatives was caught by a park ranger and issued a citation for making out, with her pants down, with a male member in the House. She resigned from the ethics committee.	Did not seek reelection
Angela Wozniak	R	In 2016 this member of the New York State Assembly admitted to an extramarital affair with her legislative director. She was censured by the legislature's ethics committee for retaliating against her former lover when he broke off their affair.	Did not seek reelection

scandal might be a Darwinian leveling ground for those unfortunate to get caught in one. After all, in a battle where only the strongest (politicians) survive, scandal has the power to root out those who are in hot pursuit of sex. Such politicians do not or cannot consider the consequences of getting caught and therefore allow scandal to derail their political career. Third, scandal razes the female politician's chances of building a successful political career since eight of the nine examples here put the kibosh on political-career advancement.

When we compare the average (median) age of the scandalous male politician to his nine female counterparts we notice a whopping difference. In my scandal compilation there are 125 male scandals. I found the ages of 117 politicians at the time of their scandal through online searches. The average median age for men was 52, with the youngest scandal sufferer at 32 and the oldest at 74.

Even though there are only nine examples of scandal-suffering women (with ages obtained for eight of them and an age range of 24–52), it's worth pondering reasons behind the male/female age gap. As I began considering possible explanations for why the median age for women *scandalers* was 39.5 and 52 for men *scandalers*, I reached back into my memory for a conversation I had with a gender scholar in 2008, when Sarah Palin was the Republican vice presidential candidate. I was making the goofy argument with this gender scholar that maybe we'd have—finally!—our first female political sex scandal of a national caliber since Palin seemed to court controversy. My conversationalist wondered, if such a scenario were to unfold, would the media portray Palin as the seducer or as the woman who succumbed to (presumably) a man who pursued her? To bring that question back to our sample of women *scandalers*, did their age make them vulnerable (i.e., attractive) to those who wanted to "know" them intimately? Were they the pursuers or the pursued? One could reasonably assume that if we apply stereotypic gender dynamics to these situations that a 39.5-year-old woman politician would be appealing to her older colleagues. Yet when we dive deeper into this sample we find that seven of the women *scandalers* had sex with—or were alleged to have sex with—people of a lower status than their own professional-social position, including sex partners who were staffers, lobbyists, and nonpoliticians. Therefore, it was the woman politician who maintained a higher professional status than the person (a man in all cases but one) of her interest. Was she emboldened by her own power? Or did the pressures of the campaign/office cause her to act out in ways that were counter to her best professional interests?

The answer that makes the most intuitive sense is the Darwinian approach. In seven of the nine cases the women *scandalers* got caught either within a year or two of assuming office or during their campaign. They had, therefore, the opposite of beginner's luck. They might have previously engaged in risky behavior that was amplified once in the public spotlight; they might have been seduced by the power of their own power; or perhaps they had a compulsion they could not control.

Of the 125 male politicians we spot 22 cases of men (17.6 percent) who had a scandal within a year or two of assuming office or while running their campaign. Therefore, while the women *scandalers* had a higher rate of women who got caught in scandal during those key moments of running for or assuming office (77.8 percent), what's striking is that women *scandalers* had a higher percentage of political failure when their scandal occurred during that time frame than their male counterparts. I found that 77.3 percent of men and 85.7 percent of women had political failure when their scandals occurred as they were seeking, or new to, office. What are we to make of this? I argue that *scandalers*, regardless of gender, might not have enough political capital or clout to survive a career-crushing scandal when their political career has not yet reached cruising altitude. Perhaps they don't yet have enough people in their corner fighting for them because either they are an unknown or untested political entity, or they haven't had the time and means yet to accrue favors owed to them. And of particulate note, even from our small sample of nine, women caught in scandal have only the slightest chance of moving beyond their catastrophe. Instead, their private romps consume their public office and shatter in nearly all cases their chances of political survival. At least at the time of writing.

With male politicians caught in scandal, the chance of survival overall is still unlikely. I found that 72 percent of men overall have political failure when caught in scandal (compared with 89 percent of women); that 58 percent of men who have a scandal beyond their first two years in office face political failure; and that 28 percent of men caught in scandal do not face political failure. The takeaway? If you're a man, your chances of political survival are much better if you can hold off at least two years before getting caught in scandal. Try to build up political capital first.

CHAPTER 3

What a Joke: Philandering Politicians Get the Cartoon Treatment

A politician's sexual foibles are prime material for political cartoonists. After all, if there's a unifying language to political cartoons, it's the visual skewering of newsworthy people and events. Political cartoons are "visual/verbal, non-narrative commentary, typically in single-panel form, created by a staff member or a newspaper or appearing originally on the editorial pages of a newspaper."[1] Cartoonists rarely play nice. And when it comes to a politician's sexual missteps, the gloves quickly come off. But for these critics, it's all in a day's work. "Cartoonists are not expected to be fair to the figures they choose to draw. The essence of the cartoon is satire, a distortion of the truth."[2] To satirize, cartoonists employ stereotypes, hyperbole, and ad hominem attacks.[3] There's no mercy for life in cartoon motion. According to political cartoon scholar Joan L. Conners, "To be in a cartoon commentary is to be a target."[4] And to laugh at what the cartoon provokes, or invokes, is to share common cultural norms with its creator, the cartoonist. "Both the visual itself and the humor it provokes are culturally coded,"[5] writes communication scholar Juana I. Marín-Arrese.

The cultural codes in political cartoons include representations of gender that reflect the dominant frame of male power in the political sphere. "Because cartoonists must use gender in a manner relevant to readers' social experiences, cartoons provide a window into pervasive cultural attitudes about gender,"[6] according to Janis L. Edwards, who has written extensively on this medium as well as on gender and politics more broadly. Political cartoons represent an area worthy of probing for two main reasons: First, as a site for analysis, these cartoons typically reduce complex events to simple visual images that are based on stereotype—a cultural shorthand to convey key information to readers. And second, men dominate this field, which further justifies the necessity to study gender representation in political cartoons.[7] When studying how political cartoonists lampoon those caught in sex scandals, we have a unique opportunity to reveal how a field dominated by men, which deals in stereotypes as its language, presents scandal-tarnished political elites, who are overwhelmingly male. Specifically, this chapter asks the following questions:

1. Which metaphors do cartoonists employ in scandal cartoons?
2. How do political cartoons on sex scandals *do* gender?

Before describing my cartoon analysis, including how I selected the cartoons and what their imagery revealed, I will first flesh out each of these questions.

WHICH METAPHORS DO CARTOONISTS EMPLOY IN SCANDAL CARTOONS?

"Symbolism is the heartbeat of caricature," write Martin J. Medhurst and Michael A. DeSousa, authors of an iconic, scholarly 1981 treatise on the rhetorical functions of political cartoons.[8] "Cartoons 'work' to the extent that readers share in the communal consciousness, the available means of cultural symbology, and are able to recognize that shared locus of meaning as expressed by the caricature."[9] If symbolism represents the pulse of caricature, which includes political cartoons, then metaphor represents its backbone. A "metaphor is an identity relationship between two phenomena that, in the given context, belong to different categories."[10] The process of conceptualizing one idea in terms of another embodies communication through metaphor.[11] For instance, the visual image in a political cartoon featuring a scandal-tarnished politician about to step off a cliff uses metaphor to show that his political life is over. Cultural critic Diana E. Popa views metaphor as consequential "to understand and experience the intangibles of culture" and argues that metaphors are central to politics "not only at the verbal level but also visually."[12] Therefore, in answering this question, I hope to reveal how cultural metaphors connect to political embarrassment, infidelity, and powerful men losing their grasp on power.

HOW DO POLITICAL CARTOONS ON SEX SCANDALS DO GENDER?

This question pays homage to the classic 1987 article by Candace West and Don H. Zimmerman, published in *Gender & Society*, titled "Doing Gender."[13] West and Zimmerman counter the long-held, deeply ingrained belief that men and women are categorically different and that their psychological and behavioral proclivities can be determined and predicted on whether they have female or male reproductive parts. The scholars turn this notion on its head. Instead, "We argue that gender is not a set of traits, nor a variable, nor a role, but the product of social doings of some sort."[14] Therefore, if we conceptualize the "social doings" of gender and gender performance, how do political cartoons *do* gender within the context of politicians acting out sexually? Do cartoon reproductions of gender differ depending on the type of scandal (the sex act at its center) and whether it involved sexual contact or insinuation with another man or another woman?

For her 2001 article on the 2000 presidential election, Edwards—the cartoon scholar—identified five leadership traits reinforced in political cartoons of the 2000 presidential campaign. These traits of masculinity include character, viability, competency, charisma, and independence.[15] Building on her work, I will attempt to establish traits of male politicians in scandal cartoons. By crafting this typology, I hope to understand how cartoonists not only take aim at scandal-tarnished politicians but also how they categorize their masculinity within scandal scenarios.

SELECTING SCANDALS FOR CARTOON ANALYSIS

In 2014 I began to compile a list of political sex scandals at the national and local levels dating back to mid-20th century. This list, which was discussed in chapter 2, includes 134 scandals. Since I am interested in post–Bill Clinton cartoons for my cartoon analysis—an inclusion of Clinton cartoons would certainly overwhelm all other scandals—I began by searching Cagle.com, described as "one of the most extensive online collections of contemporary editorial cartoons," for each national-level politician, post-Clinton, on my master list.[16] National-level politicians include elite public servants who hold the positions of presidents, vice presidents, members of Congress, governors, and candidates running for such positions. I then searched Cagle.com for cartoons on each scandal-suffering politician. To make sure I found as many relevant cartoons as possible, my search parameters extended for six months following initial news reporting of each scandal. I located a total of 136 cartoons featuring 12 politicians (table 3.1).

I conducted a qualitative thematic analysis of the 136 cartoons, comparing and contrasting each cartoon with its counterparts within each particular scandal and among all scandals, to determine which broader themes emerge in cartoon analysis.

Table 3.1   Politicians Caught in Scandal Who Get the Cartoon Treatment, Post-Clinton

Politician	Year	Position	Scandal Info	Number of Cartoons
1. Mark Foley	2006	Florida congressman	Sexted with male congressional pages	7
2. David Vitter	2007	Louisiana senator	Had sex with female prostitutes	2
3. Larry Craig	2007	Idaho senator	Attempted to solicit sex from male undercover cop in airport bathroom	13
4. Eliot Spitzer	2008	New York governor	Had sex with female prostitutes	16
5. David Paterson	2008	New York governor	Admitted that he and his spouse had affairs	2
6. John Edwards	2008, 2010	Presidential candidate	Had affair with campaign videographer with whom he had a child in 2008; denied paternity until 2010	6
7. Mark Sanford	2009	South Carolina governor	Had affair with woman from Argentina	5
8. Eric Massa	2010	New York congressman	"Tickled" male staff	2
9. Mark Souder	2010	Indiana congressman	Had affair with female aide	1
10. Chris Lee	2011	New York congressman	Sexted with women	1

(Continued)

Table 3.1 (*Continued*)

Politician	Year	Position	Scandal Info	Number of Cartoons
11. Herman Cain	2011	Presidential candidate	Accused of sexual harassment by multiple women	41
12. Anthony Weiner	2011, 2013	New York congressman and New York City mayoral candidate	Sexted with women	40

METAPHORS IN SCANDAL CARTOONS: UNDERWEAR

The images of scandal-suffering politicians standing alone—and vulnerable—in their underwear represented a recurring metaphor in 19 cartoons. The underwear metaphor emerged in six scandals belonging to Mark Foley (one underwear depiction), Eliot Spitzer (six depictions), John Edwards (one), Mark Sanford (two), Herman Cain (two), and Anthony Weiner (seven). Cartoonists drew red hearts to embellish the boxer shorts of all politicians. Anthony Weiner, the former New York congressman of sexting notoriety, was subjected to further humiliation because cartoonists depicted Weiner in "tighty-whities" in five of the seven cartoons showing him in underwear. Politicians dressed in their unmentionables offer a strong visual disconnect between the way a male public servant should appear in public (fully clothed and suited up) and how scandal actually devolves a politician's appearance within public view. He is stripped of his sartorial status and reduced to a man in his skivvies, harkening to the cultural trope—or nightmare—of appearing before a crowd in one's underwear.

In most of these underwear cases, the scandal-bereaved politician is drawn half dressed. In these instances, the politician dons some combination of a suit jacket, tie, and dress shirt with heart-decorated underwear covering his nether regions. The contrast reveals the politician's "authentic" sense of self through his exposed underwear. While he may play politico "dress-up" by throwing on a suit jacket, it cannot hide what's underneath—the heart-motif underwear showcasing his playboy ways. The underwear and

©Taylor Jones - all rights reserved.   caglecartoons.com

The cartoon "Weinerwear," by Taylor Jones, was published on June 2, 2011. (Courtesy of Cagle Cartoons)

suit dichotomy shows that the politician is attempting to maintain his slipping grasp on power following news of the scandal. For example, Bob Englehart's cartoon features a down-and-out Eliot Spitzer with a five-o'clock shadow coloring his face. His expression is steadfast, like a bulldog's, as he points to a sign at a podium that reads, "Client 9," referring to the alias that the prostitution ring, The Emperor's Club, delegated to the New York governor. His pants are on the floor around his ankles, and his bony and hairy knees poke out from his heart-adorned boxers. "That's Governor 9," asserts the embattled politician.[17] The governor may be down and out, and a ridiculous spectacle who is half dressed in this cartoon portrayal, but he deserves the respect his office demands, gosh darn it!

We see the same dynamic replicated in a cartoon about the John Edwards scandal, where cartoonist John Darkow features "Two Americas"[18] through two cartoon panels. In the first panel, we see an old woman with an angelic halo above her head. Her lips are closed but upturned. She is "the Faithful." In the next panel, we see John Edwards with his coiffed hair, his face overtaken by a disingenuous grin. He is dressed in a suit jacket, dress shirt, a tie, and heart-speckled boxer shorts. His "loverboy" boxer shorts send a clear message that Edwards is "the Not so Faithful." We see this phenomenon repeat itself with Anthony Weiner. Here, through Taylor Jones's cartoon representation,[19] the politician's dress shirt and tie cover his private parts (he's pants-less). The hair on his legs stands at attention and his knees are angling toward each other. The white tube socks reveal a less-than-trendy appearance. Where is his underwear? My goodness, the tighty-whities droop from his nose!

It is worth mentioning here the Anthony Weiner microtrend of the tighty-whitey. I just referenced the example where Weiner wears a dress shirt and tie while his white briefs dangle from his proboscis. In three other examples, the politician (actually) wears the tighty-whities around his loins where they belong, and in a fourth instance that underwear is used as the white flag of surrender to announce his resignation from office.[20] The tighty-whities are a riff on the photos that went viral during his scandal that featured "Not Safe For Work" "crotch shots" of Anthony Weiner's aroused package, barely contained by his briefs. While his underwear in these real-life sexts was grey in color[21] and was more boxer-brief than brief, the tighty-whitey cartoons show Weiner as a self- and genitals-obsessed, nerdy, unappealing person. For instance, in the cartoon "Anthony Weiner Forever,"[22] cartoonist Daryl Cagle features the politician peering into the contents of his white underwear, which include a miniature Weiner holding open his tighty-whities and doing the exact same thing. We see four Weiners, each one successively smaller but equally distracted by what his tighty-whities contain. The self-centered vanity represented here is a riff off of the politician who was caught in multiple rounds of sexting scandals. He, quite literally, cannot seem to keep his hands to himself or his thoughts off of his underwear and its contents.

The tighty-whitey subtheme also casts Weiner as a bit of a "jerk." In the first cartoon example, the politician is naked except for his (now) trademark white underwear and socks. He's taking a picture of his nether region. A black arrow points to his crotch and declares, "Joke." A second black arrow points to his upper body and categories the politician as "Jerk."[23] The cartoon undercuts Weiner's worth, taking aim at both his manhood and his character. In the second example, the politician's body is transformed into a hot dog—which is plainly overcooked. In fact, you might as well just "stick a fork in him," as the cartoon text instructs. The Weiner dog/Weiner politician is sizzling and dripping with grease. His tighty-whities (tacked onto the hotdog) are steaming as well.[24] Cartoons of politicians in their underwear conflate their character with their sexuality, positing one's manhood as a "joke" within the larger context of the politician as a "jerk."

METAPHORS IN SCANDAL CARTOONS: BILL CLINTON

A cartoon version of Bill Clinton appeared in six of the cartoons. While that number is not overwhelmingly impressive, it's worth visiting how his cartoon representations cement his role as the Grandfather of American political sex scandals, especially since none of the scandals actually involved Clinton but his metaphorical presence plays a noticeable role. A cartoon "Bill" appeared in three Mark Foley cartoons; one Eliot Spitzer cartoon; one John Edwards cartoon; and one Herman Cain cartoon. As the Scandal Don, his presence embodies both partisan schadenfreude and the occurrence of wayward sexual behavior in the nation's capital. Often depicted as an overly plump hedonist, cartoon "Bill" demonstrates that when it comes to scandal, he represents the point from which all other scandals spring. Let's take a closer look at his cartoon appearances in other people's scandals and what they mean.

Clinton as Hypocrite

In Gary McCoy's 2006 cartoon, "Acceptable to Democrats," Bill Clinton embodies the sexual hypocrisy of Democrats defending misbehavior if it involves one of their own.[25] The cartoon takes aim at the Mark Foley scandal, where the congressman admitted to acting inappropriately with teenage boys through electronic communication. In the first panel, we see a dorky-looking teen boy in a baseball hat, his face marked by freckles (or pimples?), at his computer. In the next panel, we see a woman's rear end—in a blue dress representative of Monica Lewinsky—sticking out from underneath a desk. President Bill Clinton is seated at the desk, a bold reference to the sexual relationship between intern and president. The cartoon states that in the eyes of Democrats, an "interaction with underage subordinate" is "unacceptable" when it involves the boy at his computer. But an "interaction with 'under-desk' subordinate" is "acceptable." In this cartoon, Clinton's bulbous face appears enormous—a fat nose protrudes from a fat face, and fat, pink lips reveal his hungry and licentious demeanor. The cartoon doesn't reveal why Democrats deem the interaction with a teen boy "unacceptable" but the interaction with a female intern "acceptable," yet one can reasonably deduce that the acceptable/unacceptable divide is determined by party allegiance. Both sets of behavior should be categorized as "unacceptable," but party ties prompt people to make excuses for their members. What remains clear is the well-fed and well-sexed appearance of Bill Clinton in a Mark Foley cartoon that makes no explicit mention of Mark Foley or offers any visual representation of Foley. Eight years after the media firestorm of Clinton's intern scandal, this cartoon represents an example of how he continued to embody the hypocrisy, overindulgence, and partisan schadenfreude of scandal.

Clinton as Liar

During his presidential campaign in 1992, Clinton notoriously said he tried marijuana but "didn't inhale."[26] That phrasing quickly became a national punchline, a shortcut to indicate—wink, wink—that a person engaged in illicit behavior but justified the action by saying that he or she only "partook" peripherally. Cartoonist John Cole visualizes this dynamic in his 2008 cartoon, "Edwards Affair"[27] to show the former presidential candidate as a liar and someone who's a bit cockamamie in the head. Cartoon Clinton looms over Edwards in size. He has a massive, rotund face with tiny, squinty eyes. Clinton is jolly as if nothing in politics should be taken seriously. "But I didn't inhale," reads his dialogue bubble. Next to him is a much smaller Edwards, nervous in appearance and dripping in sweat. His eyeballs appear as if they're about to pop out of his head. His grin is wide but unsteady—all chattering teeth on display, a stark contrast to the porky, self-assured Clinton. "And I didn't impregnate!" declares Edwards. It would take another two years (until 2010) for Edwards to admit that he fathered a child with his campaign videographer with whom he had an extramarital affair.[28] Nevertheless, back in 2008 when the cartoon appeared, Clinton's presence delegitimizes Edwards's claim that he "didn't impregnate" his mistress.

Clinton as Nonthreatening "Deviant"

Clinton's overall appearance in each of the cartoons as a rotund, over-sized man with bulbous facial features, squinty eyes, and a goofy grin lends the impression that he is your friendly, not-to-be-feared "deviant." Indeed, he is "Expert Deviant Bill" in the 2006 cartoon about Mark Foley by cartoonist Gary McCoy.[29] In this illustration, a donkey—emblematic of the Democratic Party—wears a white lab coat and holds a clipboard. The dialogue bubble above his head reads, "Mark Foley is a sexual deviant. It's even been confirmed by our resident expert on the subject." Who is this resident expert? Why it's an overly round Bill Clinton in a robe cinched at his ample waste! He holds a cigar in one hand and a copy of *Playboy* in the other, a cad who is more Hugh Hefner wannabe than former president. The message of the cartoon is that there are "sexual deviants" in both parties, and that while Democrats may be gleeful that it's a Republican caught in scandal this time around, Democrats are not a political party of sexual purists either. In this cartoon, Clinton is depicted as a lazy hedonist, enjoying his cigar (an allusion—of course—of how he turned it into a sexual device with his intern, Monica Lewinsky).

Clinton's goofy-guy persona is replicated in a cartoon about the Herman Cain scandal in 2011 by cartoonist Rick McKee.[30] In it, Clinton holds out a "pass for sexual harassment" to presidential candidate Herman Cain. Clinton is wearing a plaid suit jacket with a tie. His unbuckled pants are slouched around his ankles, revealing a pair of heart-stamped boxer shorts. He looks happy, with an open grin, a fat chin, and squinty eyes, lending the impression of a contently sated man. A lipstick kiss is planted on his cheek. "Oh, go on . . . take it! We Democrats have a ton of 'em!," says Clinton about the hall pass.

While emblematic of partisan schadenfreude and the pervasive nature of sexual impropriety across political parties, the Clinton metaphor also offers something uniquely him: a licentious but nonthreatening papa figure who is goofy, well fed, and appears as if he doesn't have a care in the world. His presence reinforces the nature of hypocrisy in scandal. Clinton possesses a "joie de vivre" in these cartoons, perhaps because his scandal—as iconic as it was—didn't succeed in toppling his presidency. While it certainly colored his legacy and defined parts of his presidency, Clinton himself has a Teflon toughness that, post-presidency, has allowed his own sex scandal to become more of a light-hearted joke and historical footnote than a deleterious and threatening phenomenon that delegitimized him.

FALTERING MASCULINITY IN SCANDAL CARTOONS

In an effort to catalogue how cartoonists take aim at scandal-tarnished politicians and how they skewer their masculinity and gender representation, I followed in the footsteps of cartoon scholar Janis L. Edwards. She investigated cartoon representations of politicians on the presidential trail in 2000 and came up with five leadership traits, but I wanted to identify other traits that were referenced repeatedly in scandal illustrations. After all, traits highlighted in scandal cartoons are representative of broader cultural stereotypes of the scandal-suffering politician. Speaking generally about cartoons and cultural norms, Michael A. DeSousa and Martin J. Medhurst, who've written extensively about the social implications of political cartoons, assert that "the cartoon generally functions not as a change agent, but as a statement of consensus, an invitation to render cultural values and beliefs and, by implication, to participate in their maintenance."[31] The predominant traits with which cartoonists categorize scandal-suffering politicians should make cultural sense to their readers, enforcing broader notions of how we think about these politicians. After all, assert DeSousa and Medhurst, "The cartoonist does not create from whole cloth, but, instead, articulates a frame from the artist's unique percept to the shared experiences of the readers."[32]

In order to catalogue these character traits in scandal cartoons, I began by searching for ways that cartoonists represented the scandal-suffering politician. A pattern quickly emerged through a constant comparison method of all cartoons. The top scandal traits are included in table 3.2.

I determined the character traits in scandal cartoons by the following criteria:

Ignorant to demise: References to politician's narcissism and inability to see that his campaign or political stature has taken a hit in the wake of scandal

Idiot: References to the politician as a goof of the highest order; as ignorant, stupid, or dumb to his situation; and blissfully unaware of the missteps that landed him in this scandal

Down and Out: References to the politician as disheveled, dazed, and out of sorts; unkempt

Prompts disgust/outrage: References to the politician as prompting disgust or outrage from other characters in the cartoon, including bystanders and political figures

Hypocrite: References to the politician as disingenuous, lacking integrity, and preaching one thing but acting in a contrary manner.

Before taking a more in-depth look at each of the scandal's traits, one needs to explore the reasons why two politicians—Herman Cain and Anthony Weiner—received more cartoon attention (see table 3.1) and therefore were coded more frequently in terms of scandal traits than their counterparts. The Pew Research Center reported in December 2011 that President Barack Obama represented the top newsmaker that year.[33] Meanwhile, presidential contender Herman Cain's ongoing sexual harassment scandal made him the third top newsmaker of 2011, with Anthony Weiner in the 10th slot. Additionally, Pew reported that Cain represented the most covered presidential candidate by the news media in

Table 3.2   Traits of Scandal-Suffering Politicians

Trait	Number of Cartoons with These Traits
Ignorant to demise	42
Idiot	32
Down and out	23
Prompts disgust/outrage	21
Hypocrite	19

2011—in advance of the 2012 presidential elections—with Weiner the most covered Democrat following Obama.[34] The Cain sexual harassment scandal was repeatedly in the news in fall 2011. Indeed, negative news coverage about him typically represented the top story for weeks in a row in November of that year.[35] His scandal represented the lead story in all media sectors, including cable, network, radio, and online news.[36] During Anthony Weiner's scandal in June 2011, the Pew Research Center reported that Americans followed stories about the economy and Weiner's resignation more than any other stories that month.[37] It's clear that the intensive media coverage and public interest contributed to the prolific cartoon treatment of Cain and Weiner.

It's worth noting that John Edwards—the presidential candidate mired in scandal coverage in 2008—didn't receive nearly the same number of cartoon representations as Herman Cain did. A simple explanation can be that John Edwards dropped out of the presidential race in January 2008. He didn't admit to his affair until the following summer, when he was no longer in elected office nor running for office.[38]

EVALUATING THE SCANDAL-TARNISHED POLITICIANS

Ignorant to His Demise

This trait was not spread evenly across all politicians. Cartoonists depicted Herman Cain as the most intractable politician with his drawn-out scandal, followed by Anthony Weiner, Larry Craig, and Eliot Spitzer (see table 3.3). The remaining politicians received a smattering of this trait—if at all. This trait paints the offending politician as hanging onto the last manifestations of his power and position, lacking self-awareness to such a degree that it's over even as the court of public opinion and members of the media have long declared it so. Political failure is a foregone conclusion, clear to all except the politician himself. This disconnect, perhaps fueled by narcissism or a general refusal by the politician that he can't right the ship, exposes a sharp contrast between the politician's presumed handle on the scandal situation—and his hopes to overcome it—with the actuality that it is not surmountable. For each of the politicians mentioned here, his ignorance regarding his dire situation is noticeable because each politician did end up succumbing to the drumbeat of his political collapse in the end:

- Herman Cain ended his presidential campaign in December 2011 due to the onslaught of sexual harassment charges against him.

Table 3.3 Number of Cartoons Featuring Each Scandal Trait per Politician

Scandal	Ignorant to Demise	Idiot	Prompts Disgust/ Outrage	Down and Out	Hypocrite	Total Number of Scandal Traits
Mark Foley					1	1
David Vitter	1			1	1	3
Larry Craig	7	3	1	1	3	14
Eliot Spitzer	3	5	1	6	6	21
David Paterson		1				1
John Edwards	1	2	2	2	3	10
Mark Sanford			2	1	1	4
Eric Massa		1				1
Mark Souder					1	1
Chris Lee			1			1
Herman Cain	20	2	5	3		30
Anthony Weiner	11	18	10	7	3	49
No. of cartoons with this trait	**42**	**32**	**23**	**21**	**19**	

- Anthony Weiner resigned from Congress in June 2011 in the immediate media frenzy surrounding his sext-tweets, and he lost in the 2013 primaries during his run for mayor of New York City.[39]
- Larry Craig of bathroom sex-solicitation notoriety announced his resignation and then decided that he would not resign immediately but would not seek reelection in 2008.
- Eliot Spitzer resigned from office only days after news broke that he had sex with prostitutes.

Regardless of the politician's eventual resignation or acknowledgment that the scandal had overtaken his political aspirations, cartoonists depicted these politicians as ignorant to the damage that their respective scandals wrecked on their "brand."

In political cartoons, Larry Craig is depicted as an oblivious tap dancer. He's dancing a jig with "jazz hands" and needs to be yanked off stage by the stage manager. The tap dancing references his alleged foot tapping in an airport bathroom stall to gain the sexual attention of a man in the next stall, a man who turned out to be an undercover cop. The tap dancing and jazz hands also take aim at, and mock, Craig's sexual identity. Craig has adamantly denied being gay, despite being arrested and charged with a disorderly-conduct misdemeanor after his alleged sex-solicitation of another man.[40] In the police interview transcript following the incident, Craig tells the arresting officer, "I am not gay; I don't do these kinds of things."[41] He publicly reiterates this point at his televised press conference two months after his arrest, with his wife standing next to him. He states, "Let me be clear: I am not gay. I never have been gay."[42] Nevertheless, the cartoonists ignored Craig's assertions by depicting him as a tap-dancing, jazz-hands performer who refuses to exit stage right.[43] He is, quite clearly, ignorant to his demise; the curtain has descended because, for him, the show is over.

In contrast to Craig's jazz hands and tap-dancing feet, Eliot Spitzer appears gruff and tough. He is afforded a more masculine depiction because of the distinctly heterosexual nature of his scandal. Indeed, the New York media covered with glee the slinky, pouty social-media and personal photos of Ashley Dupré, a prostitute who had sex with Spitzer. Regardless of his gruffness, cartoonists still painted Spitzer as a man ignorant to his demise. "I am shocked! Shocked! To discover federal prosecutors in my private life!," says Spitzer, lying in a bed surrounded by the American and New York State flags as TV cameras capture his startled expression.[44]

The "ignorance" of Craig and Spitzer, however, pales in comparison to Herman Cain and Anthony Weiner, according to cartoonists. Depiction after depiction showed Cain and Weiner refusing to grasp the severity of their scandal situations. Cain is depicted making excuses, declaring victory, unsure why his campaign is even faltering; he's in denial and downplays the severity of his sexual advances toward women.[45] In one cartoon, Cain stands at a podium addressing women angrily pointing at him, saying, "Ladies, ladies! Please stop harassing me, so I can continue my campaign."[46] The presidential candidate is clearly oblivious to the harm that these "ladies" have caused his character and campaign. It's worth noting that while Herman Cain is black, only one of his 41 political cartoons makes direct reference to race.[47]

Like Cain, Anthony Weiner cartoons show the politician attempting to persevere despite public and media consensus that his candidacy has deflated. Weiner is shown as someone who keeps sexting long after he should have stopped; as someone uninterested in altering his behavior;

and as someone thinking—wrongly!—that he has the situation under control, that he can make it right, and that the public will give him a second chance.[48] For instance, cartoonist Christopher Weyant depicts the politician as encased in a hot dog (complete with bun and mustard) that is larger than his body. Weiner holds up a sign, tiny in comparison to the oversized hotdog, that reads, "Integrity."[49] It's clear that Weiner's private parts—and what he's done with them—overshadow any attempt at damage control. The politician is ignorant to his own demise even as the public and media long since have cemented their damaging views of him.

Idiot/Goof

Cartoonists lampoon politicians as idiots, as goofs of the highest order, as nincompoops whose scandals are indicative of their idiot status, or as louts whose idiocy awkwardly manifests itself in their handling of the scandal fallout. The idiot/goof traits are not evenly distributed across all scandal cases. Anthony Weiner receives the brunt of cartoonists' scathing critique as a world-class idiot. But he has company. For instance, Eliot Spitzer is an idiot who wears an "I Love New York" thong upside down on his head, so that his forehead looks like butt cheeks poking through the underwear.[50] He is also a moral crusader, decked out in a knight's body armor despite having forgotten to close his zipper[51] and put on pants.[52] Larry Craig, as previously described, is the tap-dancing goof who doesn't acknowledge his own demise. Once he does clarify that he will leave the political system by serving the remainder of his term without seeking reelection, he is depicted as moving at a snail's pace toward leaving political office. Quite literally, a miniscule snail pulls Craig on a skateboard as Democrats and Republicans alike cheer his exit.[53] Herman Cain is the idiot with a paper bag over his head as he addresses the public, offering every possible excuse for his behavior, and he is the martyr who—literally—shoots himself in the foot with a pistol to show that he is the victim of character assassination.[54] Eric Massa is an idiot addressing the media, with a crew of Massa clones behind him, all whispering different reasons why he is leaving office.[55] And finally, Anthony Weiner is, perhaps, the ultimate idiot who can't keep his underwear on, can't take responsibility for taking it off, can't stop photographing his private parts, and can't figure out the way privacy settings work on social media—and he doesn't even get the benefits of an actual physical encounter with his paramours.[56] He is, according to cartoonist John Cole, "the hyperloon."[57]

Prompts Disgust/Outrage

A number of cartoon illustrations featured unnamed and unknown figures—stand-ins for everyday American civilians—reacting with disgust and outrage to the scandal-tarnished politician and details of his sordid behavior. Anthony Weiner cartoons prompted more disgust and outrage than any other politician, with remaining cases scattered equally throughout other scandals. Some of these cartoons play with the object of disgust, linking public reaction not to Anthony Weiner's nudie texts but to things like the federal budget. "Eww!" shriek two women in RJ Matson's cartoon, "More Indecent Exposure." "Some Congressman just exposed his big federal budget cuts on Twitter!" Another echoes her horror: "What was he thinking?!"[58] In a related example, a curvy young woman looks at her phone and reacts in revulsion at what is on the screen. "That's horrible!" she declares. In the corner of the panel, we see a deflated, confused President Obama. "Strange," he says, "Anthony told me chicks dig this stuff," as he snaps a photo with his phone of a large document titled "Obamacare."[59] In a separate example, a cartoon Mark Sanford appears shocked and cowed when a middle-aged man representing the state of South Carolina (as emblazoned on his t-shirt) screams, "You can take that 'hike' now!" in reference to Sanford's excuse for his disappearance, that he was hiking the Appalachian Trail, when he was really frolicking with his paramour in Argentina.[60]

Down and Out

This trait shows politicians not so much regretting the behavior that landed them in the scandal swamp in the first place, but as down on their luck, "shlumpy," and unkempt in their physical appearance. For the "down-and-out" theme, politicians have become resigned to their reduced standing. Expressions are downturned, faces feature five-o'clock shadows, and postures reveal rounded shoulders. The politician oozes matter-of-fact chagrin. RJ Matson depicts this dynamic in "What I Did on My Summer Vacation," which shows an elephant—emblematic of the Republican Party—arriving in an airport terminal. He runs into a buttoned-up donkey, a Democrat. The Republican elephant's pants are unzipped. A long elephant snout hangs out of his zipper, emblematic of the penis. "Don't ask," says the elephant.[61] Moving beyond the metaphorical, cartoonists depict Eliot Spitzer as covered in facial stubble;[62] John Edwards in a garbage can surrounded by flies;[63] Sanford a crying mess;[64] Herman Cain with chickens squatting on his head (representing sexual harassment allegations that have literally "come home to roost"),[65] and Anthony Weiner as a sullen, shlumpy, skinny—and often decrepit—man.[66]

Hypocrisy

Hypocrisy in scandal cartoons—as elsewhere—reveals the double-sided nature of politicians as a distinct flaw in their character DNA. The hypocrisy trait was lightly sprinkled throughout most cases. There was hypocrisy on the level of the political party, with Clinton's Oval Office sexual exploits deemed "acceptable" (perhaps because they involved a female intern who was of consenting age), while Congressman Mark Foley's online sexting scandal—which didn't involve actual touching but did involve explicit messages to underage congressional male pages—was considered "unacceptable" by Democrats.[67] Cartoonists also lampooned the Republican double standard with the Larry Craig and David Vitter scandals. When Vitter had sex with female prostitutes, it became a case of "boys will be boys." Yet when Craig attempted sex solicitation with another man, the Republican Party reacted with a panicked, "BOYS? BOYS?" and ran in fear from Craig.[68] Meanwhile, a cartoon depiction of President George W. Bush (who was president during the Larry Craig and David Vitter scandals) shows him echoing former Iranian president Mahmoud Ahmadinejad, who once notoriously declared that there were "no homosexuals" in Iran. "We don't have homosexuals in GOP!" declares cartoon Bush.[69] The hypocrisy trait also is lobbed at scandal-tarnished politicians. Eliot Spitzer, according to cartoonist John Cole, cleaned up New York, "By meeting my prostitutes out-of-state!"[70] And a Democratic donkey declared with glee that "I'm with holier-than-thou hypocrite Christian adulterer," referring to then governor Mark Sanford as embodied by an irate elephant (with its pants around its knees, revealing heart-decorated boxer shorts).[71] Cartoonist Nate Beeler took aim at then congressman Mark Souder's hypocrisy for having an affair with a female staffer while simultaneously espousing a conservative Christian philosophy on extramarital sex, by depicting the congressman as saying: "America's teens should abstain from sex until marriage . . . That holy . . . Eternal . . . Neverending . . . Joyless bond between one man and one woman who is not a congressional staffer."[72] Whether on the party or individual level, hypocrisy allowed cartoonists to easily fillet the double standard that politicians created for themselves.

CARTOON DEPICTION OF POLITICAL WIVES

Political wives were shown in eight cartoons. They were portrayed as tough, shrill, angry, conniving, and superior to their "goofy idiot" husbands. In cartoon, Hillary Clinton wears oversized male suit pants, while her husband and Eliot Spitzer stand undressed in heart-decorated boxer shorts;[73] Silda Spitzer belies her calm, supportive presence at her husband's press conference announcing his resignation from political office in a cartoon that shows her chasing him with a knife into the shadows;[74] Elizabeth Edwards stands confidently with her arms crossed across her chest, declaring her toothy-grinned husband "swine;"[75] Gloria Cain is reduced to a bunch of irate symbols, emanating from a cell phone, indicating her ire directed at her husband. A staffer says "Mr. Cain, sir, It's Mrs. Cain. She wants you to feel her pain."[76] Jenny Sanford calls her philandering-traveling husband a "tramp" and orders him to "Take another hike!" upon his return from Argentina;[77] Huma Abedin—Anthony Weiner's wife at the time of the 2011 and 2013 scandals; she announced her separation from him in 2016 following a third round of sexts—is the victim of his rampant sexting when he opens her pants to take a snap. "I need to expand my voter base," he tells her.[78] And then there's the single instance of two political wives cast as conspiring together. Huma Abedin has served as Hillary Clinton's longtime advisor. Abedin first began working for Clinton as her intern in 1996.[79] So it's no surprise that the news media—and cartoonists by extension—further connected the women since both have suffered through the public and high-profile philandering of their political spouses. "You know, Huma," a cartoon Hillary confides to her younger confidante, "In a perfect world, women would rule, and their men would be eunuchs."[80] Huma Abedin's toothy grin in Taylor Jones's cartoon indicates acceptance of her mentor's articulated utopia. (This cartoon takes on heightened meaning in retrospect because e-mails belonging to Abedin were found on Weiner's computer during the 2016 presidential election, prompting the FBI to reopen the previously closed case about the (mis)use of Hillary Clinton's private e-mail server. Law enforcement officials found those emails during an unrelated investigation into Weiner's sexually explicit exchanges with a 15-year-old girl in North Carolina.)[81]

The cartoon depictions of political wives, as a cohort, serve to further diminish and humiliate the offending politician, but this doesn't make them likable. Instead, the wife is a piler-on, heaping insults onto the idiot/goof of a husband-politician who prompts outrage and disgust among those around him. Just because the cartoonist derides the scandal-politician and depicts the wife as kicking him while he's down doesn't mean the wife comes across as either sympathetic or likable. Cartoon scholar Janis L. Edwards found in her 2007 study of the genre that "traditional sex-role expectations are heightened in these cartoons, as cartoonists routinely 'discipline' political wives for transgressing the boundaries of their subordinate roles by speaking out on just about any subject."[82] While Edwards did not write in the context of scandal—where one could reasonably presume that a humiliated political wife might be granted some slack by cartoonists—I found that wives were leant no sympathetic illustration.

MAKING SENSE OF HOW CARTOONS "DO" GENDER

A man created each of the 136 cartoons that I analyzed for this chapter. It wasn't hard to figure out. Traditionally masculine names like Adam and Bob and John and Gary populated their bylines. In the two instances where a cartoonist boasted a possibly gender-neutral first name—such as Taylor and RJ—a quick Google search revealed them to be male. In a field that is overwhelmingly dominated by men, "Ideal masculinity is defined in opposition to what is feminine," writes Edwards. And, by extension, "Ascribing female characteristics to a male candidate is a reliable way to debunk his suitability" for office.[83] But when I examined cartoons within a specific scandal focus, I did not find cartoonists ascribing feminine traits as a way to castrate scandal-tarnished politicians. Instead, the scandal traits that emerged cast them as lesser males, faltering in their masculine status—not because they were acting in a feminine manner but because they were acting overwhelmingly as idiots. Indeed, if we take the five traits that emerged in scandal cartoons and flip the traits so they are defined by their opposites, we see the emergence of ideal male traits. In this way, "Ignorant to demise"—when flipped—is self-awareness. "Idiot/goof"—when flipped—is intelligent. The opposite of "Down and out" is smart in appearance and maintaining control. The opposite of "Hypocrisy" is integrity. And when you flip "Prompts outrage/disgust," you suddenly have respect and admiration. Therefore, if we consider only the flipped traits, we have quite clearly a list of ideal masculine traits for any man, including politicians:

- Demonstrating self-awareness
- Possessing intelligence
- Exhibiting a clean-cut and handsome appearance
- Possessing integrity
- Demanding respect and admiration

Ultimately, cartoonist representations of scandal-pocked politicians show these politicians as faltering men who fail to uphold their ideal masculine traits of character. Instead of possessing self-awareness, intelligence, a handsome appearance, integrity, and respect, they are ignorant of their social standing, idiots, down and out, hypocrites, and disgusting. While they are still portrayed as men, they are not masculine. They are bad-news fellas who are ill-suited for political leadership. They are laughingstocks.

Political wives, by contrast, are not direct subjects of cartoon ire because they were not caught in scandals themselves. Regardless, they make a limited, supporting-role appearance. They are presented in a wife-specific manner that is straight out of central casting: shrill in tone, angry in demeanor, piling on trouble for an already burdened husband-politician, and conniving for their own aspirations. This depiction, while stereotypic, at least provides an alternate portrayal of political wives as a cohort that unwavering "stands by their man," a theme I will explore in depth in chapter 5.

Ultimately, the politicians' biggest liability—as depicted in scandal cartoons—is not the fact that they engaged in behavior that is unscrupulous but that such behavior revealed masculine-degrading traits of slovenliness and idiocy that elicited public revulsion. Cartoonists quite literally stripped offending politicians down to their briefs, to humiliate them in betrayal of their position and their power. With a few artfully maneuvered pen strokes, cartoonists helped the public see that when the emperor has no clothes, no amount of bravado or posturing can help cover up the idiocy of his actions.

CHAPTER 4

When Mistresses Become Media Starlets: The Ascension of the Political Sex-Scandal Celebrity

Unlike the ignorance and goofy "idiocy" that defined cartoon representations of politicians in the previous chapter, news coverage of two prominent scandal mistresses revealed a Yin and Yang dual identity for each woman. Articles in the *New York Post* and *New York Daily News* painted Ashley Dupré (a prostitute involved with now former New York governor Eliot Spitzer) and Sydney Leathers (a woman who sexted with now former New York congressman Anthony Weiner) as "slutty shape-shifters." In news coverage, both women possessed the same character traits: women who had strayed from their formerly wholesome roots to become conniving and sexual troublemakers.

Similar to an analysis of political cartoons, an examination of newspaper tabloid coverage of these women offers a glimpse into broader cultural values and norms in highly readable, entertaining—albeit reductive—form. The *New York Post* and the *New York Daily News* both quickly depicted these women as caricatures in their respective scandal stories. The type under investigation in this chapter is reflective of a familiar cultural character—the scandal mistress as exploitative, self-involved, self-destructive, and ultimately damaging to others—a gold digger in the truest sense of the word. Her worth can be measured only by the physical and visual value that men extract from her.

Media scholar S. Elizabeth Bird uses a "hall of mirrors" metaphor to connect tabloids to a broader culture and the character types found within. "The suggestion here is that cultural phenomena are indeed interconnected, but that each does not exist in some objective space. Rather, everything reflects off everything else in ever-repeating images."[1] In other words, the way in which *New York Post* and *New York Daily*

News stories paint Dupré and Leathers mirrors and enforces the social stereotype of a scandal mistress. But a closer examination of both women in these publications shows a nuance that, once revealed, is inescapable: the woman who actively seeks the spotlight in the midst of this media frenzy is mocked and torn to pieces. Yet the one who does not grant interviews to these publications in the immediate aftermath of scandal—but chooses to wait for the storm to pass, seeking to balance the media's interest in her as a one-dimensional sexpot with her own aspirations for a life not categorically defined by sex—is cast as the more desirable and less desperate scandal mistress. Leathers's eager interaction with the news media made her unattractive to them, and they punished her for it—which will be made clear in this chapter. In contrast, Dupré only granted a brief interview to the *New York Times* as the scandal unfolded in March 2008.[2] Besides that, she was mum for the time being as related to official media channels. Eventually, Dupré would grant high-profile interviews to *People* magazine and Diane Sawyer on ABC's *20/20*, but by then it was November 2008, and eight months passed since the story broke about her role in Governor Eliot Spitzer's resignation. Dupré had a chance by then to cast herself anew as a mistress worth listening to, ensuring a certain level of intrigue mixed with the already established notoriety, unlike Leathers, who had little new to offer media producers and consumers because she was repeatedly in the news. Spitzer's and Weiner's respective sexual ties to the come-hither Dupré and the social-climbing Leathers did not boost their likability among the public or media mavens. In fact, their connections to these "other women" only succeeded in further demoting the politicians as "idiots," even in the case of Spitzer, who cavorted with a sultry, in-demand prostitute. What we see in news coverage of Spitzer and Weiner, throughout the pages and photo spreads of the *New York Post* and *New York Daily News*, is a parade of clowns, reminiscent of the popularly recurring theme of political cartoons ("Idiot"). As a refresher from chapter 3 on political cartoons, I categorized cartoons under an "Idiot" theme if they referred to a scandal-suffering politician as a goof of the highest order—ignorant, stupid, or dumb to his situation. Similarly, it was not uncommon for the *New York Post* and the *New York Daily News* to place unflattering photographs of scandal-suffering politicians next to the women they pursued. Ultimately, these newspapers offer a dynamic where the hot "other woman," who is hesitant about her suddenly public position, is considered more alluring than the fame-chasing scandal starlet who freely mocks the politician that brought her notoriety in the first place. And Weiner and Spitzer, regardless of their assignations to the hot-or-not women, are depicted, plainly, as dopey losers. For the women, it's a simple metaphor of prostitution: if you pursue media coverage, you're prostituting yourself and the public may enjoy you for some no-strings fun. But they will never take you seriously. The irony is that Dupré, who shunned early coverage of her scandal role, actually worked as a prostitute. Meanwhile, Leathers—who never even met Weiner (let alone had sex with him)—pursued media placement. For the politicians, there is no dichotomy. News reports saw them only as targets to be devoured through persistent mockery of their manhood, their political ambitions, and their decrepit track record as husbands.

THE NEWSPAPERS

The *New York Post* and *New York Daily News* are based in "the city that never sleeps," and their daily circulations rank them as among the top 10 print newspapers with the highest circulations in the United States. The daily circulation for the *New York Daily News* is 338,944 and the *New York Post's* is 262,570, which places them 7th and 10th, respectively, according to 2014 data.[3] Known for their boldface, double-entendre headlines in all capitalized letters and photographs of underdressed women, the *New York Post* and *New York Daily News* pursued stories on Dupré and Leathers with unrestrained enthusiasm. For these tabloids that trade in caricatures, it was clearly the case of the sluts versus the (politico) *schlubs*. A Lexis-Nexis search of "Ashley Dupré" and "Sydney Leathers" for the year of each scandal, 2008 and 2013, respectively, revealed 75 stories in the *New York Post* and *New York Daily News* on Leathers and 32 stories on Dupré. The difference in the number of stories for each woman can be attributed to the fact that Leathers aspired to—and did—become a media personality, with an active Twitter account and foray into the adult industry, and readily spoke to news reporters. Meanwhile, Dupré generally did not grant interviews or establish herself as a public personality during the year of the Spitzer scandal.

THE WOMEN

Sydney Leathers, a 22-year-old from Indiana when the sexting scandal broke, is part of the second iteration of the Anthony Weiner scandals, this one occurring in 2013. As background, in 2011 Weiner resigned his New York congressional seat after admitting to sending sexts and illicit photos to young women via Twitter. Weiner returned to the public stage in May 2013 when he announced his candidacy for New York City mayor. That

summer, his sexts with Leathers—which began in the summer of 2012—
were published on thedirty.com, a gossip website as its name so implies.

Weiner and Leathers—their last names alone are enough to make them
fated to each other—became acquainted on Facebook in 2012, a year after
his resignation from Congress. News accounts vary about who reached
out to the other first. Regardless, their online romance, fueled by "kinky
messaging, steamy phone sex, and mutual declarations of love," was soon
initiated.[4] But it was not meant to be. The summer romance had fizzled by
fall. Contact between them ceased until April 2013, when Weiner needed
those hot texts deleted—and stat—with his pending mayoral announce-
ment. "Do me a solid," Weiner messaged Leathers. "Can you hard delete
all our chat here?"[5] Leathers said "yes." But what she really meant was
"no." Leathers ultimately released their chats to thedirty.com and vaulted
herself into the scandal stratosphere as a media sensation and personality as well as a Twitter presence—with upwards of 20,000 followers. The
attention and exposure accelerated her career as an adult film star. But
before the rise of her celebrity, there were the sexts themselves, her entrée
into a world of notoriety. Weiner's sexts are—in the words of one *New
York Post* writer—"enough to make a porn star blush."[6] The married former congressman messaged his online paramour, describing a fantasy: "I
slide my c—k in you slow at first, then harder my b—s are slapping your
a—. With each thrust you squeal a little. I start to f—k you so hard your
t-ts almost hit your face. You reach behind and spread you a—."[7] With the
release of the sexts, Leathers roared onto the public scene as an eager and
frequent media presence, offering her uncensored opinion about Weiner
as a terrible person, husband, and politician. She chided him publicly
with glee. "The part that's most annoying is that I was 22 years old and in
a bad place, but if anyone asked him he would say the same thing about
himself, yet he's an adult."[8]

Ashley Dupré, from New Jersey, also was 22 years old. She was an aspiring pop singer who used MySpace to showcase her musical repertoire
when the scandal broke, which immediately "outed" her as a prostitute
whose regular client was New York governor Eliot Spitzer. Yet interactions
between Dupré and Spitzer were presumably very different from Leathers's
"relationship" with Weiner. One may assume that while physically sexual
together, Dupré and Spitzer had a business agreement. Dupré was paid for
her sex work with Governor Spitzer—a reported $1,000 per hour.[9] She
contracted work with a company, although an illicit one, known as The
Emperor's Club. There were no personal text messages shared between
the two, at least none that media outlets could get their hands on. Dupré
might have sought wealth and riches, as many news accounts described

her motivations for working as a prostitute, but none described her as *fame-seeking* or as exploiting her involvement in a politician's downfall to ascend the celebrity ladder. In the wake of the scandal, Dupré did not grant media interviews—except one to the *New York Times*, where she was quoted in an article published the day after Spitzer's resignation as saying: "I just don't want to be thought of as a monster."[10] Dupré was not charged with any crime. Nor did she construct a public personality immediately post-scandal. Instead, she tried to manage her existing profiles on social media, such as MySpace and Facebook, while under a barrage of media and public interest. While Dupré's MySpace account gained significant traffic in the scandal aftermath from a curious public and a devouring media, her only allusion to the scandal were the words "Yeah, I did it,"[11] which she posted to her account on the day the scandal broke in March 2008. Her Facebook account was a private one. In an attempt to manage the scandal fallout, Dupré asked members of a Facebook page devoted to her high school class, "Do me a favor and don't try to cash out . . . thanks."[12] In fact, in the scandal aftermath, Dupré vacillated between deleting her social media accounts and then reactivating them, leaving CNN to ask two days after the governor's resignation, "So does Dupré want the attention that comes along with this scandal or not?" (As if a person who is vaulted into a jarring international spotlight should know how to handle this highly unusual—and unwelcome—experience with certainty and aplomb.)

As for a Twitter presence, Dupré didn't have one until March 2009, according to her own Twitter account (@AshleyDupré), which hardly comes as a surprise. After all, only 300,000 tweets were sent daily the year of the Spitzer scandal in 2008. By the time Leathers burst onto the (social media) scene in 2013, upwards of 500 million tweets were sent each day, and she was an active contributor to that eye-popping number, a willing participant in the world of social media—just like Weiner, whose careless social media postings initiated his political demise.[13]

It's not just the nature of (social) media that's a marked difference between these two political sex scandals, both rooted in New York and both involving 22-year-olds as the "other women" to married politicians. Nor is it the difference in whether the illicit relationships were actually physically consummated. When it comes to media exposure involving Dupré and Leathers, a key difference lies in the extent to which they divulged private details of their sexual encounters with their respective politicians. Although Leathers never actually had physical contact with Anthony Weiner, nor even met him, she was readily forthcoming to the media about their online and on-the-phone sexual interactions.

And Weiner was found wanting in his sexual skills, according to Leathers. "[He] would orgasm in 30 seconds,"[14] and "he would get off and she would be [left] hanging."[15] Weiner was incessant, desperate, and insatiable in his sexual needs, calling Leathers "five times a day to have phone sex"[16]—or, by other news accounts, "talking sometimes twice a day,"[17] or even a mere occurrence of "at least twice a week."[18] That information was part of her scandal currency, the carrot she dangled before a hungry media horde—before they collectively turned around to beat her with the stick once they were sated with the snack she offered. In comparison, Dupré divulged no sexual details about her encounters with New York's 54th governor, just the admission on her MySpace page that "yeah, I did it," which she quickly changed to "thank you all for your support, it means a lot to me."[19] She had much personal firsthand information about her paramour to offer the salivating media, but she wasn't playing that game—at least not in the scandal's immediate aftermath. No doubt she had legal ramifications to consider during the federal investigation that shuttered the Emperor's Club following the Spitzer scandal.

What united these two women, at least in terms of news coverage, is the dichotomy of *good girl* versus *money-grabbing prostitute* that exists in *New York Post* and *New York Daily News* articles, yet this is hardly a new trope.[20] To historicize their role in a long lineup of political sex-scandal mistresses, let us first visit the construction of "media whores" and female publicity within the political-scandal genre before proceeding with a media analysis of Dupré and Leathers specifically.

FEMALE PUBLICITY IN SEX SCANDALS

Sociologist Joshua Gamson offers an incisive historical review, dating back to the 19th century, of various mistresses whose sexual connections to high-profile men in the United States seized media attention. That list won't be reviewed here, because it's worth reading Gamson in the original. But I will emphasize his point that "in the midst of remarkable change in gender structures and the movement of feminist ideologies into the mainstream of American life, [scandal mistresses] . . . have skitted along musty virgin-whore and victim-vamp axes that have gone almost nowhere for centuries."[21] Gamson in 2001 pinpointed the gendered connection between female sexuality, publicity, and notoriety, which continues to hold true today. His argument represents a useful template for analyzing the media-shy prostitute Ashley Dupré, as the more desirable "scandal icon,"[22] and Sydney Leathers, the sexting star who did not have actual sex with Anthony Weiner but "prostitutes" herself nevertheless as she "cashes in on her notoriety."[23] According to Gamson:

> A woman who enjoyed the limelight, these stories began to imply, was a woman who employed and enjoyed sex; women's celebrity pursuit itself, even when sex was not directly used to get there, was analogous to prostitution. The role of female "innocent," or victim of male sexual aggression, became less available the more a woman was shown to find pleasure in fame.[24]

Perhaps it's no coincidence, then, that news accounts never described Leathers, who appeared to seek and embrace her scandal notoriety, as an "innocent." Let us now take a look at *New York Post* and *New York Daily News* coverage of these two scandal mistresses.

Ashley Dupré

How did this "wholesome" woman, who one year prior to the 2008 scandal was "planning a traditional Catholic wedding to the man of her dreams," become so "secretive?" So ponders an article in the *New York Post* less than one week after Eliot Spitzer resigned the governorship.[25] A second *Post* article, published the same day, argues that even as an alleged "party person," Dupré led a secretive life. As the "high-priced hooker" who was partial to "boozing it up" with men in finance, her party pals were unaware of her lucrative and illicit profession. "She's a nice person," a hedge fund manager said of Dupré. "I had no idea she was a high-priced call girl."[26] Implicit in his statement is that a nice person can't be a prostitute, or that if he was aware that she was a prostitute, he wouldn't consider her to be so nice. A woman who socialized with Dupré said that her profession "never occurred to us." And another man in the finance industry who knows Dupré offered this backhanded compliment: "She's got her heart in the right place, but maybe not her head."[27] A different acquaintance took a more hard-line approach. This unidentified source described Dupré's sartorial choices on the club scene as a dead giveaway to her nighttime profession: "She was wearing a silk shirt as a dress. You could see every body part. She looked like a hooker."[28] This article encapsulates the push-pull dynamic presenting Dupré as the sweet young woman gone awry who also is a duplicitous prostitute out for financial gain. The two descriptions are incompatible.

Another *Post* article echoed the Dupré duality, arguing that "two alternate pictures are emerging of Ashley. In one, she's a survivor—of abuse, homelessness, and drug abuse . . . In another version, she's a spoiled brat

Ashley Dupré attends a restaurant grand opening in Los Angeles in 2011, three years after the Eliot Spitzer scandal dragged her into the national spotlight. (AP Photo/Rex Features)

whose stepdad bought her a Porsche that she wrecked. So she ran away from home at 17."[29] When the scandal broke, Dupré's grandfather told reporters who came to his New Jersey home that his grandchild is "very nice. She's a beautiful girl."[30] Yet the same article quotes a pimp who employed Dupré in 2005 and sampled the goods for sale: "This was probably the sexiest, hottest girl I had." Of her work as a prostitute, the pimp said: "She thrived on it, like a fish in water."[31] This duality of a beautiful innocent versus a sex-crazed wild-child mimics Dupré's double identity as a prostitute where she donned aliases ("Victoria" and "Kristen") during work hours as an escort. Even her last name of "Dupré" represents a double identity, since she was born with the last name "Youmans."[32] So who's the real Ashley? The good girl—or the money-seeking prostitute?

Making good use of her new it-girl status, Dupré "steps out at hot club" for her 23rd birthday, less than two months after the scandal.[33] Is she a typical young woman looking to have fun or a hypersexed wild child? The article paints her as both. She wears a hoodie and wants to "stay inconspicuous" in the club but she still manages to turn heads in her sweatshirt that's "three sizes too small, and also, her boobs were popping out,"[34] which generated long stares from club goers. She is uncertain about how to bask in this limelight. "Dupré couldn't seem to make up her mind about wanting attention—alternately hiding behind her hoodie and getting up on the back of her banquette and waving her arms."[35]

The "Luv Gov" prostitute scandal turned Ashley Dupré into a celebrity, at least in New York. She is "suddenly turning up everywhere," according to the *New York Post*, much to the chagrin of other entertainment celebrities who do not like having their VIP sections invaded by a scandal mistress.[36] The negative attention from the scandal did have an upside for Dupré: attention to her musical aspirations, which is what brought her to New York City in the first place. Two of her recorded pop songs, which she placed online, made "an estimated $200,000" and were downloaded 300,000 times by a curious public only three days after Spitzer resigned as New York governor.[37] It wasn't just Dupré's music that was suddenly in demand. Her body, or at least images of it, was eliciting a high price from skin magazines. *Hustler* offered her $1 million for a nude photo shoot and *Penthouse* followed suit.[38] Porn producers were also attempting to cash in on Dupré's sudden notoriety by offering her that same figure to star in an adult flick.[39] Yet the Dupré dichotomy prevailed in the attempted commodification of this suddenly famous woman. Her attorney stated that Dupré "was upset over the media's exploitation of her."[40] Yet others speculated that there was no end to the "Benjamins" that Dupré could command following the Spitzer scandal. According to one New York PR professional, "Dupré could cash in on commercials, tabloid-TV shows, a sexy clothing line, perfume, and more."[41] Her work as a prostitute, it seems, led to different types of offers for Dupré to commodify her image and body in a more public way that is still sexual but not through physical interaction—at least not with the public. With people speculating about book deals[42] as well as sponsorships from alcohol companies[43] and with the *Post* naming Dupré as the 19th most powerful woman in New York City, her future seemed, if not bright, then at least lushly lucrative. Her dream to get rich seemed to have materialized—if only she wanted it. It's not that Dupré totally shunned the "opportunities" that notoriety afforded her. But she took her time in mulling over them. Ultimately, she did pose nude for *Playboy* magazine, where she had the cover story in May 2010.[44] And, in an ironic twist, she became an advice columnist in December 2009 for the *New York Post*,[45] a weekly gig she kept for two-and-a-half years. But more on that later.

Sydney Leathers

While Dupré is cast in news reports as an innocent young woman from South Jersey with a secretive, sex-fanatic side that was hidden prior to the scandal, Leathers is framed with a different duality. She is the small-town young woman, a "progressive activist," but one who is also hell-bent on using her sexting savvy—and ultimately her body as a porn star—to become famous.[46] In news accounts, Leathers also said she was in love with her politician (albeit briefly), but her feelings for Weiner soured once he lost interest in her. She became driven to publicize the degradation of Anthony Weiner as a cheating spouse and a sexting maniac. While Leathers was never described as an innocent or even a "good girl," the love trope offered Leathers motivation to embrace the limelight. She was a woman scorned. Therefore, in early reports, before she embraced opportunities to perform in the porn industry, Leathers implied that it wasn't the limelight itself that she craved but catharsis—gained by using the media as a bullhorn—since she felt used and tossed aside by Weiner. "This was a bad situation for me, because I really admired him," Leathers told thedirty.com, the online site that published their sexts. "Even post-scandal [in 2011], I thought he was misunderstood. Until I got to know him. I thought I loved him. Pretty pathetic."[47] While it's not entirely clear what happened to turn Leathers against the former congressman, one *New York Post* article alleges that Weiner promised Leathers a job at the online news magazine *Politico*, as well as a condo in Chicago so they could become physically intimate together.[48] But such assurances were never met. "I'm disgusted by him," she said, a stark shift from her earlier professed feelings of love.[49]

Like Dupré, Leathers saw her celebrity rise in the immediate scandal fallout. She "has taken on representation and is busy booking gigs," including an appearance on Howard Stern's radio show and scheduling modeling gigs for leather clothing lines.[50] She used money earned from her new celebrity to enhance the size of her breasts, preferring clothes to show off her newly acquired cleavage.[51]

News coverage of Leathers revealed a familiar duality. She is a "Midwest . . . kind-hearted girl"[52] who is also a "heavily tattooed, high school dropout hell-bent on becoming famous."[53] She is "a political junkie" and "nerd," who also has a profile on a dating website "seeking 'sugar daddies.'"[54] She has aspirations to obtain a paralegal certification "when her life settles down"[55] but in the meantime defends her decision to star in porn films with Weiner lookalikes—even as she faced an HIV exposure scare. "My whole thing is, even if I'm cashing in my body, it's my body to cash in on. It was my choice,"[56] said Leathers. That may be true, but the newspapers made sure Leathers paid for that choice by making fun of the body that brought her notoriety in the first place. Photographs of Leathers in the *New York Post* and *New York Daily News*—at least those featuring her fully dressed—reveal a physique that is more Main Street than Hollywood. (The underdressed photos reveal a recently enhanced bosom.)

And the publications don't let Leathers forget that her body type leans more toward curvaceous, and dotted with cellulite, than it is sleek and svelte—at the very moment when Leathers is seeking the media spotlight as an emerging public personality. For instance, Leathers is "a bathing 'booty,'"[57] according to a headline—she's certainly not a *beauty*—on the beach during a California vacation. The photograph features Leathers midstride, from behind, on a beach in a two-piece bathing suit. Her head is turned over her shoulder so we can also see her face in addition to her backside. Fat rolls along her mid-back are clearly visible as is cellulite on the back of her legs. It's

Sydney Leathers waits outside of a bar in New York City hoping to encounter democratic mayoral hopeful Anthony Weiner before he makes his concession speech in 2013. (AP Photo/Donald Traill)

not an unflattering photograph overall—but it does reveal her physical imperfections. The written text emphasizes what the image implies: in her bathing suit, Leathers looks "more like a frumpy schoolmarm than sultry sext kitten."[58] The bathing suit, according to the article, "was clearly meant to evoke a vintage 1940s glamour. Instead, Leathers looked like she was wearing the swimwear equivalent of 'mom jeans' as she frolicked and posed in the California surf."[59] The photo op for Leathers, therefore, ended as a judgmental disaster. And it continued. Three days later, the *New York Post* noted that Leathers "has a new gig"[60] modeling leather clothes for the clothing line Apparel NY. The article paints her as an awkward and amateur model struggling with body issues. The owner of the clothing line told Leathers to "be more edgy"[61] and said he wanted Leathers to pose topless with her hands covering her bare chest. Leathers said she couldn't oblige. "Nor would she agree to show her stomach in a midriff-baring number because, she told us, the media have been calling her fat."[62] However, she did eventually consent "to undo a few buttons on her blouse."[63] The corresponding photo to the "Leathers Models Leather Pants" article shows the sexting-star model in a form-fitting, black mini-dress that hugs her body. With her left hand on her hip, a slight bend at the right knee, and her head cocked ever-so-coquettishly to the right, Leathers appears happy and open—more curvy cheerleader than lusty seductress.

Less than a week after her unenthusiastic and unsexy modeling gig, Leathers released an online adult video, via Vivid Entertainment, that shows her "touching herself in front of cameras . . . and documents a photo shoot with frontal nudity, backside shots, and south-of-the-equator footage."[64] That foray into the porn world quickly netted Leathers a new level of recognition. "It's happening more frequently now," said Leathers. "In passing the other day, someone said, 'Oh, there's the Weiner girl.'"[65] While Leathers unwaveringly embraces her public personality, the extent to which she feels comfortable baring her body seesaws. She fluctuates between consenting—if barely—to undo a few buttons of her shirt to masturbating in front of the camera. The media picks at her less-than-toned body throughout. They declare that her "15 minutes are officially up."[66] And they note that only a handful of patrons came out to a club where Leathers was making an appearance following the release of her adult video, but "she refused to dance onstage or on laps."[67] Few would pay $20 to take a picture with her.[68] As for her adult video, it's unclear how popular it was. While the founder of Vivid Entertainment said he was "really happy"[69] with its sales figures, he wouldn't comment on the number of times it was downloaded. Her body, apparently, was not a hot commodity.

THE SEXPOT VERSUS THE SEXTER

Despite articles declaring that Leathers's 15 minutes of fame were up and that she's "worn-out,"[70] the persistent sexting mistress assured everyone that "I'm not going away!"[71] It was as if the newspapers were trying to put the kibosh on her starlet status while Leathers refused to exit stage left. Her declaration to stay put was a successful media maneuver, since it resulted in continued coverage. Media outlets and Leathers had a contentious relationship built on their need for each other. One sought readers and the other sought attention. Despite the mean tone of news coverage, the media/Leathers relationship was almost symbiotic. A double-entendre headline mocked Leathers's porn video, asserting

"Hard to Get XXX-Cited."[72] While some photographs showed Leathers as eagerly embracing the camera lens as she showed off a toothy smile,[73] other photographed moments depicted Leathers in a less-than-flattering light. Like when she appeared peeved and caught in an awkward mid-stride stance on a coffee run.[74] Even when she is described as a "vixen" or a "winner" it appears that the joke's on her, because the corresponding photograph shows Leathers in a clumsy or unwieldy pose that belies the written text. Indeed, when the *New York Post* listed Leathers as a "winner" one week, the reason she was selected is hardly flattering: "Weiner online sex pal collected enough from porn film to buy new boobs."[75] The corresponding photograph shows Leathers with a plunging neckline looking as if she's about to gag.

In contrast to Leathers, who is often shown as attractive but not sexy when the media is playing nice, Ashley Dupré appears as the genuine seductress who offers readers pouty lips and bedroom eyes. Photographs of her rarely feature a smiling face. She offers no cheerleading, toothy grin. Dupré does not look directly at the camera. Rather, her eyes are downcast, her long bangs graze her eyes, obscuring her gaze.[76] She appears coy, purring for those who look upon her to "Come hither." The *New York Post*'s cover story the day after the governor resigned calls Dupré "beautiful."[77] Two days after Spitzer's resignation, the same newspaper offered a cover story that jumps to an alluring "photo exclusive" of the woman at the center of the prostitution scandal, her hands covering her underdressed chest, the exact pose that Leathers could not do during her modeling gig. (The photo credit of these three racy photographs belongs not to a *New York Post* photographer but to an external photo agency. Following their publication in the *Post*, Dupré's attorney said she did not agree for those photographs to be published.[78]) Additionally, a headline in the *New York Daily News* declares of Dupré, boldface and in all caps, "Hottest Girl I Had."[79] The corresponding photograph features a sunglasses-clad Dupré sitting, with her legs open, in a teeny-tiny white bikini on a yacht. It is this "hotness" that made Dupré a contender as one of "The 50 Most Powerful Women in NYC," according to the *New York Post*, two-and-a-half months after Spitzer's resignation. She was ranked No. 19—right before Silda Spitzer at No. 20—because she is the "destroyer of governors."[80] Her power lay in her sex appeal that was hot enough to level a governor. She was not a political operative, but her sexual skills were enough to access elite levels of political power—and crush it. Through sexuality and physique, she held power over the governor, the linchpin of New York power brokers. Perhaps Spitzer thought he could compartmentalize his time with Dupré. But ultimately he underestimated the public and the media's appetites for tales of drama, sex, and schadenfreude as the most powerful narrative of all that can tear down a powerful man and reconfigure public opinion and media accounts as the systems in charge of his fate.

POLITICAL CLOWNS

The narrative, cultivated in Hollywood, of dorky guy frolicking with hot girl, typically bodes well for the guy's reputation and his sexual stature. But while some may say politics is Hollywood for ugly people, the real-life role of the political wife undercuts the acquisition of any points an average-looking politician may obtain from his sexual connection to an attractive woman—if the attractive woman is not his wife. Society hates cheaters, and the New York Post and Daily News gleefully pummel Spitzer and Weiner for stepping out on their wives. They reduce these men to clowns, those who cannot and should not be taken seriously as politicians or as men (thereby conflating their political power and their gendered power) because of an entrenched idiocy that led them to believe they could get away with sexual disloyalty. The newspapers' easy comparison of the two politicians to each other was also heightened by the fact that in summer 2013 we saw both politicians in the news for their reemergence campaigns. Weiner was running for New York City mayor just as Spitzer was seeking political redemption as the city's comptroller. While the second iteration of the Weiner scandal happened in July 2013, a mere two months before they both lost in the September primaries, it foreshadowed the politicians as irredeemable losers—politically and personally. For instance, the newspapers cast both men as two peas in the same scandal pod in four front-page stories and a fifth story inside the paper. Consider these two examples. "Even THIS creep thinks Weiner's a bad husband!"[81] So shouted the Daily News on its front page just four days after Weiner and then wife Huma Abedin held a press conference in July 2013 to address the latest round of explicit tweets and messages that had emerged into the public domain.[82] Corresponding photos on the front page showed the indeed creepy-looking Spitzer, with uncombed hair but smiling broadly, wearing an oversized white t-shirt that read, "Buffalo Police Athletic League." (For a New York City crowd, the word "Buffalo" no doubt cues an uncool upstate vibe.) Inset sat a thumbnail photo of Weiner, his cheeks puffed like a blow fish, looking as if he was about to exhale. The Daily News presented a hierarchy of creeps on its front page, with Spitzer dragged into the newspaper to validate the even more egregiously creepy Weiner. It's a clear example of misery loving company, and that the only power Spitzer holds post-scandal is to reinforce his dorky-guy, bad-guy status in service to other scandal-suffering politicos. In another front-page example that links both politicians, consider the *New York Post*'s instructions to the reader: "POT, MEET KETTLE." The subhead declares, "Spitzer: Weiner too pervy for mayor."[83] The corresponding front-page graphics show two tea kettles, each one with a politician's faced etched into it. Spitzer's forehead is wrinkled, and he looks to be caught midsentence. Weiner appears as a total doofus—his mouth is shaped into an exaggerated frown with pronounced frown lines, and his forehead is wrinkled as well. Again, Spitzer—as the authority on sleaze—is used to further excoriate Weiner, who is cast as even the sleazier of this lot. They're united in their sexual skullduggery, but even losers face a hierarchy of judgment. They have both fallen from power—but still believe, incorrectly, that they can reach the precipice of power again. The newspapers send a not-so-subliminal message affirming: not a chance. And the public obviously agrees, dashing hopes of a political comeback by voting for their opponents in the primaries. Neither Spitzer nor Weiner hold elected office at the time of writing.

Even though Spitzer and Weiner acted out sexually, news coverage in the *New York Post* and *Daily News* derides these politicians seeking reputation redemption for fancying themselves in a sexy and sexual manner in their private lives. The irony is that these men were caught in scandal because their sex lives weren't "vanilla"—but existed outside the bounds of socially accepted (and expected) monogamy. News accounts mock them for being antisexy and repulsive in a clownish way that undercuts the possibility of even thinking about them in a sexual manner. For instance, during the unfolding Weiner scandal in 2013, the *New York Post* featured a standalone photo with corresponding caption of Spitzer, midstride, wearing another oversized white t-shirt with black shorts and black loafers. He's wearing chunky glasses, and he's sockless. He is, "The love gov known for rocking black socks in the sack during trysts with hookers [who] went sans stockings yesterday before hitting the [campaign] trail."[84] In this account, the photo and caption serve to not only desexualize Spitzer but also to mock his appearance as off-putting and unattractive, thereby directly linking his unsexy body to his (in)competency as a candidate. This link between (unappealing) sexuality and paternalism in politics connects to the physical embodiment in political culture.[85] "Power becomes articulated through a masculine code that is positioned in terms of national interest through the family structure," writes cultural studies scholar P. David Marshall.[86] Yet the occurrence of scandal reveals that the persona the male politician presented on the campaign trail, as a man of family and integrity, was a fabricated myth. Apparently, the smiling photo ops with his "adoring" wife and children were little more than a campaign construction. While chapter 7 dives deep into this contradiction, it's worth noting here that scandal dethrones the politician for cheating on his wife and duping the public. Public shaming involves a skewering of the masculine code that helped him ascend to power. It's like catching your dad at a trendy club with "another woman." His sexuality on display is cringeworthy, and any authority he held in the family is instantly crushed.

LIFE, POST-SCANDAL

While this chapter focused primarily on media coverage of Ashley Dupré and Sydney Leathers as their scandals unfolded, let's now turn the lens toward how both fared post-scandal to understand how their proximity to media frenzies shaped them after public and media interest in their lives dissipated.

Dupré's life after the 2008 scandal took a positive turn professionally and personally. The *New York Post* recruited Dupré to write a relationship column for the newspaper, which she did for two-and-a-half years. In the debut column less than one year after Spitzer resigned from office, the introductory paragraph announcing the new column both admonishes the former escort and elevates her for her inimitable set of life experiences.

> Sure, she's made some mistakes. But now Ashley Dupré, the former escort who brought down Gov. Eliot Spitzer, is sharing what she's learned in her new sex, love, and relationship column—exclusively in the *New York Post*. Is your husband cheating? Is your daughter on a dangerous path? Our readers asked—and Ashley fired back with her no-nonsense advice.[87]

After all, if anyone would know whether a husband is a cheat or a young woman is at risk it would be Dupré, who's had intimate experiences with cheating husbands and who was described as at risk herself. But after more than two years of advice giving, Dupré set off for a new, more domestic chapter of her life. She opened a boutique selling lingerie in New Jersey the same month that she penned her last *Post* column in May 2012. She gave birth to a daughter that fall and married the child's father the following year in Paris. Her husband is described as a "construction magnate." "She got the fairy tale,"[88] according to the *Daily News*, describing her wedding as a posh but private affair that was held at the Four Seasons in the City of Light. Less than three months later, the Spitzers would file for divorce, nearly six years after the scandal broke—and after 26 years of marriage.[89] In her post-scandal life, Dupré (finally) took advantage of the public and high-profile opportunities that scandal presented. She posed nude on the May 2010 cover of *Playboy*. If the theme of her life in the immediate wake of scandal was that of a sexy young woman who couldn't decide whether to welcome or shun the media spotlight, now she offered to the public and media what it initially demanded all along: her nude body. But it was as if this big reveal was an act of penance. She was contrite in the cover story. "'Yeah, I was an escort,' she admits. 'As much as I wish I could make that go away, I can't. I'm trying to take that as a lesson learned. I'm not proud of what I've done.'"[90] And while Dupré assured *Playboy* readers that "I love sex and I'm very good at it," she now is saving herself and her sex skills "for my future boyfriend from now on."[91] In other words, her life as a professionally promiscuous woman is "finito." While *Playboy* readers can look and appreciate her nude physique, it's not for purchase any longer because she's changed her life and her outlook about sex (still good!) and who can access it from her (only her significant other). Dupré continued to play the contrition card in an article for a local New Jersey news site that interviewed her about her lingerie boutique. "I made a bunch of mistakes when I was younger, and I feel like, for the first time in my life, I'm growing into an adult, and I'm really excited about that," she told the local blogger.[92] Post-scandal Dupré had to pay for her sins as a prostitute who felled a powerful man, as a woman who chose a life of sex and seduction for money. Post-scandal she altered course, publicly denouncing her work as a prostitute while simultaneously continuing to profit from that paid (sex) work by posing for *Playboy*, writing a relationships advice column for the *Post*, and opening a high-end lingerie boutique. While admonishing her "mistakes," Dupré managed to create a successful personal and professional life that flirted with scandal. She did not reject it entirely—or even at all—but she tamed it for her benefit. When she announced in 2015 that she was closing her lingerie boutique, known as Femme by Ashley, she did so—she said—"because I will not get another chance to raise and enjoy my children," according to the boutique's Instagram page.[93] Therefore her growing family—and not a business built upon lingerie—became her focus and life's work. With the shop's closing, she cut money-generating ties to scandal and moved on to a children-centered life.

Unlike Dupré, who crafted a life for herself that was shadowed but not overwhelmed by scandal, Sydney Leathers continues to make her involvement in the Weiner texting scandal front and center of her public persona. Indeed, the bio on her Twitter account reads "18+ only! Student. Cat lady. Writer. Sometimes I do porn."[94] She has 20,000 followers and posts photographs of herself that feature ample cleavage, breasts, and lacy lingerie.[95] In the year following the scandal, Leathers enrolled in college classes to study radio and TV production while also pursuing work in the adult entertainment industry, according to a USA Today article. "The porn industry is a happy, welcoming place,"[96] she said. In 2015 Leathers got looped into another political sex scandal when a state lawmaker in Indiana, Justin Moed, sent nude photographs of himself to Leathers's phone. Their sexting interactions were outed by the New York Post and Moed subsequently issued a public apology.[97]

In contrast, Dupré's Twitter page, with more than 12,000 followers, features photo after photo of herself with her young children, tasting chocolate, baking, building snow people, and snuggling at home. It's a study in contrasts: a domestic life centered around young children, in what appears to be a very luxe home, versus Leathers's tweets about porn, her schooling, sexual innuendo, and references to continued news coverage of her life. Dupré's Twitter bio is left blank—only offering a dead link to her now-shuttered lingerie boutique. Leathers, meanwhile, offers her e-mail address, the contact for her agent, and a link to the website that houses her porn. Yet despite the homey nature of Dupré's tweets and photos, her Twitter photo is a black-and-white glam shot—she's dressed in a fur coat, her hair is windswept, her glance cast askance, and her décolleté bare. She remains kissed by scandal; but when she frames it, Dupré makes it look luxurious and oh so posh, like Old Hollywood.

FEMALE PUBLICITY AND SCANDAL

Unlike the male politicians whose bodies became immediate laughingstocks—not only for their idiocy but also for fancying themselves as sexual beings—these "other women" had the potential to be valued for their bodies and physical appearance, if they offered the public a sexually pleasing visage, and if they didn't talk too loudly and hog a proverbial bullhorn. Dupré was ultimately valued for reining in her voice and speaking about her scandal role at carefully selected moments that did not appear to value the pursuit of celebrity over a type of elegant, controlled voice. Whether through luck or strategy, Dupré massaged her involvement in an American scandal into the American Dream. She rose above her crushing circumstances, she found a man of considerable wealth with whom to build a marriage, she had children, and she appears—from the outside at least—to have secured the financial comforts and luxuries that lured her into prostitution in the first place. Her public persona (as much as one can call posting on Twitter a public act) is buoyed by her adoration and admiration for her domestic life and children. Because she didn't demonstrate pleasure in notoriety in the wake of her scandal, she could play the innocent card in scandal's aftermath, according to Gamson. "She may say she doesn't want it," writes Gamson of scandal mistresses generally, "but her subsequent behavior proves otherwise."[98] We see this dynamic with Dupré, who refrained from baring all during the scandal, and who had her attorney state publicly that she did not agree for illicit photographs of her to be published in tabloids, but who posed nude in *Playboy*—apparently on her own terms—once the scandal dust settled. The contrast of her words (that she was sorry for working as a prostitute, that she made mistakes, and that she's now reformed) with her nude photographs allowed Dupré to straddle the innocent/whore dichotomy with aplomb. She gave the public what it wanted—and apologized for it in the process. She didn't revel in the attention. But she negotiated a position that coalesced "sexual relations with men and relations with media."[99] So take a look, fellas, and let's move on.

Unlike Dupré, who ultimately gave in to the demands of the media and public but framed her consent as an act of contrition, Leathers actively, unabashedly, and directly presented herself as an independent and sexual woman who reveled in baring all—whether or not the public and media welcomed such an unrobing. She willfully connected her publicity to sex and was unapologetic in doing so. There were no sexy apologies of *I've been a bad, bad girl. So just take one quick peek as I pull down my thong for you . . .* Instead, Leathers embraces her role in the porn industry and has built a career on her role as a prolific sexter, even as she positions herself as an independent and fully realized individual. Regardless, "the woman who seeks out media attention is a harlot—the independent woman, even when she is of the 'out-of-my-way-mister, I'm-on-my-own' variety, is easily absorbed back into the role of prostitute."[100]

The irony, of course, is that Dupré actually worked as a prostitute, but cloaked her work in that field in a robe of contrition, making a distinction between what she did and who she is. Leathers could not make such a distinction because she didn't want to—and because she presumably enjoys the attention she receives as an 18+ entertainer. The scandal starlet who never actually had sex with her politician ended up thriving on her proximity to illicit sex, while the other scandal starlet—who was a prostitute—figured that if she gave in to the media's and public's perceptions of her, she could gain control of her narrative and life, and retreat—as much as possible—into her new chapter as mother, wife, and tweet-happy homemaker.

CHAPTER 5

Political Wives, Scandal, and the Double Bind: Press Coverage through a Gendered Lens[*]

The sexual transgressions of male politicians in the United States are paid special attention by the media, often with front-page and top-of-the-hour news coverage. Major contemporary sexual scandals have always involved men—not women—as the politically and economically powerful individual in the sexual dyad.[1] From 2004 to 2014 alone, we have seen numerous media frenzies involving scandal-tarnished politicians, including former New Jersey governor James McGreevey, who admitted that he is gay after his male sex partner threatened to "out" him (2004); Louisiana senator David Vitter, whose name was found in the little black book of the D.C. Madam (2007); Idaho senator Larry Craig, who attempted to solicit sex from a male undercover cop in an airport bathroom (2007); Florida congressman Mark Foley, who sent sexually explicit texts to his male pages (2006); Foley's successor, Congressman Tim Mahoney, who paid hush money to a staffer with whom he had an extramarital affair (2008); former New York governor Eliot Spitzer, who had sex with prostitutes (2008); former senator John Ensign, who had an extramarital affair with a campaign staffer (2009); former South Carolina governor Mark Sanford, who had an extramarital affair with an Argentinean woman (2009); former California governor Arnold Schwarzenegger, who fathered a child with his housekeeper in 1997 while he was married to his wife (2011);

*This chapter originally appeared as the following journal article: Hinda Mandell, "Political Wives, Scandal, and the Double Bind: Press Construction of Silda Spitzer and Jenny Sanford Through a Gendered Lens," *Women's Studies in Communication* 38, no. 1 (2015): 57–77. Reprinted with permission.

former New York congressman Anthony Weiner, who sent private Twitter messages of his erect penis (2011, 2013, and 2016); former CIA Director David Petraeus, who had an extramarital affair with his biographer (2012); and Louisiana congressman Vance McAllister, who was caught on video making out with his female staffer in his district office (2014). While this list offers ample evidence of cheating male politicians, it certainly is not exhaustive, and any attempt to make it exhaustive would be an impossibly Herculean task doomed to fail.

While male politicians may be at the heart of these scandals/transgressions/media frenzies, taking time to study how the press constructs the image of political wives fills a gap in the research on gender and political sex scandals. A study of Silda Spitzer and Jenny Sanford, situated within an analysis of their husband's political sex scandals, can reveal the extent to which press coverage depicts these women in sex-specific ways, even though their public roles as wives took different directions. The news media placed both political wives within the confines of a double bind of presence/absence: press accounts criticized Silda Spitzer (who ultimately divorced her husband in 2013) for her silent support of her husband at his press conference, while coverage of Jenny Sanford took issue with her for acting independently of her husband, who she divorced immediately after the scandal. An analysis of media reports reveals not only this presence/absence double bind but also how two high-profile, privileged, and powerful women were stripped of their own individual traits, each reduced to her position as a wife. This study's findings indicate that press coverage of both wives constructed them as symbolic figures, ultimately removing their distinct differences and casting Silda Spitzer as the "good" wife and Jenny Sanford as the "independent" wife. Examining this coverage illustrates the hegemonic role of the news media, which both perpetuates an idealized role for political wives whose husbands are in public crisis and criticizes a political wife when she attempts to fulfill that role.

BACKGROUND ON POLITICAL SEX SCANDALS

Examples in recent years of married, political elites behaving in sexually promiscuous ways are plentiful. Indeed, the presence of sex-scandal coverage in the news appears regularly in today's media. Scandal is defined as "breach of virtue exposed," which subsequently causes disapproval among a group of people.[2] The frequency of scandal coverage today marks a distinct upswing since the landmark Watergate scandal.[3] From this atmosphere of political distrust emerged the press's attention to ethical misconduct—and in a new development, sexual misconduct as well.

No longer were sexual adventures of presidents and other political figures considered strictly off-limits to the press corps or, by extension, the American people.[4]

News coverage of political sex scandals in the United States partly focuses on the besieged politician's wife. Scandals may be about systems of power,[5] but the wives, as less powerful individuals due to their subordinate social and professional position, become a part of the event's scandal and media narrative. In scandals, one can locate a consistent narrative or "common script."[6] Repetition of a process, or the routinization of an act, enforces and reinforces expected norms surrounding reoccurring events. Cultural scripts, therefore, need to be analyzed rigorously to discover how press coverage of such events reinforces or subverts norms around power and gender. The purpose of this textual analysis of scandal news coverage is to examine how wives of scandal tarnished politicians are presented by the news media. This study focuses exclusively on two political wives: Silda Spitzer and Jenny Sanford.

Silda Spitzer was the wife of former New York governor Eliot Spitzer. Governor Spitzer resigned his office in 2008 when news reports revealed him to be a client of high-priced prostitution services. Jenny Sanford was the wife of former South Carolina governor Mark Sanford. Governor Sanford confessed in a tearful press conference in 2009 that he was engaged in an ongoing love affair with an Argentinean woman. While Mark Sanford did not resign during his scandal, he left office once his term expired in 2010. (He is currently, at the time of writing, a congressman from his home state.) Jenny Sanford divorced her husband that year. The Spitzers divorced in late 2013, nearly six years after Eliot Spitzer resigned his governorship.[7]

While there is a lack of academic research on political sex scandals, there is even less research that provides an analysis of the role of gender in press coverage. A gendered lens focuses on the role of gender construction in analysis, contributing to our understanding of the (re)construction and (re)production of masculine and feminine behavior.[8] A gendered lens also adds to our understanding of sex-trait attributes associated with men and women. While there is a significant body of research on the social construction of wives and "wife-work" (a term coined by writer Susan Maushart),[9] we need more research examining political wives beyond the categorical subset of First Ladies and more analytical (rather than biographical) studies.[10]

By focusing exclusively on two distinct cases that received significant press coverage within one year of each other, we can see the extent to which the press treated and covered these two political wives differently.

Silda Spitzer and Jenny Sanford are connected by both notable similarities and marked differences. Each woman's husband was governor at the time of his scandal, and both political wives had high-profile, white-collar careers prior to opting out of the workforce and assuming the responsibilities of a political wife.[11] Despite these similarities there are also important differences between them. Silda Spitzer remained married to her husband for nearly six years after the scandal, while Jenny Sanford filed for divorce almost immediately. Silda Spitzer attended the press conference where her husband announced his resignation, but she did not speak publicly about the scandal or her marriage. In contrast, Jenny Sanford was absent from her husband's press conference, was frequently quoted in press accounts, and released a book, *Staying True*, in 2010 about her marriage. Considering the wife's role in the scandal "script"[12] prompts key questions guiding my inquiry: According to press accounts of political sex scandals, what does it mean to be a "good wife" to a politician who admits to sexual transgressions? Does press coverage of these events (re)circulate a "good wife" double bind for political wives whose husbands are caught in scandals? How does the news media, as a hegemonic institution, expect a political wife to behave in times of public, marital strife? The gendered lens guides an examination of the prominent ways in which news coverage focuses on Silda Spitzer and Jenny Sanford, including the extent to which they are quoted and how they are written about, analyzed, and constructed.

Because this study focuses exclusively on two specific political wives, attempts to generalize beyond the scope of Silda Spitzer and Jenny Sanford are questionable. However, the enthusiastic media coverage of both scandals—resulting in daily news updates, news features, and trend stories—offers unique opportunities for analysis and can lay the groundwork for future studies examining the construction of "wifeness" in the public sphere by considering additional political wives whose husbands face scandal.[13]

SCANDAL AND WIFENESS

At the center of this research are two key concepts: scandal and what I have termed "wifeness."[14] Scandal, as a salacious subject, is often criticized as an unsuitable topic for rigorous research. Critics of scandal may range from everyday news consumers who are upset with the media's turn toward sensational content to academics who dismiss scandal research as incompatible with loftier intellectual inquiries.[15] However, an emerging cluster of "scandalogists" insists that studying media coverage of scandal can produce a distinct understanding of social and political forces at play within the U.S cultural system.[16] This research provides an analysis of scandal that can shed light on the media's role in society,[17] moral issues within a social system,[18] privacy concerns,[19] and the manifestation of power.[20] And while some news consumers and academics may be critical of scandal as a social phenomenon, the popularity of these news events as a point of discussion among the public and the continuous coverage the media gives to scandal events not only justifies this research but also makes it necessary. Because scandal is a mainstay in the current media and news industry, scholars need to provide a rigorous analysis of its elements.

In addition to the core concept of scandal, the second key subject of this study is my term of "wifeness." Wifeness[21] refers to the act, practice, and social expectations associated with women who are wives. The husband-wife dyad represents the bedrock of U.S society.[22] Indeed, Americans are fascinated with marriage and the pairing of two individuals, each with a personal history and set of life experiences, who come together in a conjugal relationship.[23] No relationship is more personal and intimate than marriage. At the same time, no relationship is surrounded by so many cultural prescriptions, fables, myths, traditions, laws, and taboos. To be married is to be placed in a special relationship to another person—a relationship whose acceptable boundaries have already been established and whose general shape has already been determined.[24]

For this study, "wifeness" has the added dimension of being on public display during a time of marital strife, and expectations surrounding wifeness are present in the scandal script because press coverage includes stories about what role—if any—a political wife should play in her husband's scandal fallout. Wifeness therefore features prominently in press accounts of political sex scandals, whether the political wife attends her husband's scandal press conference or is absent but releases a statement about it.[25] While the socially acceptable heterosexual roles within the traditionally gendered pairing of marriage are neither equal nor natural, they are often at the center of press coverage on political sex scandals. No doubt this is because the media is a hegemonic institution, and these traditional marital roles—the passively natured wife as caretaker, homemaker, and child rearer and the aggression-oriented husband as the breadwinner—are deeply rooted in shared norms across Western society.[26] The unequal marital roles underlie the inequality of power that is reflective of heterosexual male and female relations in society.[27]

Is it a coincidence that all of the transgressors in American political sex scandals are men? These male politicians have behaved boldly, independently, and sexually aggressively, which are all socially embedded, gendered characteristics of men.[28] There has never been a major political sex scandal where the powerful, central transgressor is a prominent woman.[29] Thus far, women have been involved in these public transgressions but not as traditionally powerful agents. Rather, they more typically hold the socially subordinate position of mistress or wife. These scandal events reinforce a script wherein a powerful man, who holds a privileged position as a public figure, cheats on his wife.[30] This gender gap in political sex scandals can be explained in part by the overall gender gap in U.S politics. Male politicians still outnumber female politicians in the United States, despite the enthusiastic attention that Republican female candidates received in summer 2010 for their increased presence in the political realm.[31] The writer Lane Wallace noted that even if women are in a minority in Congress—with about 18 percent of congressional seats belonging to women—there are no recent examples of female politicians in Congress getting caught in a sex scandal.[32] (Of course, female Congress members may engage in "scandalous" sexual activity in private but, if so, public scandals have yet to emerge from them.) Wallace argued that this can be explained, in part, due to the sexualization of male power and the desexualization and defeminization of women in power. The fact remains that, thus far, in political sex scandals it is most typically the male politician who is caught in compromising positions. Therefore, men receive the overwhelming majority of political sex scandal media coverage.

MEDIA COVERAGE OF POLITICAL WIVES AND POLITICAL WOMEN

Political wives entrenched in their husband's sex scandal—with the prominent exception of Hillary Clinton—have received lackluster academic attention. However, the popular press pays significant attention to these women. Therefore, public conversations of political wives ensnared in scandal are taking place within media coverage and are worthy of rigorous study. Journalists Joe Garofoli[33] and Mike Celizic[34] both describe, in the San Francisco Chronicle and USA Today, respectively, a recurring script of the political wife often standing next to their husband at a press conference, where the politician acknowledges his marital infidelity. Yet writer Anushay Hossain[35] argues in the Huffington Post that political wives have moved beyond victim status. She points to Jenny Sanford, the now exwife of former South Carolina governor Mark Sanford, for her refusal to attend his press conference. Rachael Larimore, comments in doubleX, Slate.com's woman-centered blog, that political wives are constantly judged: the public criticizes the political wife if she attempts to benefit financially from her husband's scandal, and the public also criticizes the political wife if she stands next to her scandal-tarnished husband at a press conference.[36] Indeed, political wives are caught in a double bind because they receive negative media attention both when they appear to support their scandal-suffering husbands—as they "stand by" them—and when they do not. Thus, public commentary on political sex scandals and political wives in the popular press comprises an ongoing discussion that features a spectrum of views, critiques, and criticisms relating to key issues at stake. It also solidifies the need for academic attention to this subject to catch up to ongoing public deliberation in the popular press.

In contrast to the research gap on wives and scandal, robust studies on political wives outside of the scandal sphere have received the attention of scholars, prompting an examination of the ways in which media coverage of presidential and vice presidential candidates' wives is categorized according to sex-specific traits.[37] Gender scholars Asa Kroon Lundell and Mats Ekström have argued that the media "gender" political women in a way that heightens sex-specific stereotypes such as "sexualization, objectification, passivity and otherness."[38] Gender communications scholar Betty Houchin Winfield[39] noted that media coverage of First Ladies fits into the categories of "an escort with her husband; a protocol role for leading fashionable, ceremonial, and social events; and a noblesse oblige role with charity works," as well as a "policy-making role" and a "power role."[40] Winfield and Barbara Friedman's textual analysis of news reports on candidates' wives during the 2000 U.S presidential election found that the most popular media frame was the "escort role."[41] This term refers to the wives' presence alongside their husbands at campaign events. The second most popular frame in media coverage of political wives in the 2000 presidential election was the "anti-Hillary [Clinton]" frame. Candidates' wives positioned themselves as supportive of their husbands' political policies, but these women made it clear that they were not cocandidates.[42] In contrast, Hillary Clinton, in her role from 1993 through 2001 as first lady, made an effort to establish her own political career, receiving much public backlash, perhaps because she pushed the boundaries of gendered roles in politics. First Ladies of the United States are expected to remain within the boundaries of their position and refrain from asserting their own political agenda to the detriment of their presidential husbands.[43]

In addition to gender, race is another dimension of difference in media coverage of political wives. Writer J. Swan's[44] content analysis of American newspaper coverage of Cindy McCain and Michelle Obama, the wives on the presidential ticket in the 2008 elections, drew attention to race in discussions of media representation. Michelle Obama, as an African American woman, was coded as more masculine in news coverage than Cindy McCain, a white woman. However, these women's sartorial choices received more media attention than their races. Both Michelle Obama and Cindy McCain were the objects of significant media coverage for their personal style and fashion, reinforcing gendered norms in the media coverage of both of these women.[45]

While this study focuses on two political wives, briefly visiting how the news media covers women politicians helps situate the literature on political wives within the broader conversations about the double binds that women face (including both political wives and women politicians) within the male-dominated sphere of politics. When the political candidate herself is a woman (and therefore not "just" a wife), traditional gender norms, including the media's focus on such "feminine" topics as personal style, prevailed in news coverage of female candidates. Scholars[46] note that female political candidates receive significant media attention for their clothing, hairstyles, and accessory choices while male political candidates do not. Indeed, a female candidate's change of hairstyle or outfit can prompt a media event featuring eager analysis of her appearance and its consequences for her political campaign.[47] Female political candidates are gendered in ways that their male counterparts are not. The visual communication scholars Lundell and Ekström describe "gendering" as an action that emphasizes an individual's gender when such information is irrelevant to the situation. Lundell and Ekström[48] argue that women are gendered in opposition to the public's perception of a politician's necessary traits: media representations of female candidates focus on them as emotional as opposed to the preferred traits of a politician as steadfast, unwavering, and strong. In fact, scholars have referred to the double bind that female candidates face, finding that those whom the public consider too feminine are deemed an inappropriate fit for the job but noting that those considered competent are labeled unfeminine, also a negative attribute for women.[49]

Political communication scholar Kathleen Hall Jamieson explores the constrictions women face in her book *Beyond the Double Bind: Women and Leadership*.[50] She outlines five double binds and uses a case study of Hillary Clinton (a campaigner for her husband's presidency at the time the book was published and, ultimately, a first lady) as "a surrogate on whom we projected our attitudes about attributes once thought incompatible, that women who were smart were unwomanly and sexually unfulfilled, that articulate women were dangerous."[51] Jamieson argues that what made Hillary Clinton so exceptional is that she "did not live in a world of either-or, however, but of both-and. The Yale-educated wife of a powerful man, she had earned the respect of the nation's lawyers while raising a child and managing a career."[52] The former first lady's double bind, therefore, was that she could not be both feminine and competent[53] and that she was seen as the "ball-breaker."[54]

Even in 2008, a landmark year for women in politics, with Hillary Clinton vying for the Democratic nomination for president and Sarah Palin running for vice president on the Republican ticket, stereotypical constructions continued to dominate news coverage of these women running for the highest and second highest office in the country.[55] For instance, the news media often reported on Palin's physical attractiveness while focusing on Clinton's dowdiness and "cankles."[56] Other scholars have noted that media coverage that stereotypes female candidates can prevent them from achieving election victory.[57] Scholar James Devitt cited the media coverage of female gubernatorial candidates as a barrier for their political ascension.[58] He reported that only 10 percent of U.S. governors are women, which is noteworthy because governorships are often key positions to secure on the way to the U.S. presidency.[59] These aforementioned studies indicate that news media cover women in the political realm differently than men. This coverage reinforces sex-specific stereotypes, hinders individual female advancement, and places women within the constraints of a double bind whether they do or do not meet these gender-based standards.

For the women who are entrenched in the political sphere as "wife" but not "candidate," marital circumstances are rooted in the concept of a "two-person, single career" marriage.[60] This concept refers to the unpaid work that a wife does on behalf of her husband to advance his image and help propel him forward in his chosen profession. "The 'two-person, single career' pattern is fully congruent with the stereotype of the wife as supporter, comforter, backstage manager, home maintainer, and main rearer of children."[61] In the political world, male politicians' wives often campaign with their husbands, participate in photo opportunities, conduct volunteer work, and organize donor events—all in an effort to further the husband's image as a family (and therefore reputable) man.[62] While these women are not themselves running for office, they work (often unpaid) as an image maker for the husband.[63] While Papanek, the scholar who advanced the theoretical problem of the "two-person single career," cites the wives of corporate executives as the prime example of the "two-person, single career" phenomenon, she also mentions the work of male politicians' wives: "The rejection of such public roles by the wife requires considerable effort and is generally seen as injuring the husband's work performance."[64]

A wife's apparent support of her husband-politician when he is caught in scandal continues to play a role in media coverage, just as it does when she campaigns for him, or appears next to him, in more hopeful times. However, the issue of a wife's loyalty to her husband after his apparent betrayal of her is complicated when the wife figuratively and literally stands by her spouse in press events where the accused husband confirms or denies his guilt. Why would she continue to play the role of "good wife" when her husband has failed at his role of "good husband?" This chapter lays bare the social norms surrounding how a political wife is expected to act when her husband, a public and therefore powerful figure, is caught in a scandal. This research is rooted in the belief that social reality is constructed through the habituation of routine, social institutions, and established norms that are shared across different groups of people within the same social system.[65] Drawing on the works of critical theorists, this study views media, broadly speaking, and the press more specifically, as an institution reflective of dominant ideologies.[66] The political wife's construction, therefore, also reflects dominant gendered ideologies about a wife's position in relation to her husband.

METHOD

Guided by grounded theory, a textual analysis of Silda Spitzer and Jenny Sanford press coverage was conducted. Articles were taken from *USA Today*, the *New York Times*, the *Washington Post*, the *Albany (N.Y.) Times Union*, the *State* (Columbia, SC), and CNN.com. This study focuses on nationally circulating newspapers and the largest papers in the politician's home state, as well as CNN.com, to investigate how daily publications cover all news developments associated with each scandal. CNN.com was selected as a popular online publication, as people increasingly consume news coverage online[67] and ranks third in popularity among online news sites.[68] The most popular online news site is *Yahoo! News*, which is a news-aggregating site and not a news-publication site; the second most popular online news site is *BBC online*, which is based in the United Kingdom. Therefore, the top two online news sites were eliminated in favor of CNN.com.

After conducting a search on LexisNexis and CNN.com of "Eliot Spitzer and wife" and "Mark Sanford and wife," a total of 272 articles were retrieved. These included 106 articles on the Eliot Spitzer scandal and 166 articles on the Mark Sanford scandal. Table 5.1 provides a quantitative breakdown of where these articles were found. As shown in table 5.2, the time frame of coverage for the Eliot Spitzer scandal was from

Table 5.1 Origins of Articles Used in Study Analysis

Scandal	New York Times	Washington Post	USA Today	Local Paper	CNN. com	Total Number of Articles
Spitzer	40	17	8	30	11	106
Sanford	27	31	5	94	9	166
Total articles	67	58	13	124	20	272

Table 5.2 Dates of Scandal Coverage

Scandal	Press Conference Date	First Date of Coverage	Last Date of Coverage	Additional Round of Coverage
Spitzer	March 10 and 12, 2008	March 10, 2008	April 15, 2008	
Sanford	June 24, 2009	June 23, 2009	August 20, 2009	December 1, 2009–March 1, 2010

March 10, 2008 (the date of his first press conference), through April 15, 2008, when news coverage of the event tapered off. The timeframe of coverage for the Sanford scandal was from June 23, 2009 (the day prior to his press conference, when news accounts emerged that he was "hiking the Appalachian Trail"), through August 20, 2009, when news coverage tapered off. The Sanford scandal also has a second round of coverage, from December 1, 2009, through March 1, 2010. This second round marks the divorce of Jenny and Mark Sanford and the release of Jenny Sanford's book, *Staying True*.

I approached the study as a feminist who believes women's experiences need to be heard and privileged in a social system that structurally makes women's worth subservient to men's. This study of textual representations of political wives was guided by questions that attempt to systematically document the way in which these women are constructed by press accounts of them. The methodological framework is grounded theory, with a coding scheme at first open to "all possible theoretical directions" of the data.[69] Later, I entered "a focused, selective phase that uses the most significant or frequent initial codes to sort, synthesize, integrate, and organize large amounts of data."[70] There are four main aspects to grounded theory that informed this work as it progressed. First, I collected data from extant texts—in this case press accounts—and analyzed data continuously. Second, I coded data from themes that emerged from texts and not from previously established hypotheses. Third, I made comparisons between and among emergent themes throughout all stages of analysis. Fourth, I developed theory on political wives during data collection and analysis. The goal of textual analysis is to lay bare latent assumptions and representations of some aspect of a text.[71] In textual analysis, texts are believed to be constructed objects that represent messages from a larger social environment and are not objective because they stem from a specific context.

Articles were analyzed until saturation was reached, which happened when "no new properties of the pattern emerge."[72] Emergent themes were examined to determine how the wives were represented in press coverage of the scandals. By analyzing and interpreting texts, it is possible to illustrate how society views and values a particular issue, group, or event as well as which views are more dominant. Texts also provide a record of how societies make sense of an event.[73] Common interpretations are gleaned by taking into account other texts in the series, the genre of the texts, dominant discourses reflected in the texts, and intertexts.[74] The nature of qualitative work is exploratory without rigid guidelines directing research. This research uses commutation and exnomination techniques. The commutation test makes clear assumptions that are embedded in a text. For instance, if a text lingers on a lengthy description of a wife's appearance, it is possible to switch the subject's gender and reread the text to see if an article would linger in the same way on a husband's appearance. The exnomination technique exposes dominant ideas and groups that society has taken for granted, which helps us realize that the phrase "political husband" is less used than "political wife," since historically there have been more male politicians than female politicians. For the textual analysis of printed text, manifest and latent representations of the wives were considered. (Please see Appendix B for guiding questions.)

THE IDEOLOGICAL CONSTRUCTION OF THE SYMBOLIC "GOOD WIFE"

The overarching script to emerge from news coverage of Silda Spitzer and Jenny Sanford was the construction of the political wife as a symbol rather than as an individual. Her symbolic status played a more prominent role in news coverage than even physical descriptions of her body.

Therefore, analysis will focus exclusively on the former theme. Despite differences between Silda Spitzer and Jenny Sanford in relation to their husband's respective scandals, the media spotlight ultimately removed differences between them by constructing them as possessing feminine "sameness." The press did this by placing both women within the confines of an absence/presence double bind. Although the press criticized Silda Spitzer's presence at her husband's press conference, they also, ultimately, criticized Jenny Sanford for distancing herself from her scandal-suffering husband and speaking out against him. This conflicting coverage of these two women prompts the question: what is a political wife to do when she faces criticism for either "standing by" or "stepping away" from her husband?

The news media protested what appeared to be Silda Spitzer's "good wife" fulfillment, her stereotypic public attendance and support of her scandal-tarnished husband. In part, the news media's frequent and vocal reactions may stem from changing values surrounding women's work and wifeness in the United States. However, the news media continued to construct even Jenny Sanford—initially labeled as a mold-breaking political wife—as a subservient, passive, and supportive figure.[75] For instance, in the later stage of press coverage, Jenny Sanford was described as one of five critical reasons for her husband's political rebound.[76] Therefore, even Jenny Sanford, who divorced her husband in 2010, was upheld as a stereotypic wife who "stood by her man." In addition, journalists' unease with Silda Spitzer, as a political wife who upheld gender norms within marriage—is undercut by their deeply embedded construction of wives in the manner they detest: voiceless, clingy, and without agency. Jenny Sanford was outspoken, and news commentators often took issue with her deviation from gender expectations. Perhaps this explains why, toward the end of Jenny Sanford news coverage, she is recast in familiar gender frames as a supportive wife doing her part to help her husband. This phenomenon bolsters theorist Stuart Hall's argument about the constant and unconscious reproduction of ideology.[77] Hall argues that while people individually act in ideological ways and make ideological statements, ideologies are not consciously reproduced by the individual.[78] Rather, ideologies are transmitted collectively by members of a society in mostly unintentional and unconscious ways. This phenomenon also supports Barthes's argument that people will ultimately fall in line with dominant ideological narratives for the sake of maintaining social order.[79]

Silda Spitzer represents the ultimate "good wife." Literally, she was the inspiration behind the eponymous hit CBS show.[80] Figuratively, she was a "good wife" because she was present—and silent—at her husband's press conference in 2008, where he acknowledged extramarital affairs. As a silent-but-present (and therefore supportive) "good wife," Silda fulfilled her role as the female spouse as well as her cultural script.[81] The press subsequently treated her in a more feminine way than Jenny Sanford, who was absent from her husband's press conference yet vocal about his apparent betrayal of their marriage. Through the feminine representation of Silda Spitzer, an ideological construction of a married woman who is not in control of her own experiences within the scandal emerged. Her experiences and feelings, whether they included betrayal, humiliation, anger, or fear, were taken from her and broadened to the female public as a whole. In this way Silda Spitzer became the ultimate symbol of a wife scorned even as she stood next to her husband at his press conferences as a "good wife."

Yet even Jenny Sanford, the woman who broke the political wife mold as a spouse who did not literally stand next to her husband during his public acknowledgment of infidelity, and who divorced her husband and spoke vociferously against his actions, was ultimately painted by media accounts as a symbolic good wife. This occurred even when Jenny Sanford appeared to deviate from her traditional sex-specific duties of wifeness. Therefore, both political wives are constructed by press accounts in a similar manner, even though their actions in the wake of the scandal were different. Their gender and position as wives superseded their individual and specific actions. Ultimately, as in the case of female politicians, the hegemonic media institution lowered Jenny Sanford's position when she broke the mold. This upholds the dominance of male politicians by reaffirming his masculinity in contrast to the wife's expected femininity.[82]

Silda Spitzer's silent role in the public eye, as she stood next to her husband at both of his press conferences, prompted 10 stories about fidelity, forgiveness, and women "standing by" their men. It is clear from news coverage that when the general public follows the unfolding narrative of political sex scandals, the events and their consequences are not isolated to the transgressor and his wife. Instead, the political wife becomes a symbol for the pain women endure that is inflicted upon them by men. "Look at his wife! Look at her! Explain this to me, honey. Explain it. *Why do men do this?*"[83] This excerpt from the *Washington Post* article headlined "In One Man's Fall, Bruises for All," explores the wide-reaching effects of the Spitzer scandal. The article continues: "The reverberations of Eliot Spitzer are showing up in relationships everywhere we look."[84] At the press conference, women see the political wife publicly standing next to her husband-politician after he appeared to have betrayed her, and they fear her situation as humiliated victim. Silda Spitzer's presence becomes the visual symbol of male transgression.

The *New York Times* article headlined "Public Infidelity, Private Debate: Not My Husband (Right?)" details the threat of male infidelity in a post-Spitzer world. The article asks what type of infidelity wives might tolerate:[85]

> What type of infidelity is forgivable in a marriage? What triggers an exit strategy? So ran at least one of the many hair-splitting strains of mesmerized chatter this week among women, especially current and former wives in the New York area, as they watched yet another pale, drawn woman standing by her husband's side, trying to withstand the gale force winds of his sex scandal. What will she do next? Leave? Stay? For how long? If my husband hired a prostitute? the chatter went.[86]

It was the Spitzer scandal, and the public relationship of Silda and Eliot Spitzer, that sparked that "chatter." The questions in the excerpted article illustrate how easily a political wife becomes a symbolic figure whose predicament is broadened to the concerns of the (female) public. Silda Spitzer's situation serves as a vehicle through which members of the public reflect on their own marital lives.[87] It prompts discussions about what Every Woman would do in Silda Spitzer's place. These personal questions are initiated by "yet another pale, drawn woman standing by her husband's side," in other words, Silda Spitzer.[88] Therefore, Silda Spitzer—or any political wife prompting public discussion—becomes a catalyst and ultimately a public symbol of infidelity's consequences.

It is clear from the Spitzer case that individual scandal is quickly broadened to the level of symbolic "phenomenon" via trend stories to become part of a pattern wherein an individual political wife represents something larger than herself as a person. In a *Times Union* piece, a commentator asks why "famous, power-hungry men" always have to have their wives "super-glued" to their side at such press conferences.[89] Another *Times Union* article argues that "Silda's presence at the press conference was bad for women everywhere."[90] Whether Silda Spitzer decided on her own to stand next to her husband at his press conference or her attendance was a result of spousal negotiation, her presence is construed as a stand on the larger issue and reflects on the state of women "everywhere."

The political wife's difficult situation, in which her personal actions are broadened into a trend story issue, is indicative of women being objects of attention. While women are typically objects of the (male) gaze, here women are objects of public opinion. Just as women's physical and outward appearances are scrutinized and looked upon as entities for inspection and visual pleasure, so too are her experiences in a time of scandal co-opted from her. They do not belong to her alone, just as her body does not belong to her alone. It is an object of desire and criticism.

JENNY SANFORD BREAKS THE MOLD

In contrast to Silda Spitzer, Jenny Sanford is vocal in her experience as a political wife caught up in her husband's scandal. News coverage of Jenny Sanford pitted her against her political-wife "predecessors," noting her new and independent path from the women who came before her.[91] A *Washington Post* op-ed headlined "Jenny Sanford, Role Model" sets apart this political wife. In the initial stage of press coverage, Jenny Sanford becomes the foil for the good wife by standing independently as a woman. It is during this initial stage that she is constructed as an agent in control of her experiences. Therefore, her symbolic status as a scorned wife is lessened at first. Here, *Washington Post* columnist Ruth Marcus categorizes the different political wives in her op-ed:[92]

> In one [scandal scenario], the wronged wife stands, looking stricken, by the side of the cheating pol as cameras whir. See Silda Wall and Eliot Spitzer, Suzanne and Larry Craig. In another, the wife is not on display but issues a supportive, if unnervingly euphemistic, press release. See Darlene Ensign: "Since we found out last year we have worked through the situation" and "our marriage has become stronger." Since we found out? Seems to me that one of us knew earlier about that, um, situation.[93]

In a similar example in the *New York Times*, news writers recall the list of political wives who follow a scandal script, in contrast to Jenny Sanford:

> Few could forget Hillary Rodham Clinton's sitting next to her husband, Bill Clinton, as he acknowledged to "60 Minutes" that he had caused pain in his marriage; or Dina Matos McGreevey, looking half dazed as Jim McGreevey detailed a homosexual affair and resigned the governorship of New Jersey; or Silda Wall Spitzer, posing just behind Gov. Eliot Spitzer of New York as he discussed hiring expensive call girls, her jaws clenched so tight that she could have cracked steel bars.[94]

Jenny Sanford is the political wife who strays from the good wife script and brings relief to a press accustomed to covering scandal stories with a repetitive narrative: husband admits wrongdoing, and his wife shows her unquestioning support. In contrast, Jenny Sanford comes across as a different type of political wife.[95] The headlines alone make it clear that she's carving an independent path for herself. For instance, the *Washington Post* headlines declare "Jenny Sanford, Role Model," "In Hubby's Time of Trouble, She Can't Be Bothered," and "In S.C., the Governor's Wife Is 'the Hero in the Story.'"[96] Meanwhile, the *New York Times* notes that "Political Wife's Hard Line Strikes Chord" and "In Storm, Governor's Wife Is Hurt but Unbowed."[97] The *State* announces that "Jenny Sanford Breaks Pattern of Betrayed."[98] This political wife, according to headlines, is different. Indeed, Jenny Sanford is not only quoted in about one-third of the articles on her husband's scandal, she is also quoted significantly in each article. For instance, in 10 articles, she is quoted more than seven times in each story.

This outspokenness, often directed against her husband, resonated with women in general, according to news coverage. The *New York Times* reports that "for thousands of women, responding on the Internet and Twitter, Mrs. Sanford's decision to hold her husband accountable provided a catharsis, a kind of public exorcism of the ghosts of political wives past."[99] Yet this resonance ultimately casts Jenny Sanford as a new type of symbol—one who is vocal and puts her personal needs before her husband's. Therefore, even as a political wife who breaks the mold, Jenny Sanford cannot escape symbolic status. A *Washington Post* writer elevates the position of Jenny Sanford: "Wow. Maybe this is a new role model for all wronged spouses, not just political ones."[100] That statement reinforces the point that political wives represent more than their own personal experiences.

The experiences of political wives are co-opted by the general public to suit the circumstances of their own lives. However, Roger Cohen, another *Washington Post* writer, cautions against using their experiences in this way.[101] He argues that hoisting these political wives to a symbolic role diminishes their private experiences when they become part of the public domain. Cohen is the lone writer who warns against objectifying these women by turning them into symbols of the "scorned wife":

> From the start, both Silda and Jenny were being used as symbols in different ways. To some commentators, they were not real women with real and very painful dilemmas but symbols to be manipulated to make both a personal and general point: One was a weak enabler while the other was a proud and independent woman who did what all women should do when humiliated by a lout of a husband. Between the lines, although in screaming italic, was a warning to the men in their lives that Jenny was the role model: Pay heed, darling. I will do the same.[102]

The writer warns against essentializing Silda Spitzer and Jenny Sanford by denying them their personal experiences: "[T]hese women are not vessels for the problems and anxieties of others nor exemplars of how, in some sort of emotional vacuum, these scandals should be handled. If anything, they should evoke humility. Life overwhelms us all."[103] Cohen recognizes these women as individuals, yet the public and most news writers use political wives as conduits to explore broader issues around fidelity and marriage. Because political wives whose husbands are scandal-tarnished rarely divulge the intimate details of their experiences, these women are largely unknown to the public and those who write about them. That may contribute to the ease with which their experiences are turned into symbols and cautionary tales, thereby erasing the individual contours of their predicaments.

Jenny Sanford interacted regularly with the news media and was quoted often. The quotes paint a picture of a woman who was bruised by her husband's actions but not devastated by them. She comes across as strong, confident, and independent of her spouse—traits that are traditionally ascribed to men. Jenny Sanford's "masculine-leaning" traits come through most strongly in articles in the *New York Times*, the *Washington Post*, and the *State*. Three days after Mark Sanford's June 24, 2009, press conference, the *New York Times* featured a front-page story of Jenny Sanford with the headline, "In Storm, Governor's Wife Is Hurt but Unbowed."[104] The accompanying front-page photo features a relaxed standalone of the first lady with her hand resting on her face. The jump photograph features the first lady standing with her dog, facing a cluster of photographers on her beachfront property. Her posture in the latter photograph is tense; her legs are in a wide stance (as opposed to the more feminine position of ankles touching, knees at an angle). She wears sunglasses so her eyes are not visible. The written text captures a woman who does not need a husband. "'Am I OK?' Mrs. Sanford repeated, from the driver's seat of a vehicle. 'You know what? I have great faith and I have great friends and great family. We have a good Lord in this world, and I know I'm going to be fine. Not only will I survive, I'll thrive.'"[105] The confident answer, the assurance that she will "thrive" in the face of scandal and the description of her in the "driver's seat," positions Jenny Sanford as in charge.

However, this independence and toughness can also be construed as uncaring toward her husband. A *Washington Post* headline—"In Hubby's Time of Trouble, She Can't Be Bothered"—indicates the gulf between this political wife and her politician-husband. Here, Jenny Sanford lacks warmth expected of most wives: "The wife has responded with calibrated contempt for his behavior, a grudging offer of Christian forgiveness, and the relaxed wardrobe of a regular at Canyon Ranch."[106] Denied a name in this aforementioned excerpt, Jenny Sanford is merely the cold "wife" who is distant, slightly cruel, but looking good. The article notes that Jenny Sanford was absent from her husband's press conference, which "denied the public record the usual 'aggrieved wife' photograph, one in which she is standing alongside her husband looking gaunt and tired."[107]

The masculine attributes describing this political wife emerge in the *Washington Post*, noting Jenny Sanford's "investment-banker steel,"[108] another article describing her office as the "war room,"[109] and a third article commenting on the fact that she "seized the role of stage manager" with her husband's political campaigns.[110] Other masculine constructions of Jenny Sanford are less direct but still place her outside the bounds of female warmth. She is not husbandcentric. One article in the *State* quotes Jenny Sanford as dismissive of her husband's career, post-scandal: "His career is not a concern of mine. He'll have to worry about that."[111]

While Jenny Sanford initially brings relief as a counterexample to the coterie of supportive political wives and is therefore cast in masculine terms because of her gender deviation, news coverage of Jenny Sanford also takes issue with the ways in which she broke the political wife mold. Columnist Ruth Marcus of the *Washington Post* wanted Jenny Sanford to more aggressively break the mold. Yet two other columnists, Maureen Dowd of the *New York Times* and Jane Herlong of the *State*, were irritated by this political wife's voice. Dowd labeled her "passive aggressive;"[112] while South Carolina columnist Herlong criticized Jenny Sanford for seeking out too much attention with her "media blitz ad nauseum."[113] Perhaps their backlash against her represents pushback for Jenny Sanford's refusal to play by the political wife script. Jenny Sanford's voice clearly irks them. Perhaps it is because she is outspoken. This is evidenced by Dowd's praise of Silda Spitzer's tacit nature in the same column where she takes issue with Jenny Sanford. In contrast to Jenny Sanford, Dowd lauds the "dignified Silda Spitzer silence."[114] Extending Dowd's logic, if there is "dignity" in a woman's silence, then speaking out must be indicative of undignified behavior.

PRESS RECONSTRUCTION OF WIFENESS

For women participating in the political sphere—whether as a politician or political wife—it is clear that press coverage of them is often categorized by a significant focus on their gender and fulfillment of their gender expectations. This happens when women fulfill their gender norms as well as when they break them. The implications of such double-bind depictions are twofold. First, news coverage reinforces a homogenization of women in politics, whether such female agents are directly involved as elected officials or on the periphery as political wives. Either way, these women are often reduced to a symbolic type and denied an individualized set of experiences particular to their own histories. What results in the case of political sex scandals is the reinforcement of social scripts that depict a woman as the passive victim of her husband's actions, and the husband as the dominant actor who controls the course of the marital dyad, even when he has transgressed morally. The irony is that the public and news consumers do not welcome such depictions of aggrieved political wives. Therefore, the second implication of the double-bind depiction is that the gendered elements of scandal stories generate a significant amount of public discourse surrounding gender, marriage, and fidelity. To follow the five gendered double binds (womb/brain, silence/shame, sameness/difference, femininity/competence, and aging/invisibility) that Kathleen Hall Jamieson erected in *Beyond the Double Bind: Women and Leadership*, this study offers a sixth double bind that women face: presence/absence.

In conclusion, this research has demonstrated that news coverage depicts Silda Spitzer's public support of her husband sparking strong feelings among the general public, including feelings of panic relating to infidelity and conjugal relations. The talk that scandal generates reinforces both the moralizing nature of scandal and the way in which people personalize scandal to relate its themes to their own lives.[115] The occurrence of scandal has become so habitualized that its core characters, including the politician, his wife, and the public, know their roles within the script.[116] In some instances, the wife may deviate from this role, as in the case of Jenny Sanford. Within the institution of scandal, the public's role is to talk, debate, and share information (often garnered from various media sources) about the unfolding events. It is clear that scandals create a media discourse about its moral themes, as there is a strong moral aspect to scandal.[117] These moral themes can include the legalization of prostitution, remaining in marriage after infidelity, sharing the news of marital infidelity with children, and participating in an "open" marriage. Many of these themes can become the subject of news coverage in the form of trend stories, reinforcing the connective nature between moral discourse generated by the public and the news media's dissemination of this talk. As such, the news media plays a key role as a hegemonic institution, transmitting social norms surrounding gender.

It is no surprise that people find the moral themes of scandal compelling and want to talk about them. First of all, the narrative structure of scandal makes it easy and exciting to follow.[118] Second, scandal helps people understand systems of power and polices people who step outside social norms.[119] In addition, people are most interested in scandals that are connected to their own deep-rooted fears about sexual betrayal.[120] The success of the CBS show *The Good Wife* (loosely inspired by Silda Spitzer) indicates the extent to which the public and the press can sustain its interest in the trials and tribulations of a political wife. The political wife, therefore, has become an institution within a social institution— a recognizable character who is a "type."[121] Even though political wives such as Silda Spitzer and Jenny Sanford may take opposing approaches to fulfilling or shirking the obligations of wifeness, the press ultimately constructs both women in relation to their husbands. This reaffirms the hegemonic nature between husband and wife, with the latter as the subservient spouse within the marital dyad.[122]

Scandal is the locus within the broader American culture that regulates sexuality outside of marriage.[123] When men step outside the bounds of acceptable sexual behavior, it is the wives who have the potential to bolster their reputations (and perceived power) for the public. "The decorous woman who always knows her place, both in public and in relation to her husband, is what undergirds the masculinist regime."[124] Hillary Clinton was perhaps one of the first political wives to break the mold as an outspoken and independently minded woman, and was subsequently cast in nonfeminine terms, as a "ball breaker" and "a congenital liar."[125] In the end, however, she issued a statement of support for her husband in the wake of the Monica Lewinsky sex scandal, because her deviation from her gender's norm hurt her husband's political clout and public standing. Like Hillary Clinton, Jenny Sanford was also described in terms atypical of her gendered self because she, too, broke the mold as an independent woman.

Ultimately, political wives face the same hurdles under the media spotlight as female politicians. They are judged whether they uphold their gender norms or deviate from them: "Either they're not tough enough to be in charge, or they're too bitchy to be. Either they're too masculine or not masculine enough. If they're good looking, it's held against them; if they're not good looking, same deal."[126]

As good wives, neither Silda Spitzer nor Jenny Sanford are constructed as individuals. Rather, the ideological construction from press coverage placed them first and foremost on a symbolic platform built on "wifeness." When Silda Spitzer upheld the stereotypic "good wife" position as a present yet silent supporter of her husband, she was condemned in press accounts. Yet a year later when the scandal of Mark Sanford seized the media spotlight, the symbolic figure of Silda Spitzer returned as a "dignified" wife in contrast to the vocal and divisive figure of Jenny Sanford.

Therefore, just as female politicians suffer from double standards because of their gender, so too do political wives with scandal-tarnished husbands find themselves as the subjects of judgment. With this absence/presence double bind, political wives face criticism by the press not only when they publicly support their husband but also when they appear to shirk their wifely duties during their husband's scandal. These political wives are judged as symbols of scorned wives and always in relation to their husbands. After all, the political wife's "proper role" is a feminine figure to uphold, and not besmirch, her husband's masculinity in a time of crisis.[127] The good wife, therefore, is a symbol that embodies an impossible ideal: unerring feminine support of a philandering husband. If she stands by him she is weak and wifely; if she stands in opposition to her husband she undercuts the sole purpose of a political wife: to bolster her husband within the public sphere. The good wife finds herself unable to extricate her gender from the very female problem of the double bind.[128]

Future research can include interviews with reporters and editors who wrote the stories that were analyzed for this study, investigating the extent to which they were familiar with the absence/presence double bind in which they placed Silda Spitzer and Jenny Sanford. Feminist in approach, this future line of inquiry would follow the work of those who offers guidelines for a "transformational" experience for the interviewer and her subjects on topics surrounding gender and power.[129] Perhaps this line of inquiry could bring us a microstep closer to confronting the gendered double binds that are transmitted through and by the news media.

CHAPTER 6

Have I Got a Story for You: State Lawmakers Confront Scandal in the New York Assembly

The state legislature in New York has the unfortunate distinction of being a veritable cauldron of corruption. It's no joke that an Albany college professor has founded the Museum of Political Corruption.[1] The facts speak for themselves: leaders of both the New York State Assembly and Senate—one, a Democrat, the other, a Republican—were arrested on corruption charges within four months of each other in 2015. Both were found guilty of all charges within two weeks of each other later that same year. And then there are the sex scandals, perhaps indicative of pathological behavior—or a culture of institutionalized sexism that is slowly becoming more democratized as women fill elected seats and as assembly behavior is dragged into a more progressive 21st century. But even as more women join the professional ranks, they find themselves fighting a long history of bad behavior. The following anecdote, shared by an assemblyman, epitomizes the assembly's "bro culture." Years ago, evidently, the assembly created a wellness program for its members. Assemblymen frequently got their blood pressure checked by nurses, which sadly but perhaps predictably devolved into chauvinistic chaos. "They were . . . propositioning the nurses," he said.[2] Beyond such anecdotes are the cold facts. The *Buffalo News*[3] counted 11 sex scandals from 2003 to 2013 in the New York State Legislature that embroiled men ranging from aides to assemblymen to governors.

Previous chapters in this book have explored the contemporary scandal landscape and have examined news coverage of politicians, their wives, and the "other women" who snagged headlines. Now it's time to explore scandals' impact inside a legislative body—in this case, that of the state of New York—to understand how politicians maneuver around and through the scandal morass. Considering the track record for corruption in the

New York State Legislature, Albany's political culture offers a prime case study for analysis.

It's not that "open season on scandal" is freely permitted in Albany. A sexual harassment policy is in place; interns may not "fraternize" with members or be present at official events that include alcohol; and all interns, staff, and members receive regular sexual harassment training. A third-party, confidential hotline exists to report sexual misconduct or harassment. But cases of pathological behavior still poke through the cracks. As one assemblywoman attempted to explain the scandal phenomenon: "It is an extreme need. It's . . . [an] emotional need overcoming rational judgment. I can't explain it. . . ."

Over the course of a year and a half, from 2012 to 2014, news of scandal-tarnished New York State assemblymen received prominent coverage in New York's most storied dailies, including the *New York Times*, *New York Daily News*, and *New York Post*—not to mention coverage in local TV outlets and online news sites. The parade of male state lawmakers behaving egregiously, aggressively, and chauvinistically ultimately resulted in the resignations of state lawmakers Vito Lopez in 2013, Dennis Gabryszak in 2014, and the beleaguered apology of a third assemblyman, Micah Kellner, in 2013.

While sexual harassment continues in today's workplace structures[4]—which sociologist Joan Acker describes as inherently masculine[5]—politicians who engage in chauvinist activities that have been a part of the assembly for generations can now become a liability to the state. It is not just that they're breaking assembly rules; it's also that media frenzies embarrass both the institution and their non-scandalous colleagues.[6] Sexual harassment is also time consuming and costly to the functioning of the assembly, requiring, by assembly rules, an investigation. Additionally, during the recent trio of scandals, the assembly paid more than $200,000 to outside law firms to develop an anti-harassment policy[7] as well as $200,000 for the establishment of a hotline to aid government workers reporting sexual harassment.[8]

The three political sex scandals, all involving sexual harassment of female government employees and interns, occurred one right after the other. This chapter is composed of interviews with New York State Assembly members. In this chapter I investigate how recent male scandals have impacted members personally and professionally, when a state body is enmeshed in the distractions and legal wrangling of sexual harassment and ethics investigations of their colleagues. At the heart of this chapter are interview anecdotes that serve as a window into Assembly Chambers. (It's worth noting that seven months after

I completed my interviews with assembly members—which took 1.5 years to complete and included 23 people—a female lawmaker became the first woman in the assembly to have her own sex scandal. It's a rather seedy distinction that shows women are not immune to scandal. But a female-instigated sex scandal is still an anomaly.[9] This chapter does not include analysis of the Angela Wozniak scandal, but it is mentioned at the outset of this book.)

THE SCANDAL TAINT

Private events involving lawmakers and elected officials may occur behind closed doors, but that does not mean that the event will remain private or that it affects only the people involved in it. Scandal can taint everyone with whom it comes in contact, including not only those involved in the private event but also all who learn of it. After all, scandal involves shame, (im)morality, and a sexuality that is often exploitative and exploited. As such, scandal's contagious elements threaten to contaminate those who broach its borders directly or indirectly.[10] According to sociologist Ari Adut, scandal contamination represents the demoralization and shame of the public, which consumes news of scandal, or "the individuals, groups or institutions that hold high status in the eyes of this public."[11] As members of a scandal-tarnished institution and as colleagues to scandal-tarnished (male) politicians, the assembly members interviewed here have experienced secondhand scandal contagion. They circulate within close professional proximity to the offenders, and they were elected to a governing body believed by the general public to be corrupt. As such, these assembly members can offer their unique insights about scandal and its indirect contamination.

THE SCANDALS AND THEIR AFTERMATH

Vito Lopez (2012)

The Vito Lopez affair was the most prolonged of the three scandals that occurred in the assembly, and Lopez was the highest-ranking legislator embroiled in sexual harassment allegations. In the summer of 2012, two women who worked for Lopez, a man described by the *New York Times* as "one of the last powerful Democratic Party bosses in New York City,"[12] alleged that they were victims of sexual harassment. Then Assembly Speaker Sheldon Silver censured the 71-year-old legislator. The New York State ethics commission investigated the allegations that Lopez had "verbally harassed, groped, and kissed" the two aides and examined how the legislature handled each claim.[13] Lopez resigned his assembly seat in May 2013 and in his statement announcing his resignation declared that he would run for New York City Council in the fall elections.[14] He was fined $330,000 by the legislative ethics panel in June 2013, a sum that was described as "the largest fine in [the panel's] history."[15] In September 2013 Lopez lost in the Democratic primaries for the New York City Council. He died in November 2015.

Micah Kellner (2013)

In July 2013, roughly one year after the allegations against Lopez had surfaced, Micah Kellner, a 34-year-old assemblyman from Manhattan, apologized publicly for inappropriate online chats he had with a female junior staff member while playing Facebook Scrabble with her three years earlier.[16] The lawmaker told her in a Google Talk conversation that he hired her because he thought she was cute and that he would like to fall asleep next to her. When the staffer reported to her supervisor in 2009 that she was harassed by the assemblyman, the supervisor provided a report to the assembly's Democratic counsel. The counsel, however, did not initiate an ethics investigation and was ultimately forced to resign in July 2013 for his inaction on the sexual harassment charge.[17] In September 2013 Kellner ran for New York City Council (while still serving as assemblyman), but lost. In 2013, when new reports of the sexual harassment incident from 2009 were made public, the assembly referred the allegations to its ethics commission.[18] The Ethics and Guidance Committee's investigation stripped Kellner of his committee chairmanships, mandated that he attend additional sexual harassment training, and prohibited him from hiring any interns.[19] While Kellner did not resign his assembly seat in the wake of his scandal, he decided not to seek reelection when his term expired in December 2014.[20]

Dennis Gabryszak (2014)

The assemblyman from Buffalo resigned in January 2014 after seven female staffers alleged that he had made inappropriate remarks and sexual advances toward them via text messages, on Facebook, and in person.[21] Days after Gabryszak resigned, the female staffers he had targeted released a graphic video to the media that showed the former assemblyman alone in a bathroom stall, pretending to masturbate or receive oral sex. In the video, which he allegedly sent to female members of his staff, Gabryszak appears to orgasm, flushes the toilet, and asks, staring straight at the camera, "Is this what you wanted?"[22] At the time of this writing, Gabryszak remains out of public office.

METHODOLOGY

This project had two phases. In March 2014, while the legislative body was in session, I mailed a letter to every New York State assemblywoman. The lawmakers received my letter just as the legislature passed its budget, one of the most significant and time-consuming tasks of the session. My hope, therefore, was that my deliberate timing would allow the legislators to have at least a few minutes to entertain questions from an academic researcher. My letter did not specify a deadline, reinforcing the idea that I would speak with them at their convenience.

I focused on the New York State Assembly—and not the State Senate— because recent sex scandals had occurred in the former legislative body, which had, in the spring of 2014, 33 female legislators and 117 male legislators. The assembly also has more lawmakers and, therefore, greater legislative power. Assemblywomen accounted for 22 percent of state lawmakers within the assembly. At the time of the research in 2014, New York State ranked 33 out of 50 for its representation of women within the entire state legislature, with 20.7 percent of elected seats within the state legislature[23]—which includes both the state assembly and senate— belonging to women.[24] In comparison, Colorado that year ranked first in the nation, with 41 percent of women holding elected office within its state legislature.

My research letter identified my academic interests and university affiliation. I stated that the purpose of my study "is to explore how male scandal impacts female politicians." Also included in the letter were ways in which information from the interviews might be published and disseminated.[25] I followed the guidelines set forth by scholars who have employed interviews with members of the political elite by typing my invitation for a research interview on university letterhead[26] and applying the "golden rule" of communicating with potential participants openly and honestly about the delicate nature of this research.[27] The fruits of those interviews were published as a journal article in 2015.[28]

After interviewing eight assemblywomen in spring 2014, I opened the study to all members of the assembly. I broadened the interviews so that I could hear how male members were impacted by the scandalous behavior of their colleagues. After all, bad behavior tarnishes the entire assembly. It's not only women who suffer, although it is a particular suffering they endure with the repeated barrage of male-implicated scandal.

Therefore, I e-mailed and posted another round of research letters in May 2015 to all members of the assembly in office at that time, minus the women already interviewed. I conducted an additional 15 interviews in spring and summer 2015, for a total of 23 interviews. In 2015 the number of women in the assembly jumped to 43, with women representing 25.8 percent of seats in the state legislature.[29] This ranking pushed New York to a much more favorable rating of 20th out of 50 states (from 33) for the percentage of women in the state legislature. I conducted 14 interviews over the phone, 8 interviews at the Albany Legislature, and 1 at a restaurant. All participants were offered—and accepted—anonymity because of the sensitive nature of the topic. The average interview length was about 35 minutes.

The timing of these interviews was auspicious for one who studies scandal. In January 2015, after phase one of the interviews, veteran Assembly Speaker Sheldon Silver was arrested on corruption charges. He was found guilty and sentenced to 12 years in federal prison in May 2016. A few months after Silver's 2015 arrest, Dean Skelos, leader of the New York Senate, was arrested on corruption charges unrelated to those brought against Silver. In December 2015 he also was found guilty of all charges and subsequently sentenced to five years in prison. Because the Silver and Skelos corruption cases did not relate to sex, we did not talk about them in the interviews. But their cases no doubt informed the dynamics of the interviews.

A SNAPSHOT OF THE ASSEMBLY MEMBERS WHO PARTICIPATED IN THIS STUDY

Due to the anonymity granted to the assembly members, I cannot provide any identifying information about their work, positions, backgrounds (including professional, personal, or ethnic), or years of service within the state legislature. Therefore, I will write of this group of 23 lawmakers in the aggregate without providing any identifying information. I interviewed 18 Democrats (the assembly has a majority of Democrats) and 5 Republicans; 3 members of color; 14 women; and 9 men. The median years of service in office was 10.

ACCESSING THE ASSEMBLY THROUGH STORIES

Storytelling sits at the center of these interviews. An analysis of assembly members' anecdotes helps us better understand dynamics of power and gender within these sex-scandal stories. What are the stories they tell as they reflect on the scandals that have ripped through their place of work? What themes emerge through these stories based on the genders of the storyteller?

Through the process of narrative inquiry, we have the opportunity to study lived experience by assembly members who circulate in a governing body under fire for sexual harassment. As gripping tales that are sensational by their very nature, scandal lends itself well to a method of narrative inquiry. This is especially the case because stories connected to scandal hold significant currency in the assembly rumor mill and at the proverbial water cooler. It was not uncommon for assembly members to exchange stories related to scandal-tarnished fellow members.[30] "It is commonplace to note that human beings both live and tell stories about their living," writes D. Jean Clandinin, a professor of education at the University of Alberta, who has published extensively on the narrative inquiry method. "These lived and told stories and talk about those stories are ways we create meaning in our lives as well as ways we enlist each other's help in building our lives and communities."[31] Story, as a site for analysis, represents a portal through which a person interacts with her world and extracts meaning. "Narrative inquiry, the study of experience as story, then, is first and foremost a way of thinking about experience."[32] What's gripping about this narrative approach is that it takes an object of the everyday—an anecdote, a simple story—and privileges it as a key to understand experience and life situations. By shifting stories from the periphery to the center, we are assured of their value to unlocking our understanding of lived experience. As Clandinin writes, "The truth about stories is that that's all we are."[33]

Narrative Inquiry and Story Analysis

The three dimensions of narrative inquiry further cement it as a worthwhile approach in studying sex scandal in the New York State Assembly. These three dimensions include personal and social interactions, continuity across time and place, and situation.[34] Researchers who use narrative inquiry work within this 3-D space, along with their subjects, to compose field texts for analysis.

This chapter uses the work of Joanne Martin, a researcher of organizational culture at Stanford University, as a template for deconstructing and then reconstructing stories of organizational taboo. In a journal article on organizational taboos, Martin retells an anecdote shared by a prominent (although unnamed) male CEO at an industry conference,[35] who explains how his company is working with a female employee to time her cesarean section to immediately precede the launch of an important new product. By deconstructing the story from a feminist standpoint and then reconstructing it by changing small portions of the text each time, Martin demonstrates how the retelling of the anecdote reveals an imbalance in the power structure that eradicates a public/private divide centering on pregnancy and birth connected to the workplace. I will use Martin's approach as a tool to personalize scandal stories from assembly members who are indirectly impacted by the boundary-crossing behavior of their scandal-tarnished colleagues.

Nine anecdotes emerged throughout my interviews with 23 New York State Assembly members. These anecdotes included stories about interns, interactions with scandal-tarnished members, male members recounting how female assembly staffers acted aggressively toward them, and tales about frat-style behavior that harken back to the previous century. I have selected the following six anecdotes for analysis:

- Anecdote 1: An assemblywoman's female intern drew the attention of Vito Lopez, one of the disgraced members of the assembly
- Anecdote 2: Another assemblywoman's story about a handsome male intern, whose interactions with a female intern caused Dennis Gabryszak, another disgraced assemblyman, to bristle
- Anecdote 3: An assemblyman who was on the receiving end of female sexual aggression
- Anecdote 4: An assemblywoman who overheard male colleagues talk about the "hot" appearance of a female legislator
- Anecdote 5: An assemblyman recalls what it was like to have an assemblywoman complain that he made her uncomfortable
- Anecdote 6: An assemblyman recalls what it was like to be teased by Vito Lopez, and how he teased him in return

I selected these stories for three reasons. First, they were told in a clear and colorful manner. Second, they speak to the nature of the desiring and desirous body within the assembly. Third, they each offer varying insights into the gendered power dynamics at play within a scandalized governing body.

Martin, the researcher on organizational culture, outlines nine steps or "analytic strategies used in deconstruction."[36] I will first present each anecdote and then apply—where relevant—the various analytic strategies to unearth new layers of the anecdote and its place within the scandal ecology. However, it is first necessary to review Martin's explanation of deconstruction within this context of story analysis. "Deconstruction," writes Martin, "is able to reveal ideological assumptions in a way that is particularly sensitive to the suppressed interests of members of disempowered, marginalized groups."[37] In a governing body where the overwhelming number of scandal lawmakers have been male, deconstructing scandal stories allows us new insights into how male-led boundary violations impact assemblywomen, in addition to male colleagues who may feel tarnished by gender association. "Deconstruction peels away the layers of ideological obscuration, exposing the conflict that has been suppressed; the devalued 'other' is made visible."[38] While we may be interested in the multiple meanings and interpretations to emerge through a deconstruction, it's necessary to note that we can never assert that we've arrived at the "truth about what the author of a text intended to communicate."[39] We do not focus on intent. Rather, it is the meaning and impression that hold our attention.

Before we dive into these six anecdotes, it is worth noting a thematic difference that emerged throughout the 23 interviews—that is, how men and women responded to questions about gender and scandal. A noticeable strain of assemblymen rejected the question: would the election of more women to the New York State Assembly reduce the occurrence of scandal? While a number of assemblywomen also rejected this idea, a greater diversity of opinion emerged among female responses to that question. I am certainly not the first person to pose this question within the scandal ecosphere. In 2011, following "Round One" of the Anthony Weiner Twitter scandal, an *Associated Press* article asked, "[I]f more women were elected to office, would political sex scandals disappear?"[40] But when I posed that question in interviews, I found a gulf in answers between men and women. Men, by and large, answered, "No." Women's reactions were more mixed. Here is a selection of their responses:

Assemblywomen on Whether More Women Would Reduce Scandal's Occurrence

1. "Of course."[41]
2. "Yes, I think it would be less likely. But I still feel that we've done a decent job of getting . . . a handle on this. But it certainly could improve by having more women. I'll grant you that."[42]
3. "Well, I certainly think it could be a good reason to support women. I'm not one of those people that says we need to have more women just because they're women. I think we need to have good people

who are qualified regardless of whether they're women, men, transgender, black, white, Hispanic, Indian, whatever."[43]

4. "I really don't think electing [more] women would reduce scandal. You could have 10 women and two men . . . and you can still have a scandal occurring. So it's not that. It's about—it's holding everyone to the same standards."[44]

5. "I sincerely believe it would. I think the women are much more inclined to work in a more rational way and not allow these scandals and things to come into play. And I think women are more likely to want to find common ground. They want to make people happy. They'll look for the compromise."[45]

6. "I don't necessarily think that if there were women in those positions that would prohibit men from not being able to control their testosterone."[46]

7. "More women, more women. The culture will change dramatically."[47]

8. "Yeah, I don't think it's realistic. Sure, we want more women . . . but you know I have lots of wonderful progressive male colleagues [who] I would rather have—to me it's not a gender divide necessarily . . . Give me a good, progressive male any day of the week than a woman who's going to vote the wrong way on things that are important to me."[48]

9. "I think it helps, the more you see women in positions of authority. I do think it makes a difference. It absolutely makes a difference."[49]

10. "Yes, don't you think so? Have you ever heard anything scandalous about a woman?"[50]

Assemblymen on Gender and Scandal's Occurrence

1. "I would hope so—but I think that's also simplistic."[51]

2. "I don't think that's the reason to elect more women. I think we should be electing more women because we need . . . a broader viewpoint on things . . . Yeah, women could be in scandals as well. I don't know what makes the difference. But I've heard stories of people in legislature, judgeships and stuff like that over the years, of women being as aggressive as men."[52]

3. "The reality is scandals in general . . . are not unique just to men, males. So therefore, to counter your comment, we should only elect women because they won't commit sexual assault, sexual corruption, or sexual harassment—I don't know if I would agree with that comment. We should elect the right person, regardless of gender, who's going to serve the public's interest."[53]

4. "I mean, if the number of men in the legislature were reduced I
   don't think that would significantly reduce the number of misbe-
   having legislators. Just like if you closed banks on Fridays—that
   wouldn't cut down on bank robberies."[54]
5. "I think, a belief—a fundamental belief—that women in positions
   of power do not . . . engage in some measure of sexual exploitation
   of those who are in a less powerful position—would be misplaced."[55]
6. "There should be more women in public office not just primarily
   because of that issue, but because a legislature should be reflective
   of the people it represents."[56]
7. "I don't think one has anything to do with the other. I don't think
   more women would solve the problem. I think they'd solve the
   problem by electing better people."[57]
8. "I think that would be certainly unfair . . . I've had experiences with
   women members that are terrific, and then I've had some women
   members—and I'm just saying this—lie through their teeth. But
   unfortunately they get away with it more because of their gender,
   and it's always assumed that the guy is . . . the guilty one."[58]
9. "There [have] has been instances of female legislators coming onto
   male staffers as well. So I think it has more to do with the fact
   that . . . you are away from home and a lot of times your inhibition
   for both sexes becomes much lower. So is that an argument that
   you should elect more women, would it change if you elected more
   women? . . . I don't think so. You may actually see more instances
   going the other way—if that happens.[59]

The Gender Divide

It is clear that women lawmakers expressed a greater diversity of opinion than their male counterparts when speculating about whether tipping
the gender balance would impact scandal's occurrence. Perhaps women
suffer greater scandal fatigue than their male colleagues, since they are
forced to deal with the impact and onslaught of scandal that repeatedly
sees men bringing shame and negative media attention to the assembly,
tarnishing their positions and work by extension. In order to see how
gender dynamics and scandal play out in the assembly, let's now dive into
the anecdotes that bring these elements together. Keep in mind that in
order to maintain anonymity with the interview subjects, any statement
that would unmask an individual's identity has been deleted. Therefore,
the texts below reflect a gentle editor's hand.

ANECDOTE 1: VITO LOPEZ, HIS "ODD DUCKS," AND AN INTERN

Assemblywoman: Well, I sat near Vito Lopez, so I was always somewhat fascinated by, you know, what was going on there sociologically. There were always these new women and then young women and they were always sort of—they were attractive but they were attractive in like a funky way, like they were odd ducks, sort of. And they were always seated around him almost like an entourage, you know. And he was always very charming and very nice to me and funny. And so I'm sure that's why he was able to cast this spell or to manipulate some of these people in the end. I guess I'm speculating, but I just thought it was interesting . . . I never was in the office with him. I never saw his interaction with his staffers. . . . But just on the floor, which is all . . . public and televised. So I never saw anything other than it was just odd to me that this man always has these young women, you know, like these young women working for him and he was in his 70s. . . . I had an intern one year who was a very attractive young girl, and after she spoke in a mock session, he had his chief of staff contact me and said that he was interested in hiring her. And he said she did such a great performance, you know, in the mock session, in which she got up and read, like, four sentences. And that's when my first . . . inclination [occurred]. And then it was . . . either a year later or . . . two years later that Vito was called and it turned out that these women that were sitting around him, that were right in front of me, were the ones that were the victims. Yeah, it's pretty crazy. But he clearly—I mean—not that my intern wasn't wonderful, she was, but she was not a standout in the mock session. He was clearly seeking to hire [her] because she was really cute. . . .

Hinda: So what was your reaction then?

Assemblywoman: Well, interestingly, I contacted her, because, they asked, and I gave her an opportunity to discuss it. I met with her parents who happened to be coming to town that day because it was a mock session day, and we all went out to dinner. And her father was like, this guy sounds sleazy. I don't want my daughter working for him. So they didn't even end up calling him back.

Dichotomies: "Odd Ducks," Cuteness, and the Public/Private Divide

The first analytic strategy in a deconstruction, according to Martin, is "dismantling a dichotomy, exposing it as a false distinction."[60] By dismantling a dichotomy, we are in fact complicating the story and situation under review. The anecdote above centers on two overarching dichoto-mies. The first is the attractive/not-so-attractive distinction. The second is a public/private divide.

The assemblywoman distinguishes between two levels of physical attrac-tiveness among assembly subordinates in this anecdote. There are those who are "attractive in like a funky way"—in other words, they are "odd ducks"—and then there is her intern, "a very attractive young girl," who is also "really cute." We have a distinction between those who are untra-ditionally vs. traditionally attractive. The legislator states that her intern's traditionally attractive appearance secured the attention of Assembly-man Vito Lopez. In fact, it became *the* reason he extended an opportunity for employment. The physical marker of cuteness, therefore, can make women a target for the untoward advances and come-ons of powerful men. In this way, being "very attractive" and "really cute" is a liability for young women (especially within the context that the assemblyman sexually harassed female members of his staff). But it's not just the "very attractive" and "really cute" ones who are targeted. We also see here that "odd ducks" were employed by Lopez. Therefore, it is not merely "cuteness" that makes one vulnerable in this situation but also youth. The assemblywoman shar-ing the anecdote utters the phrase "young women" three times. She intro-duces the anecdote by saying that "there were always these new women *and then* young women" (emphasis added), and she lasers in on the parade of *young women* whom she observed with the assemblyman, "almost like an entourage." She implies that the age difference between the assembly-man and this "entourage" raised plenty of eyebrows. Ultimately, we see that a young woman, whether she is an "odd duck" or "very attractive," is a potential target of sexual harassment. Attractiveness, therefore, is the not the linchpin to vulnerability. It's youth.

The second dichotomy embedded within this anecdote is the public/private divide. The assemblywoman made clear that she never witnessed Assemblyman Lopez's sexual misconduct. "I never was in the office with him. I never saw his interaction with his staffers. . . ." Her observations of him took place in Assembly Chambers, "which is all publicized and it's public and televised." Implicit in this assemblywoman's story is a belief that she did not witness any untoward behavior by Lopez to his staff-ers, because he was in public and not within the private, controlled, and unobservable environment of his office; and that she was therefore not complicit in the violation of assembly rules regarding the treatment of employees. By making the distinction, the assemblywoman implies that she did not know—because she could not know—whether harassment actually was taking place.

Subordinate Silence

Martin's second analytic strategy in deconstructing a story is attending to silences in the story.[61] In this anecdote, one group speaks and one is silent. Those who have a voice are traditional power brokers:

- The assemblywoman who tells the story
- Assemblyman Lopez, who makes his opinion known that he'd like to hire the "very attractive" intern
- Lopez's chief of staff, who attempted to facilitate that hiring
- The intern's father

Those who do not have a voice in this anecdote include:

- The "odd duck" female aides who work for Lopez
- The "very attractive" female intern

Young women clearly lack a voice in this story. Those who possess it are the assemblywoman, her male colleague, his male chief of staff, and the intern's father. When the assemblywoman went to dinner with the intern and her parents, the father said, "[T]his guy sounds sleazy. I don't want my daughter working for him." While the intern may presumably agree with her father's position, we do not hear her articulate her thoughts using her own voice. And it wasn't the intern who declined Lopez's offer of employment; it was the family as a unit: "So **they** didn't end up even calling him back" (emphasis added), as if the job included an offer to the father as well.

Contradiction: "Odd Ducks" Who Are "Attractive"

The third analytic strategy is to hone in on contradictions. Here we have the inconsistency of women who are simultaneously "attractive" but also "odd ducks." One typically does not associate an adjective of attractiveness with "odd ducks," who are commonly distinguished by unusual behavior or appearance. The aides' odd duck status is central to this story, because they appeared to converge around a much older assemblyman, according to the assemblywoman who reminisces about her disgraced colleague. This highlights his questionable behavior and decision-making capacities, perhaps foreshadowing scandal, even as the assemblywoman admits she never saw anything blatantly wrong but merely found it "just odd" that the older legislator surrounded himself with young women of a certain appearance type.

The Age Difference

Martin instructs us to pay attention to the element "most alien" to the text.[62] Here, it's clearly the age gap between the "young women" and the assemblyman "in his 70s." The age difference caught the assemblywoman's attention and caused her to linger on the legislator and his "entourage."

Revisiting the "Odd Ducks" Under a "Spell"

The fifth analytic strategy instructs us to unpack metaphors. Here we return to the "odd ducks," the legislator's aides who were "attractive in a funky way." Their odd-duck status caught the attention of the assemblywoman, enough to hold her interest but not enough to do much more than watch them as a social curiosity. ("I was always somewhat fascinated by, you know, what was going on there sociologically.") The presence of these women with the assemblyman hinted at a professional setup that wasn't quite professional. The assemblywoman's intern, not an odd duck because she is a "very attractive young girl" and "really cute," was in danger of becoming assimilated into the "odd duck" office but was saved from such a fate by her father's protective instincts. The intern was an innocent—a pretty and "young girl" (even though she was a college student), and her body needed protection against potential violation. The assemblywoman even had an "inclination" when Lopez's chief of staff inquired about hiring her. The "odd ducks," while a curiosity, didn't appear to have such protectors. The intern, meanwhile, was delicate—like a "girl" and beautiful to boot. Protection was needed in order to keep her away from Lopez, who "cast this spell" on his staff.

The Double Entendre of the Man Who "Has These Women"

The seventh analytic step in the deconstruction of a narrative is to analyze double entendre within the text. As Martin notes in her analysis of the cesarean story, sexual undertones exist when one suggests that a man "has" a woman.[63] In the assemblywoman anecdote, the legislator describes it as "odd" that "this man always has these young women" (in his employment). One cannot deny the sexual undertone in the assemblywoman's statement, even if she did not witness any illicit behavior when she observed Lopez with his staff on the assembly floor. Regardless, an "odd" sexual dynamic was at play.

Reconstructing the Story

Martin instructs us to reconstruct the text by swapping out key elements, one at a time, with comparative substitutes. For instance, if we substitute "attractive" for "ugly" we have a story where an assemblyman surrounds himself with "ugly young women." And the intern—once "very attractive"—is now rather ugly. Yet her father still protects her from the "sleazy" assemblyman. This substitution reveals that the element "most alien" in this text—the age gap—still persists. Indeed, it doesn't matter if a young woman is attractive or ugly, the assemblyman preys on young women. We also can reconstruct the story by substituting young women for "young men." And we can reconstruct the predatory assembly member as a woman. Yet regardless of the subordinates' or assembly member's gender, we still see the age difference persisting as the "most alien" element to the text. This changes in the final reconstruction, where we substitute young women for "old women." In this iteration, we've removed the "most alien" element of the text (the age gap of an older man surrounding himself with "odd duck" women). Sexual harassment is sexual harassment, whether the victims are young or older. But this final reconstruction reinforces the vulnerability of young subordinates working in the assembly. Those who are at risk are young people—regardless of physical appearance.

ANECDOTE 2: INTERN MATCHMAKING GONE AWRY

This anecdote relates to another scandal-tarnished assemblyman, Dennis Gabryszak, who resigned in 2014. The focus is on a young male intern who worked for an assemblywoman, who shares this story:

Assemblywoman: I have a young guy that comes up from _____ and works with me there who's terrific and lovely and a gentleman and smart. I mean, he's just—you know, the young girls—and he's handsome. And lots of young women come by my office to talk to him, and he knows what he's doing and he's very helpful. He's just someone other people would gravitate toward. So this woman across the hall came over, and I saw she was there several times having coffee or whatever—because I had coffee in my office. Whatever. These are little informal offices that we have up there.

Hinda: Hm-hmmmm.

Assemblywoman: Anyway, I mentioned to Gabryszak at a meeting that I thought that—I made a joke about there was some little relationship between his intern and my intern. And he like literally turned his body from me as if I will never talk to you again, and I was like, "Whoa, whoa!" What a ridiculous—I was just being, like, cordial.

Hinda: Wow, it was like he was being very possessive.

Assemblywoman: Exactly. I read it that way right away, as did the guy that works for me when I mentioned it, and the woman didn't come back again.

Dismantling the Dichotomy of Collegiality

In this anecdote we have the dichotomy of colleagues who are cordial to each other and those who are not. The assemblywoman implies that there is a general expectation that people working within the assembly are cordial to each other and that it's a social environment. Her intern has visitors who stop by the office for a chat in these "little informal offices." She speaks cordially of her intern, praising his abilities, sociability, and appearance. The female intern has developed a cordial rapport with the male intern. Yet when the assemblywoman speaks with her colleague in a way that she thinks of as cordial ("I made a little joke," she says) he responds with hostility. Her reaction is shock—not just at the way he uses his physical body to show disregard but because she thinks she was being friendly and therefore her behavior did not warrant a hostile response. ("I was like, 'Whoa, whoa!' What a ridiculous, I was just being, like, cordial.") The fact that the assemblyman reacted with hostility to a casual conversation that she deemed "cordial" was a clue, to her, that something was amiss with her colleague.

Examining Silence

Of the four people who have a role in this anecdote (the assemblywoman, her male intern, Assemblyman Dennis Gabryszak, and his female intern), only one of these individuals does not have a voice: the female intern. The assemblywoman tells the story and also approaches her colleague about the social interactions between their interns; the assemblyman lets his opinion be known by physically turning himself away from the assemblywoman, which she and her male intern interpreted as jealousy. But we don't hear from the female intern. She had her own authority when she visited with a fellow intern, drinking coffee in the assemblywoman's office, but once the assemblywoman suggested, jokingly, "some little relationship" with the male intern, she didn't return to the office. The angered assemblyman presumably curtailed her free movement.

Attending to Disruptions: Cordiality—or Meddling?

The assemblywoman, not knowing that the assemblyman with whom she had spoken had already created a hostile environment for his female staff member, was surprised at his reaction to her comment because she was "just being . . . cordial." While it's certainly not uncommon to make casual and offhanded comments and to joke about the (potentially romantic) compatibility of two people in an office environment, such a comment may be unwelcome to interns and others. It is understandable if the interns did not want their interactions to become fodder for office gossip, even if it was good-natured. Therefore, while the assemblywoman may have thought she was acting in a "cordial" manner, it may have been unwelcome from the interns' perspective. It certainly would not be unreasonable for them to feel uncomfortable that a boss was playing "matchmaker" or commenting on their romantic compatibility behind their backs and to another superior. But we don't know.

Element Most Alien to the Text: Antagonistic Body Language

When Assemblyman Gabryszak "literally turned his body" from the assemblywoman as she joked that "there was some little relationship" between their interns, she responded with genuine surprise. It's not common for someone to use their body to express a physical manifestation of disregard when talking with someone else, especially if the subject of conversation is meant to be "cordial." The assemblyman's abrupt use of his body to signal his anger indicated to the assemblywoman that he had a problem with her casual suggestion about the "little relationship" between interns. He appeared so angered by her suggestion that his body indicated, "I will never talk to you again."

Double Entendre of "Having" Interns

In the first anecdote, we read how another assemblywoman described Assemblyman Lopez as a "man [who] always **has** these young women" (emphasis added). In this current anecdote, the assemblywoman uses "have" to describe her intern: "I have a young guy that comes up from _____." The use of "have" heightens the power and sexual dynamics of this office quadrangle, between the assemblywoman and the male intern, between the male and female interns, between the assembly members, and between the assemblyman and the female intern.

Reconstructing the Story

The gender identity of the interns doesn't affect the power dynamic between the assembly members and the interns or between the assembly members themselves. Neither does the interns' age impact the contours of the story. What does change the story—through reconstruction—is imagining the female intern, who worked for Assemblyman Gabryszak, returning to her coffee chats with the male intern. As the assemblywoman noted in her telling of the story, "The woman didn't come back again" after her abrupt interaction with an apparently jealous Assemblyman Gabryszak. The clear implication is that the assemblyman had words with his intern, forbidding her to return to those casual coffee conversations with assemblywoman's intern. But if we reconstruct the story to show that the female intern returned to these coffee chats, we see that she maintains freedom of movement; her body is not controlled by a male superior, and his jealous whims do not restrict her freedom of association.

ANECDOTE 3: GETTING "DRAGGED" INTO THE BATHROOM

In this story, an assemblyman says that women who work in the state legislature have acted sexually aggressively to him.

Assemblyman: I am a single person up here. . . . And I have had numerous instances in which I have had women be the aggressor to me. So, it's not always a one-way street. And nobody talks about that because nobody wants to label that and be seen as a sexist, a chauvinist, but I can tell you I have had women come onto me—very aggressively.

Hinda: How do you know that they are coming onto you?

Assemblyman: Literally dragging me into a bathroom.

Hinda: Yeah?

Assemblyman: Yeah, literally.

Hinda: So then do you report that?

Assemblyman: No.

Hinda: I mean it's sexual harassment, I mean—

Assemblyman: I guess if I really wanted, if I didn't like the person I probably would report it. But, you know, I was raised by my mother and my sister and we were taught to respect women, and chivalry is far from dead in my book. But that's always happened, that's happened for a long time. There used to be a cliché up here that certain staffers, their end game or goal was to bag a legislator.

Dichotomy: Maintaining "Chivalry" at All Costs

The assemblyman notes that his mother taught him to "respect women" and that "chivalry is far from dead in my book." It's clear from this story that even if a woman acts sexually aggressive to him, he wants to maintain the standard of gender relations: that a man is courteous to a woman, even as she crosses into aggressive territory. The assemblyman says, unequivocally, that he does not report this behavior because to do so would be to disrespect women. There is also the fear that he would be labeled "a sexist, a chauvinist" by speaking out against women. The following appears to be his code: if an assemblyman does not report women's sexually aggressive behavior, then he maintains a chivalrous manner and protects the offending woman from the consequences of her bad behavior. If he does speak out against a woman's sexual aggression, then he lacks respect for women. Implicit in this reaction is the belief that a man should be able to handle women, as their protectors, and that if men speak out against gender-bending women, they risk making themselves vulnerable because they acted against the expectations of their gender.

Examining Silences

The assemblyman does not say what happened in the bathroom once he was "dragged" in there. I did not inquire because (a) I was surprised that he even offered such a juicy tidbit of information so I felt off-kilter, and (b) I also felt awkward asking a man I just met, an elected official in his Albany office, about potential sex acts that he may or may not have engaged in. Therefore, I do not know what happened in the bathroom.

Attending to Disruptions: Sexism and Female Aggression

Martin instructs us to pay attention to "places where the text fails to make sense."[64] We can find such a disruption when the assemblyman speaks of women acting in a sexually aggressive manner. "So it's not always a one-way street," he says, referring to the norm of male sexual aggression. "And nobody talks about that [female sexual aggression] because nobody wants to label that and be seen as a sexist, a chauvinist, but I can tell you I have had women come onto me, very aggressively." Since he does not label the occurrence of female sexual misconduct in the legislative culture, he does not officially affirm its existence. The assemblyman does not specify who the "nobody" is when he says, "Nobody talks about that because nobody wants to label that." Is that "nobody" specific to those working within the New York State Assembly or those within our shared culture? To name such behavior, he says, would risk being "seen as a sexist, a chauvinist." Initially, the logic embedded in that assertion doesn't make sense. Why would one "be seen as a sexist" for calling out women who engage in sexual misconduct? Why is the act of naming woman-instigated sexual misconduct considered sexist? Perhaps because it bucks gender-confirming sex traits that women are pliant and demure, and by naming woman-instigated sexual misconduct then men are contributing to women's potential professional failures. What is clear is that this assemblyman views the excoriation of woman-initiated sexual misconduct as unchivalrous and disrespectful to women. It is as if a real man can handle a sexually aggressive woman. And if she diminishes his male essence—his ability to control a woman—through her sexual misconduct, then he is not man enough to handle a woman.

Focusing on the Alien Element: The Bathroom

The bathroom clearly represents the most alien element in this story, not only because there is the implication that it might have been the site of sexual activity but also because it is an unusual conversation piece in a professional interview between a researcher and a politician.

The bathroom is symbolic of boundary crossing. There are at least three specific boundaries worth noting. As previously mentioned, there's the taboo topic of talking about bathrooms in a professional interview. Its surfacing threw off my interview game. Suddenly, and for the first time throughout the course of these assembly interviews, I found a source who was surprisingly forthcoming and personal. He alluded to himself as a sex object. Second, there is the literal boundary crossing of a person being dragged across a threshold into the specific space of a bathroom. In doing so, the person crossing into bathroom space leaves a public space where people are fully clothed and where bodily functions are controlled, because the body is constructed as proper and tidy and professional. By crossing the boundary, he moves into a place where people disrobe and conduct private "business" to attend to the evacuation needs of the body. Third, there is the boundary crossing of one gender entering the domain of the other gender, since bathrooms are traditionally designated as belonging to "women" or "men." Therefore, the woman who drags the assembly-man takes him either into the "male" bathroom, thereby crossing into a territory that is supposed to be off limits to her, or she drags him into a "female" bathroom, thereby bringing a male body into a female space. The bathroom, as an alien element in the text, is symbolic of the unbalanced dynamic between a sexually aggressive woman and a man "dragged" into a sexual encounter.

The Metaphor of "Bagging a Legislator"

It's clear that in the assemblyman's world, women are sexually interested in legislators. "There used to be a cliché up here that certain staffers, their end game or goal was to bag a legislator," he said. The metaphor refers, as we know, to having sex. But the literal image of "bagging" a person is comparable to "dragging" a person. Both connote yielding power over another person who succumbs, through lack of strength or by giving in to powerlessness, to the dominating actions of the person doing the "bagging" or "dragging." In the assemblyman's story, we have the example of a man who was overcome by the strength of a woman because she was "literally dragging me into a bathroom." But in his reference to the well-known dynamic between staffers and legislators, he uses gender-neutral terms to describe this so-called end game.

Reconstructing the Story: Playing with Gender

If we swap the gender of the people who have been "the aggressor," we see that the male-female dynamic is important to this story. After all, if it were men who had hit on the legislator ("very aggressively," as was the case with women), then the assemblyman would not use chivalry and respect for women as justification for not reporting the incidents. It is specifically because women acted in a sexually aggressive manner, engaging in sexual misconduct, that the assemblyman chose to handle the incident himself. He did not want to risk the label of "sexist," or—perhaps—"unmasculine."

ANECDOTE 4: BARBERSHOP TALK IN ASSEMBLY CHAMBERS

An assemblywoman shared this story, which took place in the impressive grand hall known as Assembly Chambers. Chambers is the site where legislators conduct official business and vote on bills when they're in session. Assembly Chambers is noted for its hallowed structure, decorated in red and gold with numerous chandeliers, marble columns, and stained-glass, arched windows.

Assemblywoman: I'm listening to a conversation of colleagues, male colleagues, just literally a week ago. I'm not listening because I'm nosy—I just happen to be in the area where they were talking. And they're talking about a woman who may be running for a particular seat to replace one of the guys who was involved in the sex scandal.

Hinda: Is that Dennis Gabryszak? Or?

Assemblywoman: I won't say which one. Because then they'll know who I'm talking about when they see this.

Hinda: Oh, ok.

Assemblywoman: And so he's explaining that she's an older lady but she looks very young. And so the other guy, the other member, said to him, "Well, is she hot?" Well, that's not a question to be asking about a legislator that's coming to be your colleague. They should be asking, "Is she smart?" They should be asking, "Is she a people advocate?" "Is she going to fight for what's in the best interests of people? Is she liberal? Is she conservative?" But "Is she hot?" I'm like—that's a crazy question. Now this person already has been elected. But that's the question he asked his colleagues.

Hinda: Now the man who said, "Is she hot?"—were you surprised that he asked that question? Or does this man already have a reputation?

Assemblywoman: No. This gentleman does not have a reputation. And I'm not surprised because that's the way men talk.

Hinda: Yeah.

Assemblywoman: They talk like that in the barbershop. They talk like that in corporations. They talk like that on the train. That's how they talk to each other.

Hinda: Yeah.

Assemblywoman: One of the most important things to them is their male genitalia. I mean, that's who they are as people. That's how they talk to each other.

Hinda: Did anyone say anything to them—or?

Assemblywoman: No.

Dichotomy: Men Talk One Way, Women Talk Another

Implicit in the assemblywoman's story is that men are programmed—whether biologically or culturally—to talk in a chauvinistic way, which is distinct from how women talk. In this anecdote, the assemblywoman's commentary on the conversation, which takes aim at her male colleagues, embodies the counter-talk to the male chitchat session in Assembly Chambers: the assemblywoman poses questions that are rational, professional, and critical. In other words, her response to her male colleagues is stereotypically male. She is work focused, not motivated by the gossip and idle chatter preferred by her male colleagues. Yet she describes their conversation as stereotypically male, perhaps because it shows a disregard for an appropriateness of space and place. They're chauvinists by acting in a manner that suits them, regardless of the saucy subject of their conversation that occurred (a) in a place of legislative work and (b) within earshot of (female) colleagues. Therefore, even though they are engaging in gossip, historically constructed as a woman's activity, their tone-deaf desire to speak in an uncensored manner, without regard for nonparticipating but listening colleagues, is characteristically male.

Examining Silences

When the assemblywoman shares this anecdote, she clearly expresses strong feelings opposing both the way her male colleagues acted and their inappropriate choice of a conversation subject. But she did not convey this outrage to them directly as she listened to them dissect the "hot" appearance of a new member of the legislature. Therefore, in the original unfolding of this story, the assemblywoman was a silent fixture, in close proximity to the gossiping male colleagues but not a part of their conversation—nor openly critical of it (to them). Yet she was silently passing judgment. It is certainly understandable why she didn't interject and voice her castigation of them. She may not want to be criticized for eavesdropping, for being uptight, or for injecting an opinion where they felt she had no business to do so. In the end, her tacit presence serves as proof that just because someone is silent on a topic doesn't mean that they are in agreement with those who are speaking—or that they even condone the topic of conversation.

Elements Most Alien to the Text: "Hotness" and Male Genitalia

The element most shocking for the assemblywoman is the way in which her male colleagues spoke about the "hotness" of a recently elected member of the assembly. It's not only that her physical appearance is irrelevant to doing the people's work, according to the assemblywoman, but that it also shouldn't be a source of idle chatter in Assembly Chambers. Yet it is, because "That's how they [men] talk to each other." The assemblywoman attempts to explain this male-strain of idle chatter with the statement that "one of the most important things to them is their male genitalia. I mean, that's who they are as people." In this anecdote, we have male colleagues disregarding how their conversation might impact their female colleague sitting next to them and then the assemblywoman internalizing that disregard by reducing her male colleagues to their genitalia. By arguing that her male colleagues' genitalia represent the sum total of who they are as people, the assemblywoman collapses their minds (and brains) into their genitalia. Their genitalia represent not only the mind-brain continuum, dictating their actions and a world view that is driven by sexual need, but also represent the epitome of male identity.

Attending to Disruptions and Contradictions: "I Mean That's Who They Are as People"

The assertion that male genitalia embody who men are as people is a startling assertion. First, it succeeds in creating a shocking visual of life-size, walking and talking genitals because "That's who they are as people." Second, it is startling because it reduces men to the desires, whims, needs, and mechanics of their gendered biology.

Interpreting the Metaphor of Men as Their Genitalia

When the assemblywoman argues that the centrality of male genitalia in men's lives dominates "who they are as people," she succeeds in cutting down her male colleagues—and men in general—as those reduced to sexual instinct, function, and need. They no longer embody rationality but corporeal primitiveness. This argument also removes agency and responsibility from men, since if they are their genitalia then they have no recourse or choice but to act in a testosterone-fueled, heteronormative manner that shoves aside decorum and reasoned thought.

Reconstructing the Story with "Hot" Men and Licentious Assemblywomen

If we swap out the gender of the key players and create a scenario in which assemblywomen were gossiping in Assembly Chambers about a hot, recently elected assemblyman—with an assemblyman sitting in close proximity to his gossiping female colleagues—we are presented with a situation that is not atypical. Nothing seems particularly alien about a group of women colleagues gossiping about the attractive appearance of a soon-to-be colleague. Would they do that with a male colleague sitting nearby? It's hard to say. Would they have such an intimate conversation within the formal structure of Assembly Chambers? Who knows. Yet this anecdote shows that gossip is not limited to a particular gender and even goes so far as to democratize the nature of gossip—since it is too often used to belittle and diminish women as their idle "sport" of choice.[65]

ANECDOTE 5: GUILTY UNTIL PROVEN INNOCENT

An assemblyman shared this story, in which he outlines how he was once the almost-target of a complaint by an assemblywoman. He allegedly made her feel uncomfortable. She did not file an official complaint against him.

Assemblyman: Quite frankly, there are people out there that are very destructive and would do anything to destroy another person's character, make stories up, et cetera, et cetera. And I can tell you I had a firsthand experience with that, where someone—they didn't file a formal complaint—but they basically said they were uncomfortable being around me. And I said, "Well, that's not true."

Hinda: Did they give any more information about why they were uncomfortable?

Assemblyman: No, and that was the thing—what specifically? Well, "It was the sort of thing you said." Well, what did I say? . . . And that's the fault with some of these situations, because there are people out there—and I've had the experience myself—where they absolutely outright lied. And what do you do? And you're trying to defend yourself. You're trying to remedy all this so it goes away, because you know if it makes the newspapers it makes it ever worse because then everybody thinks you're guilty. . . . The guys are held to a different standard. It's always assumed that the guy's the bad guy and there was no culpability on the woman's end of the situation. And the situation I was alluding to earlier was a woman, shall we say, leading on or flirting with, and then she makes this comment, and then all of a sudden she rescinds the comment. But the damage—sort of, at that point—the damage is done.

Hinda: Right. Was she an intern or a staffer?

Assemblyman: No; a member, actually.

Dismantling a Dichotomy: Men Are Guilty and Women Are Innocent

According to the assemblyman, "The guys are held to a different standard." People assume that if a woman makes an allegation against a man, "The guy's the bad guy and there was no culpability on the woman's end of the situation." In the personal situation he alludes to, he describes an assemblywoman flirting with him. Then she later makes a comment that she feels uncomfortable around him. The assemblyman argues that not only does this different standard exist but that it unfairly punishes men who should not receive blame. Even when the assemblywoman rescinded the comment, "The damage was done." It is clear from the assemblyman's anecdote that he felt wronged by the assemblywoman's comment that she felt uncomfortable around him, and that there was no validity to her accusation—especially since he felt she led him on in a flirtatious manner.

Examining Silences

We don't know the nature of the flirtatious relationship between the assemblyman sharing the anecdote and the assemblywoman who said she felt uncomfortable around him. We don't hear from the assemblywoman so we don't even know if she considered herself to be flirting with a colleague.

Element Most Alien to the Text: Using Scandal as Intentional Sabotage

It is disturbing to imagine a person using scandal as a weapon, especially in the instance where the basis of a scandal is falsely conjured—as the assemblyman alleges. Yet it is quite possible for the assemblyman and assemblywoman to experience the same interactions in different ways. Perhaps the assemblyman interpreted the assemblywoman's friendly behavior as flirting when she herself did not believe she was engaging in an intimate or suggestive behavior. Or perhaps she was intentionally flirting but then stopped, and then did feel uncomfortable in the assemblyman's presence if he perhaps continued treating her in a flirtatious manner. "The New York State Assembly Policy Prohibiting Harassment, Discrimination, and Retaliation" specifically supports people who engage in "self-help." From the 2015 policy: "The Assembly encourages employees and interns to politely but firmly advise offenders that their behavior is unwelcome and request that they immediately stop. This message can be spoken or in writing."[66] Therefore it is entirely possible that the assemblywoman was engaging in self-help when she told the assemblyman that his presence made her uncomfortable. We don't know. What we do know is that the assemblyman's concern that his colleague would fabricate a complaint against him, and that his reputation would be ruined, is part of a larger cultural trope concerning fears of women filing false reports of harassment against men. Such a position casts doubt on the validity of all sexual harassment allegations by women and shrouds their motives in suspicion. However, the rates of women who file false reports relating to sexual assault or harassment are no greater than the rates for anyone who files false reports for other felonies.[67] Additionally, Catherine Burr, who has investigated hundreds of complaints of sexual harassment, says it's unproductive to think of a complaint as "true" or "false." The aim of an investigation is to examine evidence to see if a complaint can be substantiated and to what degree—or not at all.[68] Yet from the assembly-man's perspective, the informal complaint that the assemblywoman made to him represented an example of a colleague who "absolutely outright lied." It is clear that this situation made the assemblyman feel vulnerable and wronged.

Reconstructing: Doing a Gender Swap

When we switch the gender of the accuser from a woman to a man, the story falls apart. That's because at the core of this story is the assembly-man's belief that men and women are held to different standards when it comes to sexual harassment; that the woman is generally believed and the man is guilty until proven innocent. This anecdote reveals a deep fear about the harm that a woman's false allegation can cause men, and it warns listeners of the "Jezebel" figure who can cast men astray.

ANECDOTE 6: AN ASSEMBLYMAN GETS TEASED

In this story, an assemblyman recalls how he responded to regular "josh-ing" from Assemblyman Vito Lopez, a legislator known to many as a bully.

Assemblyman: He was always making comments to me about something. But it was usually about my height, about being from—[deleted to maintain anonymity] or something like that because he was very tall and I'm about 5 foot—[deleted]. And so in fact I was kidding *him* one day. I walked in and I said, "You got to be one of those really tall staff people." And it just so happens my two staff members were both shorter than I am. I had two . . . women working for me. They were both attractive.

Hinda: Yeah.

Assemblyman: They were middle aged and they're shorter than I am. So I walked [up] to him and said, "This is my staff. I have a height requirement in my office as well." So I said that—he was just, you know, kind of a smart ass.

Dismantling a Dichotomy: You Tease or You Get Teased

After the assemblyman received one too many unwanted comments about his height, he attempted to reverse the dynamic by targeting Vito Lopez. So the assemblyman took the element with which Lopez teased him (his height) and used it against him by making fun of Lopez for being tall. The assemblyman then targeted two of his female staff, using their bodies—i.e., their short statures—to show Lopez that he, too, can exploit other people's physical appearances as a means to assert his authority. And even a shorter man is still taller than two short women.

Examining Silences

We don't know how Vito Lopez responded to being teased—and whether it stopped him from teasing the assemblyman. We also don't know how the assemblyman's two female staffers felt about having their boss bring them into this dynamic.

Focusing on Element Most Alien to the Text: Juvenile Teasing

The anecdote has the air of a middle school bullying incident. A tall person bullies a shorter peer. Finally, the shorter peer gets fed up and teases the bully for being tall, and he also drags two subordinates—who are even shorter than he is—into this dynamic. We know that there is a certain amount of informality that exists in formal work structures, but this level of teasing seems more typically found in a schoolyard than at the state legislature. In this anecdote we have an alpha male who teases a beta male. The beta male then musters up his power to tease the alpha male, using two subordinate females to puff up his position.

Reconstructing with Gender

If we swap out the gender of the assemblyman's staffers, by making them men instead of women, we still have an instance of a person with greater authority using his subordinates to defend himself against a bully. But there is something distinct about a male boss talking about the physical appearance of his female support staff that fits a traditional paradigm of using women's bodies in a male game of one-upmanship. From this anecdote we learn how an assemblyman decided that the only way to take on a bully is to employ those same bullying tactics.

PUTTING THE SIX ANECDOTES IN CONCERT WITH EACH OTHER

By analyzing these six assembly anecdotes—where bodies are front and center in an assembly setting—we've identified six dichotomies. And by reconstructing these six anecdotes by swapping key elements, like gender and age, we've identified important forces at play in the assembly (table 6.1).

These dichotomies and reconstructions demonstrate a nuanced gender dynamic in the assembly. On the one hand, these anecdotes are evidence of sex-specific stereotypes. For example, we have instances of an older male politician surrounding himself with an entourage of young women. That same politician expresses interest in hiring someone else's intern based on her looks. We have examples of men (a father and an assemblyman) acting as protectors of women—to protect them from "sleazy" men or, in the bathroom anecdote, from the repercussions of woman behaving aggressively. We have the example of an assemblyman acting rudely to his

Table 6.1   Key Dichotomies and Reconstructions to Emerge from Assembly Anecdotes

Anecdote	Dichotomy	Reconstruction
1: Vito Lopez's odd ducks	Odd ducks vs. cute intern	Age difference matters
2: Intern matchmaking	Cordiality vs. rudeness	Assemblymembers have power over interns, especially when it gets personal
3: Dragged into bathroom	Chivalry vs. gender independence	Women who act aggressively may be protected by men's chivalrous intentions
4: Barbershop talk	Male talk vs. female talk	Gossip is not limited by gender
5: Guilty until proven innocent	Male guilt vs. female innocence	Men and women are judged by different standards
6: Assemblyman gets teased	Tease vs. gets teased	The only way to beat a bully is to be a bully

female colleague over intern jealousy, and then the instance of men treat-ing Assembly Chambers like a "barbershop," a place where they openly discuss the hotness of a new female colleague.

We also have examples of women acting in sex-specific ways. There's the example of an assemblywoman serving as messenger between an assemblyman and an intern who works in her office. There is the case of an assemblywoman making a cordial joke about matchmaking between interns; and there is also the example of an assemblywoman maintain-ing silence when overhearing the chauvinistic talk of male colleagues in Assembly Chambers.

What's noteworthy about this collection of anecdotes is that the three assemblywomen shared these stories as examples of assemblymen acting in inappropriate ways. Yet their response to the chauvinism is also gender specific. For instance, in the "odd ducks" anecdote an assemblyman is driven to hire an intern based solely on her looks. (And the assembly-woman telling the story passes on news of that job opportunity to the intern.) In the matchmaking anecdote, an assemblyman reacts with jeal-ousy. (And the assemblywoman expresses her shock but does not confront her colleague—but she does go back to her intern to rehash the event.) And in the Assembly Chambers anecdote, a group of assemblymen talk hotness. (The assemblywoman is outraged at their exchange but keeps quiet about it—to them.)

Assemblymen also have sex-specific responses. For instance, the assem-blyman who tells of being dragged into the bathroom by women[69] reclaims the power embedded in his gender identity by turning himself into the protector of these women. He acts chivalrously to them and does not report their misconduct, thereby restoring his power as a person in control of someone else's professional future. And the assemblyman who felt that an assemblywoman unfairly accused him of making her feel uncomfort-able alleges that men are guilty until proven innocent, since people are more likely to believe a woman than a man when it comes to accusations of sexual misconduct. He resented being placed in a vulnerable position that left him feeling powerless. And finally, an assemblyman who was often teased by a known bully in the legislature attacks the situation by becoming a bully himself: he uses others' physical appearance to bolster his position.

Perhaps the assembly members felt compelled to share these particular scandal anecdotes as a way to revisit, and add commentary to, situations that have left them puzzled, confused, angered, trapped by the confines and expectations of their gender identity, and powerless. By sharing these stories and adding judgment to them, they are able to reconfigure what happened in their own minds, perhaps engaging in their own reconstructions and story reclamations.

An analysis of these anecdotes also reveals the spectrum of power within the assembly and how power manifests itself in unexpected ways. I view power not as a material resource that one either possesses or lacks—but as a fluid force that flows through people, and that waxes and wanes based on interactions.[70] Michel Foucault instructs us that "power is neither given, nor exchanged, nor recovered, but rather exercised, and that it only exists in action."[71] Through these anecdotes, we see that interns have power over assemblymen (some of whom attempt to constrict their agency); and we see assemblywomen exercising power over men (by making them feel vulnerable or wronged). We see that there is power in observation because it forms the basis of anecdotes, shared with researchers and colleagues. We see that there is power in voicing these stories, because they are then codified in this book. As the researcher who often felt small and diminished while conducting the interviews (especially those held in Albany legislative offices) I now exercise power in writing about assembly members, and analyzing their behavior and stories.

The backdoor channels of casual story-sharing demonstrate that it is not only assembly*women* participating in what some describe as gossip but assembly*men* as well. After all, it is through a conversational process that assembly members unburden themselves with some of the uncomfortable gender dynamics within the legislative body, quiet moments that discomfited the legislators; nothing so "egregious" to report up to the chain of command but the interactions nonetheless lingered in their minds, which they eventually shared when I probed them for stories about scandal. Ultimately, it is through story sharing that we are able to peel away the layers of bureaucracy and decorum, to see assembly members as intricately connected to each other in moments of scandal crisis.

CHAPTER 7

"How Can People Be So Dumb and Still Be in Politics?" Public Response to Prominent Scandals

When a politician "gets his[1] rocks off" during a sexy escapade that excludes his wife (but may include prostitutes, mistresses, and smartphones), the cultural response is strident and clear: a political wife who supports this politician (whose cognitive apparatus has migrated from his head to below his belt) needs a lesson in acquiring self-respect.

Since I began studying news coverage of such scandals in 2008, I have repeatedly been struck by the manner in which political wives who themselves engaged in no illicit activity—or broke any marital vows or cultural codes of monogamy (as far as we know) or humiliated their spouses by resigning in disgrace or jeopardized the emotional welfare of her family—nevertheless become the target of public debate, shame, and excoriation within the political sex-scandal script. We certainly have plenty of examples from which to cull this trend. Consider how media coverage portrayed the wives of:

1. Former New Jersey governor James McGreevey, who admitted that he is gay during a nationally televised press conference (2004)
2. Louisiana senator David Vitter, a client of the "D.C. Madam," who reportedly had a diaper fetish[2] (2007)
3. Former Idaho senator Larry Craig, who attempted to solicit sex from a male undercover cop in a Minneapolis airport bathroom via a covert foot-tapping signal (2007)
4. Former Florida congressman Tim Mahoney, who paid off a staffer to keep mum about their extramarital affair (2008)[3]
5. Former New York governor Eliot Spitzer, who had sex with prostitutes while wearing his black trouser socks (2008)

6. Former Nevada senator John Ensign, who had an extramarital affair with a campaign staffer—a woman who happened to be his wife's best friend from high school (2009)
7. Former South Carolina governor Mark Sanford, currently a congressman from that state at the time of writing, who had an extramarital affair with an Argentinean woman—and then, when caught, said he would "try to fall back in love" with his wife (2009)
8. Former California governor Arnold Schwarzenegger, who, while married, fathered a child with his housekeeper in 1997 and kept that information secret from his wife (2011)
9. Former New York congressman Anthony Weiner, who sent tweets featuring images of his erect penis to women online—prior to and during his wife's pregnancy, and after the birth of their son (2011, 2013, 2016; his wife announced their separation in 2016, after a third round of sexts were released)
10. Former Louisiana congressman Vance McAllister, father of five, who was caught on his office surveillance camera embracing a female staffer in his district office—whom he fired as soon as news of their behavior became public (2014)

The cultural conversation appears abundantly clear that when it comes to "politicians gone wild," this is no country in which to stand by one's man. No doubt, the title character at the start of the CBS series *The Good Wife* is inspired by the supportive and silent image of Silda Spitzer at her husband's press conference. In 2008, then New York governor Eliot Spitzer admitted to "private failings"—his euphemism for sex with prostitutes—while she appeared perfectly coiffed and poised as his wifely chaperone at the podium when he tendered his resignation from office. The apparent paradox of her stately, groomed appearance with his public blitz of betrayal and humiliation brought to mind no image of any wife I could conjure up outside of the traditional political sphere. In a contemporary culture where women are increasingly the primary earners in their family,[4] the image of a political wife publicly muted in the face of her husband's philandering and career crash increasingly represents an out-of-touch and out-of-date relic from a different time. But here we are.

With this in mind, I was curious to explore how the general public responds to public images of slack-shouldered politicians offering canned remarks of apology to the nation with their political wives on display. In order to understand how people specifically relate to, contest, and perhaps even connect with three different wifely scenarios at scandal press conferences, I conducted an online survey in 2014, using a random sample of

adults from across the United States, to investigate how people reacted
to the sex-scandal press conferences of Eliot Spitzer (2008), Mark Sanford (2009), and Anthony Weiner (2013). Analyzing 330 open-ended
responses, I found that while respondents overwhelmingly expressed disdain toward the scandal-blemished politician and his wife, a prominent
theme of sympathy toward the wife emerged as well as an acknowledgment that politicians are "just like us." Ultimately, responses indicated
the push-pull of scandal—an admonishment for the general public to
mind their own business when it comes to the private lives of elected
officials, but, on the flip side, an awareness that private misbehavior often
can have very public consequences.

I selected these specific scandals because I was interested in the public
display associated with a news conference; and each selected press conference is distinct due to the political spouse's role, whether as the silent,
absent, or outspoken wife.[5] Each of these scandals features a husband
and wife, where the husband-politician was caught—and admitted to—
culturally unsanctioned sexual relations with other women. Each scandal
features a press conference, where spousal roles were televised and subsequently dissected by talking-heads in the media.

Indeed, political wives hold a unique distinction within the broader wife
category. They are held to the presence/absence double bind—the subject
of chapter 5—where news accounts typically blast the wife who stands
next to her scandal-tarnished husband—an impenetrable wifely avatar of
silent support. Yet news accounts also take issue with her when she acts
independently of him while his face is smeared with the dirt of scandal.[6]
These wives cannot win. And they are burdened with this double bind,
because as political spouses they are the public purveyors of the politician's responsible and family-oriented brand, selling the image of a loving
and functional family through photo ops, campaign events, and formal
functions.[7] Myra MacPherson, a journalist who was also married to a politician, knows firsthand how politicians make public use of their families
for political gain. She writes, "Professional politics and the politician's
family are intertwined realms of private and public spheres. Politicians
leverage their spouse and family to bolster their image in a post-Watergate
political landscape."[8] To prove that the husband-politician is no crook,
the political wife publicly demonstrates her commitment to him.

The political wife, in vouching for her husband's worth, cues a cultural
shorthand indicating that the candidate or incumbent is a man of valor, of
homegrown iron character. Wifely support is campaign currency; vetting
in the private sphere has cache for the public one. Therefore, the public's
and media's anger directed at a political wife whose husband is ensnared in

a sex scandal has two primary roots of disbelief. First, she potentially knew of her husband's polyamorous sexual proclivities and therefore knowingly sold the public a false bill of goods. After all, she vouched for his family-oriented character in a political sphere that commodifies select private information about politicians with public performance and presentation.[9] Or the political wife was caught off guard by the husband-politician's (s) extracurricular activities and therefore "failed" in her performance of "wifeness" and spousal surveillance skills. If the politician-husband can so easily dupe a watchful wife, the logic goes, in which ways is he capable of deceiving his constituents and disregarding *their* interests? (In this way, the public represents an extension of the political family, with the politician as the paternal figure "caring" for our interests and selecting how best to "help" us.[10]) Whatever the reasons, we often see the political wife at her husband's side during scripted news conferences. Perhaps her presence represents one more requirement of her, part of her outlined duties as a political wife doing her wifework.

To some extent, all wives can identify with, or at least have experienced, the tedium that is "wifework."[11] Political wives just do so publicly and, during an unfolding scandal, within the context of an abrasive familial and political crisis. Writer and journalist Susan Maushart makes the distinction between the difficulties of marriage and the difficulties of being a wife. "Being married is not the problem. Nor is being a parent, or at least not in the same way. The problem is being a wife."[12] It is a "problem" because of the cultural baggage that is attached to "wifeness," my term to describe the very act of being and performing "Wife," which includes wifework.[13] Maushart's coinage of "wifework" refers to the emotional and physical labor/toil associated with how society expects a wife to act. Wifework includes overseeing and taking care of a disproportionate amount of unpaid housework; taking care of the husband's emotional needs and sexual desires; managing childcare and housework; cooking meals to the husband's culinary taste and schedule; allowing the husband to set the tone and content of daily conversations; and helping him maintain, smooth, and correct his family relationships. For a political wife, the expectations are even greater, since her wifework is more public, and her private life is not only less private but is also used, twisted, and massaged for her husband's professional ascension.

Christine Delphy[14] is a French Marxist feminist scholar who sees the family unit as the source of female economic exploitation and oppression. All societies, argues Delphy, must produce goods and (re)produce humans for societal survival. Delphy is interested in women's roles in this cycle of (re)production. Since housework and childwork fall under women's responsibility, women are "serfs" working without pay for a male master who oversees this exploited workforce.[15] Society, then, is reliant on women to work without pay for their female and often home-centered tasks.

> Whatever women receive in return is independent of the work which they perform because it is not handed out in exchange for that work (i.e., as a wage to which their work entitles them), but rather as a gift. The husband's only obligation, which is obviously in his own interest, is to provide for his wife's basic needs, in other words he maintains her labor power.[16]

While Delphy provides examples from a French cultural context in the 1980s and does not address the unpaid labor of politicians' wives, her theoretical underpinnings connect in a relevant way to the argument that women who do not engage in unpaid work for their husbands' careers will be viewed as selfish and at risk of marriage failure.[17] The social expectation that women must work unpaid for the good of the family reproduces a woman's subordinate position. Wives are supporting actors in the two-person, single-career marriage,[18] otherwise known as the career-dominated marriage, where the husband's work in such fields as business, law, politics, and medicine may be the central focal point of the marriage. In unfolding news coverage of scandal, we often see this spousal disparity, with the wife working on her husband's behalf, lending her presence at press conferences to soften the blow to his public image. In the event of attempted crisis containment, the political wife does not "just" engage in wifework inside the home but also at public venues with news photographers documenting her every reaction to her husband's admission or denial of sexual misdeed. In a stunningly public moment, the image she so carefully crafted and maintained for years—or even decades—comes crashing down in front of her with the indefatigable Tammy Wynette herself in the role of marital counselor: "Sometimes it's hard to be a woman/Giving all your love to just one man/You'll have bad times, and he'll have good times/Doin' things that you don't understand."[19]

What is so remarkable about the political wife's wifework during scandal is that her labor is not working toward spousal career ascension—with its potential benefit to herself and her family—but rather her presence presumably serves as a type of human shield, the embodiment of damage control for the scandal-tarnished husband. And that is why her presence can be so maddening: with the "stand by your man" political wife, we see firsthand how the wife is treated as a mere casualty of the politician's careless, callous, and need-driven behavior. And it's unclear, with the politician's career in shambles, what benefit she can possibly derive from publicly supporting her husband. (Presumably, her presence means that if she can rally behind her scandal-tarnished husband, then the public should too. But that explanation is superficial and not believable. As a result, her presence conveys more cog-in-the-scandal machine than forgiving spouse.) Her apparent willingness to "get thrown under the bus" can be perplexing, unless she and her husband's team are acting on autopilot: she fulfills her role as supportive spouse because it's the only role she's been cast to play.

A politician serving in the New York State Assembly once told me that dignity has a price when political wives stand in support of their husbands. She said, "I think for the most part when women do that, it's because they've become part of a lifestyle and they're not willing to give up on the lifestyle. That's just the way I see it when a woman decides to humiliate herself by standing there while her husband tells you, 'I slept with whoever; I did whatever.' It's because you're willing to give up your dignity for a lifestyle."[20]

Perhaps the most iconic role of the three political wives under the microscope within this chapter belongs to Silda Spitzer,[21] then wife of former New York governor Eliot Spitzer. He was outed in 2008 as "Client

New York governor Eliot Spitzer announces his resignation amidst a prostitution scandal as wife Silda looks on in New York City on March 12, 2008. (AP Photo/Stephen Chernin)

No. 9" of the Emperor's Club, an exclusive New York City-area prostitu-tion ring. Silda Spitzer silently stood next to her husband as he resigned his post as governor at a press conference in March 2008. She filed for divorce in December 2013.

The second press conference belongs to Mark Sanford, then governor of South Carolina. In June 2009, he went missing for the better part of a week. Neither his staff nor his family knew his whereabouts. When his staff finally reached him, Sanford said he was hiking the Appalachian Trail. In actuality, he was in Argentina with his mistress, a woman he described as his "soul mate" as the scandal unfolded.[22] At a press con-ference upon his return to South Carolina, Sanford said, "I have been unfaithful to my wife. I developed a relationship with a—what started out as a dear, dear friend from Argentina. It began very innocently, as I suspect many of these things do, in just a casual e-mail back and forth, in advice on one's life there and advice here."[23] Jenny Sanford was absent from the press conference. She filed for divorce within months of the scandal. Refusing to lend credibility to her wandering husband, Jenny Sanford became the "role model" political wife[24]—at least initially, until media coverage described her as either too shrill, too independent, or too unbending.[25]

The final press conference belongs to former New York congressman Anthony Weiner and his then wife, Huma Abedin, Hillary Clinton's longtime political advisor. While survey respondents viewed a press con-ference that took place in 2013, the scandal has its roots in June 2011, when then congressman Weiner said his Twitter account had been hacked after an explicit photograph of an erect penis was released. As the scandal unfolded, Weiner said he "can't say with certitude" that the image didn't belong to him, but he did assert that he was investigating what he called a "prank."[26]

One week later, Weiner admitted to sending lewd photos to women online and also admitted to inappropriate—although nonphysical—relationships categorized by texting, sexual innuendo, and photo shar-ing. At a press conference announcing his resignation from Congress that month, Huma Abedin—who was pregnant at the time—was absent. In summer 2013, as the disgraced former congressman ran for mayor of New York City, new photos and online exchanges emerged from the depths of the Internet. Anthony Weiner, now mayoral candidate, again held a press conference where his wife not only was present but also spoke on her husband's behalf. Huma Abedin announced her separation from Anthony Weiner in August 2016, following the release of a third round of lewd sexts.

Huma Abedin stands beside her husband, New York mayoral candidate Anthony Weiner, as he speaks during a news conference on July 23, 2013, in New York. (AP Photo/Kathy Willens)

University of Cambridge Sociologist John B. Thompson offers a social theory of scandal by describing these sensational media events as "struggles over symbolic power in which reputation and trust are at stake."[27] For Thompson, the tarnished reputations belong to the politicians, but since political wives play so prominently into the scandal script—at least in the United States—and since they contribute to the symbolic ascension and demise of the politician, their reputations potentially cultivate mistrust within the American public as well. "[I]n liberal democracy, reputations matter . . . in the struggle for electoral success, good reputation is a vital resource," writes Thompson. "Hence the tarnishing of one's reputation through scandal is a risk that political leaders or aspiring leaders must seek energetically to avoid."[28]

Before highlighting the most prominent themes from the respondent survey, it is first necessary to review why character is so important within the American political system and how the illusion of a public/private divide within politics contributes to the heightened sensationalism of these scandal frenzies.

The increasing importance of one's character in the political field is closely connected to the changing role of technology and mass communication in the 20th century, especially with the emergence of a television culture. Thompson writes extensively on this topic,[29] so only a brief summary will be offered here: "The development of new communication media . . . gave rise to 'the society of self-disclosure': a society in which it was possible and, indeed, increasingly common for political leaders and other individuals to appear before distant audiences and lay bare some aspect of their self or their personal life."[30] The intimacy of the television structure, of gazing on a subject's face, often seeing the subject react in real time, appeared to reveal a previously hidden "essence" of the subject's nature and character. To reveal their character then (or at least a construction of their character) is to lift the curtain on their personal life, allowing audiences access to a flesh-and-blood politico both behind the scenes, in real time, and in visual detail. In doing so, Thompson, argues, the politician's aura of aloofness was lost. And gained? The politician's ability to present oneself as anybody else, a person with whom audiences could relate.[31] But this was no "kumbaya" relationship between the voting masses and the politician. As politicians presented themselves as "one of us," the prominence and relevance of their character grew to new heights. A lot rested on this notion of "character:"

> People became more concerned with the *character* of the individuals who are (or might become) their leaders and more concerned about their trustworthiness, because increasingly this becomes the principal means of guaranteeing that political promises will be kept and that difficult decisions in the face of complexity and uncertainty will be made on the basis of sound judgment.[32]

Integrity, sincerity, and honesty became the prized possessions of any politician. But as increasd emphasis was placed on the contours of one's character, the gutter traits of one's personality also grew in significance within the political field. There would be little room to forgive indications of a weak character or the exhibition of lying, pandering, judgment lapses, and flip-flopping. Ultimately, when a politician or aspiring politician trumpeted his strength of character as an indicator of his political skill—with his wife and family bolstering the image of the husband-father as an effective leader not only in the home but outside of it—the politician opened himself to judgment when (inevitably) less seemly aspects of his character poked through the façade. After all, we maneuver through a world where politicians don't have the luxury of letting down their guards because offline behavior can so easily be broadcast online, and online behavior meant to be private can too easily cross over into the public sphere. "Character," writes Thompson, "was an attribute by which they could just as easily be hung."[33] While a TV culture enhanced politicians' visibility, showing them performing everyday rituals like visiting diners and kissing babies—thereby offering a visual "glimpse" into their (constructed) character that gives the impression of a private, authentic self even as it is scripted for public and news consumption—the roots of character's public/private divide can be found within the Victorian era.

Why is it, in recent history, that a politician is viewed as more genuine and reliable if—he makes it known that—he prepares his own dinner every evening? "This political 'credibility,'" writes the Sociologist Richard Sennett in 1977, "is the superimposition of private upon public imagery," which arose in the 19th century "as a result of the behavioral and ideological confusions between these two realms."[34] Sennett pinpoints the mid-19th century as the origin of character authenticity in politics. The credibility of what a person said in public depended on people's perception of that person's character, "so that the truth of what he said appeared to depend on what kind of person he was."[35] Quickly, "the system of public expression became one of personal representation; a public figure presents to others what he feels, and it is this representation of his feeling which arouses belief."[36] This reliance on character, and the notion that a person's credibility hinges on whether one's character appears authentic, is all the more noteworthy because the masses attempted to conceal their true character in public during the Victorian era. There was a strong motivation to conceal any hints of their authentic selves lest they inadvertently reveal a belief that would make them vulnerable to scrutiny or judgment. (Today, writes Sennett, we understand this phenomenon when someone unconsciously says something, causing awkwardness or discomfort, as a "slip of the tongue."[37]) Therefore, beginning in the Victorian era, the public domain represented a paradox categorized by "isolation and visibility."[38] "There grew up the notion that strangers had no right to speak to each other, that each man possessed as a public right an invisible shield, a right to be left alone. Public behavior was a matter of observation, of passive participation, of a certain kind of voyeurism."[39] The communications scholar Joshua Meyrowitz writes that secrets were reserved for the private domain:

> Victorian Era—the height of print culture—was a time of "secrets." People were fascinated with the multiple layers and depths of life: secret passageways, skeletons in the closet, masks upon masks upon masks. But the fascination with these layers did not drive the Victorians to destroy secrecy, but rather to enhance it as a natural condition of the social order. To a large degree, skeletons were meant to stay in the closet, sex was to remain

behind closed doors and scandalous acts were to be hidden from peering eyes . . . Our own age, in contrast, is fascinated by exposure, Indeed, the *act* of exposure itself now seems to excite us more than the content of the secrets exposed.[40]

While Meyrowitz wrote those words in 1985, eons before the choke-hold of our digital culture, he prophesized how a change in media culture, from print to digital, would change not only personal behavior but the contours of the public/private divide. If the Victorian era privileged the privacy of secrets, the digital world (what Meyrowitz terms "electronic media") obliterated the safety of secrets. "Ironically, what is pulled out of the closets that contain seemingly extraordinary secrets is, ultimately, the 'ordinariness' of everyone. Presidents with hemorrhoids, Popes who get depressed, Congressmen who solicit sex from pages."[41]

To return to the survey at the heart of this chapter, responses convey unease in learning about politicians' secrets, a conflict between what some view as a need to know vs. a right to know vs. a firewall against knowing.[42] But what is central to survey responses is the revelation that scandal demonstrated a deficit of character, although respondents differed in what to do with this new knowledge of a politician's now-public deficiency.

SURVEY RESPONDENTS

Survey participants were recruited using Mechanical Turk (MTurk), an online survey system overseen by Amazon. Participants were paid 25 cents for completing the survey in August 2014. A user identification system prevented the same person from completing the survey more than once. Only MTurk workers living in the United States could participate in the survey. In recent years, academics have increasingly turned to MTurk for survey research, and scholars have found that those who complete surveys via MTurk "are more representative and diverse than the corresponding student and convenience samples typically used in experimental political science studies."[43] The survey directed participants to watch the scandal press conferences on YouTube of Eliot Spitzer (featuring the silent wife), Mark Sanford (featuring the absent wife), and Anthony Weiner (featuring the wife who speaks). They were then asked the open-ended question, "Please use this space to share what you're thinking right now regarding political sex scandals, politicians, and political wives." Responses were analyzed using the constant comparative method of an open-coding scheme and then getting more selective through an ongoing method of analysis.[44]

The 330 survey respondents hailed from 44 states within the United States. There were 151 women who participated in the survey and 179 men. Their median age was 33. The youngest was 19 and the oldest was 79.

MARITAL STATUS OF RESPONDENTS

- About 48 percent were single ($N = 158$)
- About 40 percent were married ($N = 134$)
- About 9 percent of the respondents were divorced ($N = 30$)
- Additionally, 5 of the 330 respondents said they were separated and 3 said they were widowed

SEXUAL ORIENTATION OF RESPONDENTS

- About 90 percent of the respondents identified as straight ($N = 296$)
- Remaining respondents identified as bisexual, lesbian, gay, or other

HOW THE RESPONDENTS REACTED

Three prominent themes emerged in my analysis of the 330 open-ended responses to three sex-scandal press conferences. The first theme suggests that respondents balked at the politician's and political wife's character (or lack thereof). I labeled this the "disdain" theme. Respondents cast serious "shade" at politicians and their wives, expressing no lack of disgust at the politico's actions and the humiliating situation he created for his wife. The fact that the most prominent of the three themes relates to the politician and his wife's tarnished character indicates a public that views scandal as indicative of a personal flaw and that disdain cast at the wife demonstrates scandal's contaminating effects.

The second theme suggests that respondents see a public-private line that has been crossed with the broadcasting of scandal. But disagreement exists among respondents about the extent to which the public and news media should mind their own business or whether public consequences should indeed exist for private misbehavior. A third theme demonstrated sympathy, mostly directed at political wives, who many respondents viewed as having been dragged unfairly into a glaringly public situation. Yet surprisingly, sympathy is also directed—although to a lesser extent—to the politicians who made a profound mistake, just like everyone else does now and then. This offers a striking counter-response to the most prominent "disdain" theme, where no politician was granted the luxury of sympathy. Let's now examine these three themes in detail.[45]

DISDAIN

Overwhelmingly, respondents reacted to the press conferences with unrestrained vitriol directed at "cheating" politicians *and* their "greedy" wives. The disdain category included a number of elements, such as the belief that politicians are selfish; that their wives are power hungry and should have known that husband-politicians are bad news; that cheating is inexcusable; that politicians should behave better and leave their wives out of their public mess; that politicians' deceit causes pain and humiliation; that it prompts disgust from the public; and that the scandal press conference is a spectacle displaying political marriages as a farce.

Within the disdain category, I will focus on the two most recurring subthemes: (1) "shade" cast at politicians and their wives and (2) the dismissal of the news conference as a charade that reveals the political marriage as a farce.

Casting Shade at Politicians and Their Wives

Overwhelmingly, respondents unleashed a torrent of disdain at the politicians *and* their wives. Oftentimes, respondents who blasted the politician also attacked the political wife in the same keystroke. For instance, a married 31-year-old woman wrote, "I think these women are nuts to stand by them. How can they stand there and smile when they were just cheated on, and in a huge public way. None of these politicians are upset they did it, they're only upset that they got caught." A divorced 57-year-old woman wrote, "To me it just makes the politician look more like a loser to have his wife alongside him at one of these events, as though he is trying to hide behind her. If I were the wife, I wouldn't think it would help at all for me to be there, and it certainly wouldn't help me." In another example, a 44-year-old married man also upbraided the politician and his wife as a cohesive unit: "I think it's horrible to expect the spouse of a political candidate caught in a sex scandal to be present for all to see while their spouse holds a press conference about it. It is cruel and demeaning and unfair to them. I can't understand how they all agreed to it." The press conferences prompted a 34-year-old married man to paint all political couples with a broad brush: "Politicians are sleazy crooks and their wives lack dignity." And in another example, a 62-year-old divorced man slammed everyone entangled in the scandal's net: "I think they are all corrupt people that just want power and nothing will stop them from obtaining that." Finally, a 70-year-old married man simply wrote, "They are all sleazy."

Within these aforementioned examples, we see instances of respondents excoriating the political couple as a scourge. The political wife who did not engage in any scandalous elements is nevertheless swept up into the scandal script for appearing to pull (at least publicly) a Tammy Wynette "stand-by-your-man" moment. The scandal-tarnished couple takes its lumps as a unit. While it's the politician's private misdeeds that dragged his family into the scalding scandal spotlight, the political wife's misdeed is rooted in her public *presence*, her very being, which conveys that her husband's deceit, stupidity, and/or licentiousness is still worthy of her corporeal presence. In an attempt to fulfill her wifely duty of stolid support, to continue in her role of political appendage so often defining her purpose throughout all stages of her husband's political life, the political wife becomes a liability to her own well-being at her husband's public shaming. She is the laughingstock who appears to have put the demanding and demeaning interests of her oafish, caddish, and carousing husband before her own basic need for dignity. Therefore, when the politician gets caught and when the wife subsequently steps into her role as defender of the realm—lock stock and barrel—she also becomes as much a target of public disdain as the man who unzipped his trousers when he should have kept them belted.

While respondents often cast the politician and his wife as emerging from the same corrupt mold, both tainted with an unflattering patina, there were other instances where the political wife received the brunt of the shade directed at the political couple. In many of these instances, respondents assert that wives should know better than to partner with rapacious men in power. What is taken for granted is the corrupt character of the male politician, specifically, and the powerful male, more broadly. So if a potential political wife is blind to the "innate" character faults of the male politician, then she is ignorant. And if she knowingly partners with someone boasting a political streak, then she is as power hungry as the corrupted spouse. For instance, a 36-year-old married man takes as fact that powerful men abuse their positions: "Guys in power abuse it all the time for money and sex. If you are married to a guy like that, then you have to know what you're getting into beforehand." This thread continued with specific jabs at the wives: a 47-year-old single male said, "I think the wives show up to support their husbands, but it doesn't say much for their integrity. I guess they want the gravy train to continue." A 40-year-old single man wrote, "Most normal people would not behave like this in these situations. It shows that the spouses are as greedy and power addicted as their husbands." And a 60-year-old married man argued that "these guys are duplicitous whores who have been this way probably since high school. If these wives claim they are surprised, they are fools."

A 39-year-old single male offered a new twist to the political wife's presence at the scandal news conferences: that the political wife wanted to be there in order to maintain a slipping grasp on power. He said, "Politicians are so greedy for power and maybe their spouse[s] are as well that they will beg with their husbands for forgiveness so they don't lose that power or chance at regaining power." Others continued this theme that political wives will denigrate themselves to maintain a plush lifestyle, which is a comment similar to the one made by the New York State lawmaker at the outset of this chapter: that a political wife will sacrifice her own dignity in order to maintain her proximity to power. According to a single, 30-year-old male: "Wives that stand by are not motivated by supporting their husband, they are motivated to stand by in order to gain political benefits by others surrounding them." And a 53-year-old married man offered this backhanded compliment, "I think political wives will stand beside their husbands through thick or thin."

Female respondents also dug into political wives who lent their presence to scandal-tarnished husbands, casting the bulk of their criticism at these wives even though it's the politician-husbands whose misdeeds precipitated the wife's presence. "I think it is ridiculous for a wife to stand up there like nothing is wrong. Spitzer's wife looked like she was ready to fall over from exhaustion," wrote a 44-year-old married woman. "This is a disgrace to women. Why stand next to a man who has hurt you?" A 33-year-old single woman echoed that sentiment. "I don't know why women would stand and allow themselves to be embarrassed by their husbands' actions. I would definitely divorce." And a 56-year-old single woman said, "Wives who support such abhorrent behavior give such acts tacit consent." Finally, a 28-year-old single woman placed her frustration squarely on the shoulders of political wives, saying she was "annoyed that these women almost seem like their husbands' behaviors are okay."

While political wives were targeted and berated for granting the "benefit" of their presence to subpar husbands, politicians were blasted for using their wives' presence for their own gain in the first place. Respondents called upon politicians to leave their wives out of their public mess. "They did the dirt, they should have to face the music themselves. Their betrayal is first and foremost against the person they married, and to the public secondly. Honestly, their wives should have a media field day on them after what they did," wrote a married, 39-year-old man. A single, 40-year-old man took issue with a politician banking on his wife's presence to pull him out of his deceitful hole. He wrote, "It just seems really awkward, intrusive, and staged to have your spouse present. Using your spouse as a political tool after you are caught cheating on them seems like piling on wrongdoing." A 34-year-old married woman backed that viewpoint, writing, "I think it is horrible for these men to hurt their wives by not only going against their wedding vows but also asking them to support them while they admit to their wrong-doing in public. It is very self-ish." A 25-year-old single woman offered the view that scandal-tarnished husbands should be forced to lie—alone—in the bed they made: "In my opinion, politicians in political sex scandals need to accept responsibility and apologize for any wrongdoings on their own since they are adults and capable of making their own decisions. Having their wives by their sides isn't going to change anything in regards to what the public now thinks of them." And a 57-year-old divorced man writes that a politician's desire to have his wife stand next to him at a news conference is indicative of his power-crazed character: "I'm amazed that these guys want power so badly that they ask their wives to stand there as a prop during these press conferences." And finally, a 37-year-old married man writes simply, "I find it disrespectful for the wives to be present."

The News Conference Is a Charade; the Marriage a Farce

The second "disdain" subtheme (following "shade cast at politicians and their wives") derides the press conference as a charade, which also reveals the political marriage as a farce. In this subtheme, respondent disdain is sculpted by the perceived efforts of politicians to dupe the public through an orchestrated display of spousal cohesion. Respondents simply don't buy it and express disdain that they're expected to believe this marital mockery, since the news conference is an insult to their intelligence. "I feel like political wives or political spouses are being forced to be there with their significant others who have cheated on them," writes a 22-year-old single man. Meanwhile, a 21-year-old single woman writes, "Almost every politician is in a sham marriage, so the wives shouldn't be surprised to be cheated on." And a 23-year-old single woman writes, "I think that politicians get married to certain people that will boost their political careers and thus have no sense of commitment to the ones they are supposed to love."

A number of respondents noted the inauthentic impression of the press conference. For instance, a 33-year-old married woman wrote, "I think that it's a ploy to have the wife sit there while he confesses." And a 40-year-old single man concurred, adding, "It just seems really awkward, intrusive and staged to have your spouse present." Then there are the allegations of "fakeness," such as those from a 64-year-old married woman, "Political life is so fake. It is filled with corruption and broken dreams," and that of a 34-year-old married man, "The relationships are fake. Everyone knows it's just pomp for the cameras." Continuing with the fakery allegations, a 31-year-old single woman wrote, "To be blunt, it's all bullshit and we need to have more honest people representing us," and a 26-year-old single man added, "Having your wife by your side is basically a PR move in my opinion, and not particularly genuine." According to a 37-year-old married man: "They [political wives] look like puppets standing there."

A number of respondents took issue with the news conference as a phony spectacle. A 35-year-old married man wrote, "I think these media apologies are ridiculous media spectacles and utterly distracting to the real political issues at hand." A 40-year-old married man mirrors that view, writing that "I think that the way these things turn into such a spectacle is appalling." A 32-year-old man added that "it's all kabuki theatre." Then, a 21-year-old single man clinched the charade subtheme in three words: "All for show."

The most prominent disdain theme showed that respondents overwhelmingly cast shade at the politician and his wife. Respondents also expressed a deep-rooted suspicion about the authenticity of the scandal press conference, which showed that the only thing believable about the political couple is their commitment to their own self-interest above all else. The prominence of the disdain theme demonstrates that respondents react first and foremost to the political couple's character issues. They fault the politician less so for the sexual betrayal than for a character disintegration that led him to act without concern for his wife. Similarly, respondents flayed the political wife not just because she showed up at the scandal press conference but because of what her presence *means*: she's more interested in preserving her tenuous grasp on power or maintaining a marital façade that's more plastic than personal, or she's deficient in sufficient stores of self-respect. The politician and wife have been examined and found to be sorely wanting in character. This infuriates respondents, who react with a tsunami of moral disdain.

THE PUBLIC/PRIVATE DIVIDE

In the second most prominent theme, respondents acknowledged a tension over what type of personal, sexual information the public has a right to know about elected officials. This theme is divided into two opposing threads that occurred with equal frequency. The first subtheme includes respondents who asserted that people should mind their own beeswax. In the second subtheme, respondents argue that there are indeed public consequences for private misbehavior. Therefore, what politicians do behind closed doors is not merely of prurient, voyeuristic interest to the public, but highly relevant because it affects the political landscape.

Mind Your Beeswax: "Sex Between Adults Is Not the Public's Business. It Shouldn't Be News"

Respondents within this category saw a clear line protecting the private behaviors of politicians. In other words, what you don't know can't hurt you, and we shouldn't know what they do that's private and sexual. "I think that there is too much emphasis put on 'sex scandals' which in the end are private matters between the couple and really no one else's business. It is a shame that in the United States it becomes the focus of many campaigns, and the ruin of, in some cases, excellent leaders and legislators," wrote a 57-year-old married woman. A 54-year-old single woman echoed that view, arguing that "America makes a laughably overblown response to discovering that people who are elected to office actually have sex like the rest of the world. It's ridiculous and has little if anything to do with the process of governance."

Others argued that as long as no illegal activity takes place the public should keep their noses out of politicians' affairs. "I have always had an issue with political sex scandals in that I don't think that, barring harmful illegal acts, the public has any business in politicians' sex lives. That is strictly between them, their wives, their dalliances, and their God," wrote a 26-year-old single woman. A 27-year-old married woman said, "I honestly think that things like this are between the married couple and not the rest of the world . . . it makes little difference to me personally, what a political figure does in his marriage . . . barring anything illegal of course." And a 33-year-old married man said, "I really don't care about people's sex lives, and I don't see why the public cares so much about it. It's their private business, and as long as they're not doing anything illegal, it should have no impact on their political office." Others saw a distinct dividing line between what a politician does sexually and what he does professionally. According to a 48-year-old married woman: "I think that what politicians do in their marriage isn't anyone's business . . . No one else loses their job because of an affair, why should they?!" A 27-year-old single man said, "I think that these scandals are far too over exposed. What these people do in their free time regarding their sexual habits should be their business." And a 32-year-old married woman wrote, "It is ridiculous that our society deals with affairs in this manner. It should be a private issue, and if it doesn't have anything to do with the job being done, it shouldn't affect anyone's career." And a single, 26-year-old man wrote, "I don't think anyone should need to resign over it, their sex life is their business." Not only is sex considered to be the private business of the politician, according to a 35-year-old married man, the politician's sex life should not be a reflection of one's morality. He wrote, "I think that the choices we make in the bedroom do not reflect the people that we are at our core. One has nothing to do with the other, and I honestly don't think it's any of my business to know."

Public Consequences for Private Behavior: "It's Absolutely Disgusting and an Abuse of Power"

In contrast, a number of respondents equated the politician's betrayal of his wife to the very real possibility that he would betray his constituents. Therefore, the public has a right to know what a politician does behind closed doors. This knowledge would help members of the public to protect themselves against a politician who might deceive them. According to a 37-year-old divorced woman, "I think marriage is personal, but his character is hurt because he [betrayed] his family and if he [betrayed] his family he would probably [betray] the country and lie to them." And a 33-year-old married woman said, "If they're willing to lie and cheat on their spouses, and destroy their own family, it's terrifying to think about what they will do to us." Related, a 35-year-old single man said that "if a politician can cheat on his wife, what does that say about what temptations he is willing to pursue over the promises he made to his constituents?"

Others drew a direct link regarding the broken trust between a politician and his wife with the trust obliterated with his constituents. For instance, a 31-year-old man wrote, "Political sex scandals can have devastating effects, not only to the people directly involved, but also to the voters who supported the politicians." A 51-year-old divorced woman said, "It breaks the trust of the people, not just the wife and family. I noticed when they get caught, the[y] say they are sorry over and over. Those apologies do not take away the fact that trust was lost a great deal." Some respondents said the public status of the offending politician trumps his right to privacy. For instance, a 42-year-old single woman wrote, "I think that these public officials let their constituents down through their immoral actions. It is their private business what they do in their homes, but at the same time, their behaviors are an indication of their character. I don't think they can be fully trusted." A 32-year-old married man said, "Politicians' personal lives are supposed to be private; however, if they cheat on the person they are supposed to love the most, they will lie and cheat on others as well. Politicians caught in scandals should immediately resign or be ousted, because they cannot be trusted." And a 23-year-old married woman conceded, "It sucks they're put more in the public eye about it than non political people, but maybe that's what they need, because they shouldn't do it in the first place." A 51-year-old woman said politicians' extramarital affairs are of greater import and impact than mere civilians.' She wrote, "Unbelievable are my words. Only in government can such things be gotten away with. I know we are only human, but these people are representing us." And a 43-year-old man sees the frequency of scandal as a reflection of our degraded national character: "So many scandals, what have we really become [as a] country?" Finally, a 26-year-old single man sees a direct effect of a politician's sexual misdeeds on his public record. "It's disappointing when something like this happens, because it undercuts all the work that the politician has done." And a 23-year-old single man said scandal-tarnished politicians will lose his vote. "I think sex scandals are despicable . . . I will never vote for someone who has had a sex scandal."

The public/private divide theme showed a clear distinction among respondents. Some people saw politicians' sexual indiscretions as private and having no bearing on the public. Others saw an urgent prerogative for the public's need to know because a politico's actions in private, motivated by his personal desires and self-interest, may also reflect (corrupt) motivations as a steward of the public.

SYMPATHY

This represents the most interesting category, perhaps because it shows a space—between the outrage—that shows politicians as human, and therefore fallible. Let's take a closer look at the two most prominent subthemes within this category. In the first subtheme, we see sympathy directed at the political wives, and in the second we see it directed at the politicians who are, after all, regarded to be imperfect like everyone else.

Wife Sympathy: "I Feel Bad for the Wives Who Have to Deal with These Situations"

In the most prominent sympathy subtheme, we see respondents expressing gentleness toward the political wives for enduring this tribulation. Some respondents sympathized with the wives who persevered through both private and public humiliation. For instance, a 34-year-old married woman wrote, "I feel sorry for the woman because it's bad enough to know that your husband stepped out on your marriage but when it becomes national news, your privacy is overly invaded." A 61-year-old widowed woman said, "I feel very sorry for Silda Spitzer. I think she did it out of duty, but it was very humiliating." A 23-year-old single woman said, "I can't help but feel bad that the wife's business is now a political thing." And a 32-year-old single man wrote, "How humiliating it must be for the wives, and for the guys caught. The guys deserve it, the wives don't."

Meanwhile, another cohort of sympathetic respondents applauded the political wives for standing in support of their scandal-tarnished husbands, marking a distinct turn from the "disdain" theme where respondents berated and mocked political wives for their presence at the news conferences. A 44-year-old separated woman wrote, "I say cheers to the wives who continue to try and will act in a way such as Huma did." A 22-year-old single woman said of Silda Spitzer, "She was strong and resilient and though she did not agree with his actions, she supported him as a dutiful wife." A 51-year-old married woman remarked that "I think women who stand beside their husbands in situations like this are very brave and strong . . . I do admire them for doing what they did, but am not sure I could do the same." A 36-year-old married woman echoed that sentiment with, "I give a lot of credit to the wives of the two politicians who did attend the press conferences; however, if I was in their position there is no way I could do that." And a 37-year-old single woman commented that "I give her [Huma Abedin] props for standing up and saying her feelings." Meanwhile, a 28-year-old single woman respected each of the political wives' decisions: "I think that Huma has a strong relationship with her husband to go and talk to the press. I think Jenny has every right to be upset with her husband and I hope she got as much as she could get. I think Silda was strong to go as well. None of what happened was their fault, but their husband's fault." And a 26-year-old single man gave props to the political wives for exhibiting spousal support: "The political wives who attended the press conference show great strength to both themselves and their families. Even more so by speaking at the press conference as Anthony Weiner's wife did." A 35-year-old married man backed that view with, "I think it takes a great deal of strength, and grace to stand by their husbands regardless of their behavior." Finally, a 34-year-old single woman gave props to the wives. "Honestly? Those wives who stand by their husbands have my respect."

Politician Sympathy: "They Make Mistakes"

A number of respondents expressed sympathy toward the politicians, acknowledging that politicians are imperfect—just like everyone else. Their stance is that people should cut these politicians some slack, if not an outright break. For instance, a 33-year-old married man said, "These politicians can be rather perverted, but they are human at the same time." And a 31-year-old single man wrote, "Humans make mistakes and we blow these ones well out of proportion." A 30-year-old single man said that what the politicians did is "immoral, but people do make mistakes. As long as they learn from them, I understand." Other respondents argued that politicians are no different than civilians who have extramarital affairs: For instance, a 46-year-old divorced woman wrote, "It is sad that these men and w[o]men are scrutinized for what millions of Americans do every day," and a 20-year-old single woman said, "I think everyone is a human being, it's not like the citizens are holy saints either." And a 22-year-old separated woman wrote, "Cheating is all around us. It is everywhere. No one is safe and it's not just politics." Additionally, a 48-year-old married woman noted that "I think politicians, like other people, make mistakes in their marriages and it shouldn't have anything to do with the job they are doing." Meanwhile, a 24-year-old single man argued, "Unless America believed that all its citizens should be fired from their jobs when they commit 'sexual wrongdoings' then I don't see why politicians should have to resign. The politicians are just a reflection of the society no matter how morally decayed it is."

In the sympathy theme, we see respondents react with a "matter of factness" that was absent from the more prominent disdain and private/public divide themes. Indeed, in the sympathy theme we see respondents removing the political couple from their pedestal. It's as if they're saying, *These are regular folks: imperfect* (sound familiar?) *and no doubt suffering from humiliation* (who wouldn't?). But let's not forget that the most prominent theme of disdain reveals that people are quick to judge and release a torrent of vehemence when it comes to politicians caught in scandalous acts and a political wife who plays her part in his shaming and shameful script.

MAKING SENSE OF PUBLIC REACTION TO SCANDAL

This survey demonstrated that above all else people reacted to scandal press conferences with unrestrained disdain directed at the politicians and their wives. The second most prominent theme represented an acknowledged tension over the public/private divide. And the third most frequently occurring theme indicated a wave of gentler sympathy directed at the scandal's afflicted. What do we make of these three various themes?

With the destruction of a politician's reputation, we see—at least in the moment—the destruction of his credibility.[46] The occurrence of scandal causes a breakdown in character as the curtain is pulled back on a politician to reveal his/her problematic, personal traits. These problematic traits are viewed as a more authentic revelation of the politician's "true" self because they are not publicly performed for professional gain but instead are privately indulged out of need. This revelation spotlights the negative aspects of his character—that the scandal-burdened politician was too inept, careless, reckless, or megalomaniacal to successfully conceal. Scandal, therefore, decimates the transgressor's symbolic power,[47] which represents one of the most effective tools in a politician's war chest. Thompson, the scandal sociologist, points to (1) the decline in the party system and (2) an increased focus on individual politicians in a post–World War II era, as contributing to the rise in scandal occurrences:

> People become more concerned with the *character* of the individuals who are (or might become) their leaders and more concerned about their trustworthiness, because increasingly this becomes the principal means of guaranteeing that political promises will be kept and that difficult decisions in the face of complexity and uncertainty will be made on the basis of sound judgment.[48]

A person's integrity sits at the center of one's trustworthiness. Integrity is a character issue, and the greater import we bestow upon it—in the political context—the greater power and relevance we also give its underbelly: human weakness, foible, deception, and self-interest. "Viewed in this light," writes Thompson, "we can understand why a scandal concerning the private life of a politician is seen by many people to have broader political significance: it is not so much because they believe that politicians should adhere to strict moral codes in their private life, but because they are worried about what this behavior tells them about the integrity and credibility of the individual concerned."[49] Therefore, when respondents reacted with sympathy (in the third most frequently recurring theme) they readily acknowledged that politicians are imperfect just like everybody else. They did not expect them to uphold normative moral practices, just as Thompson suggests. But the power of respondent disdain strongly trumped the sympathy theme, and it also indicated a powerful expression of disgust and resentment directed at the political couple. It's as if the collective disdain responses bellowed in unison: *How dare you, Mr. Politician, with your oozing self-righteousness who readily casts judgment on others, who upholds yourself and your family as moral beacons for public consumption, engage in the activities you've excoriated in others?* Once this bubbling of resentment rises to the surface, there is no holding back the tide of public disdain, and the politician's position becomes "untenable."[50]

Therefore, scandal bulldozes through the public/private distinction. The acts may have occurred in private, but once the scandal trigger is released, there's no shoving them back into the proverbial closet. Private events become issues of public concern because—just like in the Victorian era—the private nature of an individual is viewed to be a central aspect of one's authentic self. And in politics a depleted reputation diminishes political power. "Contemporary society is apparently held together by a suspicion and a distaste for public life," writes media historian Jean Seaton. "Prurience has rarely been more powerful than it is at present."[51] The marriage of the public's scalding view of politicians, coupled with a general curiosity about their private lives, is catastrophic for scandal-prone politicians. Indeed, two communications and journalism scholars wrote in 2011 that when compared to 2001, the public increasingly expects the news media to examine the private lives of politicians, and the public is less likely to think the news media pays too much attention to politicians' private lives.[52]

Ultimately, for politicians whose public persona mightily conflicted with their private behavior, or for those who lacked enough stores of political power in the first place or who cultivated enemies more powerful than friends or who were simply unlikable to begin with and therefore even more unlikable post-scandal, there's little hope of bouncing back from scandal's destruction as the masses consume news of a politician's breathtaking fall. In a surveillance society, the public of millions (or billions!) has the potential to gather and disseminate sensitive information about the elite few, just as those running government, media, military, and commercial systems use our data against us.[53] This dilemma of mediated visibility demonstrates the vulnerability of politicians in the digital age. Backed by disdain and disgust, the public is armed with the power of public opinion that can truncate a politician's career once scandalized. The force of disdain reveals that respondents react personally to scandal. Their expressed vehemence demonstrates that they take intimate offense to the philandering actions of the politicians and the presence of the political wives. Perhaps this is a natural extension to the gendered nature of power in politics. The public is angered by a character betrayal that cuts so deep it's almost familial.

New media scholar P. David Marshall notes the cultural trope of politicians whose leadership traits are linked to constructions of family, masculinity, and paternalism.[54] "The homologous relationship between the familial and the nation, the father and the political leader, is a form of affective transference: the acceptability and the 'warmth' conveyed by a 'good' and 'strong' family structure becomes a legitimate model for structuring the organization of the political sphere."[55] Accordingly, power is expressed through a code of masculinity that hinges on the connection of virile politicians to the national interest and subsumed under the familiar functioning of the heterosexual family structure.[56] Respondents who protested the publicization of a politician's private behavior perhaps were decrying it as beyond the bounds of reasonable information for the public to consume, just as children protest learning about their parents' sex lives.

Politics symbolically blurs the line between candidate, family, and constituent. The politician's/candidate's family is present at all key points of the electoral process, from major campaign announcements to successful elections and stalwart concessions. According to Marshall, the new media scholar: "Although these connections to the familial appear to be natural, they must also be seen to be techniques that provide the sentiment of a common bond with the people."[57] It's not that we, as members of the public, believe the politician to be our actual father—or the political wife our mother—but we take umbrage that a political couple who so easily slipped into those roles and campaigned as the most perfect version and vision of themselves now seeks easy forgiveness under the guise of national theater, which is embodied in the sex scandal press conference. The power tables have flipped, and as a public collective we can now control the political fate of these one-time "parents" who sought to legislate our best interests. They capitalized on the construction of politics as personal and familial. But you know what? The public/politician dynamic represents a double-edged sword that cuts both ways. When a politician betrays his polished presence, the public can—and often will—make him pay. (I intentionally use the gendered pronoun.)

Ultimately, the revelation of scandal rips that common bond apart by revealing that the politician (1) betrayed his protective, paternal role to his public and (biological) family; (2) could not uphold the moral standard that carried him on the stump; and (3) was, in the end, not worthy of the trust that he asked his family and public to bestow upon him. His character was, therefore, either too weak or too deceptive, and his wife—the polished political appendage—was too much of the same. In politics, where affective, emotional power represents a hallmark of its functioning,[58] there is no such thing as a public/private divide, as much as we speak about things that occur without our knowledge and those things that happen in plain sight. Once knowledge of a private act becomes knowable through media coverage, there's no sending it back from whence it came, because that information, which is both highly personal to the politician and also triggers a personal response from the public, is too valuable a key into the politician's soul—however kinky, perverted, and dumb it may be.

CHAPTER 8

In Sickness and Scandal: Married Couples Navigate Scandal in the News

When I watch a political sex scandal press conference on television, I am overwhelmed with one thing beyond all else. What must it be like to stand in front of the cameras as part of a scandal-tainted couple, to live in a moment of private shame metastasized into public spectacle, to be placed under a microscope as one endures the crush of cameras and the searing lights? And that's just the beginning. One has to contend with becoming fodder for late-night jokes and water-cooler conversations, to be pilloried by magazine covers and gag gifts and TV shows, and to be reduced to the contemporary cultural cliché of the horn-dog politician and his staid wife. The sheer force of the humiliation, to have a lurid transgression ripped open so publicly, begs the question—what would it feel like to stand at the center of a media firestorm centered on your spouse's genitals? It doesn't require much of a cognitive leap to then put oneself in the unenviable position of the politician and spouse: *If I were that sorry politician, would I feel buoyed by my spouse standing next to me, sharing the hot glare of the lights and the public's dissection of a most intimate moment?* And, *If I were the scandalized spouse, would I consider lending my presence, so valuable in scandalous times—perhaps my last valuable asset in the marriage—to a person whose actions resulted in public humiliation of Old Testament proportions?* I know I'm not alone in pursuing these thoughts, because I hear colleagues and friends posing them to each other after every blockbuster scandal.

This chapter attempts to answer some of those questions by posing them to everyday married couples in an effort not only to grasp the cultural effects of political scandal beyond media coverage of these events but also to gain new insight into sex scandals as a gendered phenomenon. This chapter represents my attempt to systematically answer the questions that are in the social ether mid-scandal. By revisiting the video images of select sex-scandal press conferences during interviews with everyday couples, it is possible to excavate their emotional reactions to these events as they relate to their own conceptions of marriage, (in)fidelity, what is forgivable, and what is not. These discussions can lead us to new pathways of knowledge about how we process scandal and the extent to which we place ourselves into these scandal narratives, since the themes of scandal are so personal and universal. "An image is a bridge between evoked emotion and conscious knowledge," writes Chicana theory and gender scholar Gloria Anzaldúa, "words are the cables that hold up the bridge. Images are more direct, more immediate than words, and closer to the unconscious."[1]

No doubt images from the sex scandal press conference, which upholds traditional marital roles even as a husband blemishes the "family" name, have drawn ire from the press and the public. As we know from chapter 5, media coverage typically slams the now hackneyed figure of a political wife who "stands by her man." But by interviewing everyday married couples, it's possible to reveal new channels of understanding by complicating what appear to be gender-normative constructions of husbands and wives in times of marital crisis. It is assumed that interviews with everyday married couples will not shed light on what the politician and his spouse went through as they ascended the scandal podium to face an aggressive scrum of news folk. But these interviews can demonstrate how people's consumption of scandal impacts the way they think about the politician and his wife. They also can help us understand the way we react to these scandal scenes as we critically approach the cultural figure of the politician, whose sex life is transformed into a public cadaver for all to dissect and poke at the inner workings of the pervy-politician's sex life. And these interviews can help us better grasp the divisive wife, the political appendage who has the potential to resuscitate a floundering career gasping for air.

As a social institution that receives ample and frenzied media attention, political sex scandals have cultivated mass-culture appeal.[2] The popularity of the CBS drama The Good Wife, which was inspired by Silda Spitzer's silent appearance at her then husband's press conference, is evidence of its commercial value. But little research exists to investigate how people react to scandal press conferences, which typically put gendered spousal roles on display for public consumption and commodification. The literary and cultural studies scholar Janice Radway[3] argues for the relevance of reception studies to challenge an intractable, homogenous understanding of ideology through public interactions with mediated texts of mass appeal. "The content of any message, whether textual or behavioral, is not simply found in that message but is constructed by an audience interaction with that message."[4] Radway's metaphor of "ideological seams" is an incisive framework to investigate how everyday couples both relate to and contest the iconic, polarizing figure of a political wife at her husband-politician's scandal press conference. Since Radway reminds us that "no ideology is a simple, uniform, organic thing,"[5] the joining of seams is not, in fact, seamless:

> To challenge the very solidity, indeed the "naturalness," of any particular patriarchal vision of the world, then, we must be able to identify the seams, as it were, those points of intersection between the discourse and practices that together constitute individual subjects (including ourselves) in particular ways and address the needs produced as a consequence of that constitution.[6]

By identifying the ideological seams within this context, one can complicate—and indeed humanize—the figure of the political wife, who appears to have been disregarded by her husband and further shamed by the public via mediated content, including opinion articles, commentary, blog posts, social media updates, and hashtags, as well as plotlines in television shows and movies. Interviews with everyday married couples can reveal the often contested and contradictory expectations of "standing by" one's husband when a husband has behaved in ways that have presumably caused emotional damage to his wife.

Media coverage of political scandal generally slams the wife's presence at news conferences, where the husband-politician typically acknowledges—but sometimes denies—a sexual affair or indiscretion.[7] While not all political sex scandals feature a press conference and while not all political wives attend their husband-politician's press conference,[8] the press conference itself has become a critical part of the sex-scandal script.[9] Certainly, the media play a key role in the evolution of scandal by publicizing its unfolding events.[10]

Scandals may be derided socially as mere sensationalism, but media scholar John B. Thompson argues it is necessary to move beyond a casual dismissal of scandal to excavate the discourses surrounding it.[11] Since scandal emerges from a particular culture, it amounts to more than empty scintillation that piques our curiosity. Scandals represent morality tales wrapped in melodramatic narratives. They become the content of moral discourse surrounding systems of (gendered) power. They emerge as a hegemonic tool to reinforce social norms and as a counterhegemonic tool that can temporarily restore power to the public, who decides whether or not an elected official, typically male, is worthy of forgiveness. Or, the public has the power to determine if his alleged behavior is too distracting and too egregious that he needs to be knocked from his privileged perch, making sure there is no pillow to soften his crushing fall.

THREE PRESS CONFERENCES, THREE WIVES, THREE ROLES

This chapter examines how 11 men and 11 women—representing 11 married couples in total—responded to three political sex scandals. Each scandal featured a press conference and was selected for the different roles that political wives played in each one. This chapter picks up where chapter 7 left off, since the interviews here offer in-depth analysis of the same press conferences belonging to Eliot Spitzer, Mark Sanford, and Anthony Weiner that 330 survey respondents viewed.

SILDA SPITZER AT NEW YORK GOVERNOR ELIOT SPITZER'S PRESS CONFERENCE

On March 12, 2008, the governor of New York, Eliot Spitzer, abruptly resigned when news broke that he was "Client No. 9" in a prostitution ring. He announced his resignation at a press conference, where his then wife (they divorced in 2013), Silda Spitzer, stood next to him at the podium (see page 136), While she did not speak at the event, her presence was noted and debated by media. The (Albany, NY) Times Union newspaper's headlines included, "A Woman Betrayed with a Future to Ponder" and "First Comes Love and Now Forgiveness?"[12] Ultimately, Silda Spitzer's silent presence was the inspiration behind the TV series The Good Wife, a fictional attempt to answer so many questions about the life of a woman who could stand so polished, in control, coiffed, and yet so silent in support of a husband who betrayed and humiliated her.

JENNY SANFORD, ABSENT FROM SOUTH CAROLINA GOVERNOR MARK SANFORD'S PRESS CONFERENCE

Jenny Sanford appeared to break the mold of a "traditional," scorned political wife when she chose to remain absent from her then husband's press conference in June 2009. At the news event, Mark Sanford confessed that he secretly fled to Argentina to spend five days with his mistress, even though he initially told his staff—and the staff reported to the news media—that he was hiking the Appalachian Trail. Jenny Sanford thus became the "role model" for a new type of assertive, self-preserving political wife.[13] She divorced her husband in the scandal's aftermath and released a memoir in 2010, *Staying True*.[14]

HUMA ABEDIN, PRESENT AND VOCAL AT NYC MAYORAL CANDIDATE ANTHONY WEINER'S PRESS CONFERENCE

On June 6, 2011, Congressman Anthony Weiner of New York confessed—reversing his initial denial and assertion that his account had been hacked—to sending pictures of his erect penis on Twitter. "In addition," he added during a news conference on that day, "over the past few years, I have engaged in several inappropriate conversations conducted over Twitter, Facebook, e-mail, and occasionally on the phone with women I had met online."[15] He held a second press conference 10 days later where he announced his resignation from Congress. His wife, Huma Abedin, who was pregnant at the time, did not attend that event. Two years later, in May 2013, Anthony Weiner—now running for mayor of New York City—said new explicit Twitter photos might surface. On July 23, 2013, Weiner convened a third press conference, where his wife stood next to him at the microphone (see page 138). After Weiner's apology, Huma Abedin addressed the audience with her prepared remarks, buttressing Weiner's admission that his actions were deceitful. She admitted that the couple had gone through "a whole lot of therapy" and that she decided to stay with him. She ended her 250-word statement with: "So really what I want to say is that I love him, I have forgiven him, I believe in him and we have said from the beginning, we are moving forward." (Huma Abedin announced her separation from her husband in August 2016 after a third round of illicit sexts was publicized.)

THE INTERVIEWS

I conducted 22 interviews from May 2014 to June 2015. Since I was interested in the dynamic between a husband and wife—specifically within the power structures of a middle- to upper-middle-class dynamic, reflective of a similar social class to the political couples—I limited recruitment to heterosexual couples within a suburb of Rochester, New York, where I live and work. I received permission from a cafe manager at a popular, suburban community fitness center to place signs throughout the café to recruit interview participants. The signs noted that participants would receive one $50 Amazon gift card as incentive to participate in an interview on "the 'naughty' behavior of our politicians"[16] and "the political wife's presence at her husband's press conference." The snowball method helped me recruit additional participants since I ended each interview asking if they knew of other couples who might be willing to participate. Husbands and wives were always interviewed separately in order to allow spouses to speak more freely.[17] Twenty-one of the 22 interviews took place at this community café; the 22nd took place at a participant's place of work per his request. All participants identified as Caucasian. The interviews lasted, on average, 29 minutes, with wife interviews clocking in at an average of 31 minutes and husband interviews at 26 minutes. A semi-structured interview guide was employed, where I asked the same core questions of all participants, while at the same time allowing the interview to move in unexpected directions, like a conversation.[18] (Please see appendix C for a list of initial questions asked of all participants.) Participants selected aliases for this research project (table 8.1).

YouTube clips of three press conferences were shown in chronological order. We began with the 2008 press conference of former governor Eliot Spitzer. Following the Spitzer discussion with the participant, where I asked the participant whether she'd attend the press conference if she were in Silda Spitzer's shoes, the participant was shown an excerpt of the Mark Sanford press conference in 2009. The final press conference belonged to Anthony Weiner in 2013.

Before playing excerpts of the YouTube clips, I provided participants with a scandal "summary." However, since each of these three political sex scandals received significant media coverage, participants rarely needed more than a basic refresher of events because they were already familiar with these news stories. All interviews were recorded and then sent to an outside company to be transcribed. My academic institution provided funding for the Amazon gift cards and transcription services through a research grant. I analyzed transcripts using the "constant comparative method" that involved a five-step approach used in research on married couples. This involved comparison within the individual interview, within the group (of wives or husbands), between the groups, at the pairs' level, and then comparing what couples said.[19]

ELIOT SPITZER PRESS CONFERENCE

Two of the 11 husbands said they would want their wives to attend the Eliot Spitzer press conference if they themselves faced that scandal as a politician. Five said "No" to having their wives present; two were "unsure"; and two husbands said that the choice belongs to the wife, but they'd welcome her presence if she really wanted to be there (table 8.2).

Table 8.1   The Interviewed Couples

	Age	Children	Profession	Political Wife Most Identify With
Bruce*	30	2	Department of Justice	Jenny Sanford
Maeghan	31		Homemaker	Huma Abedin
Ellis	59	2	Retail store manager	Huma Abedin
Bailee	59		Homemaker	Silda Spitzer
Paul	29	2	Computer programmer	Can't answer
Olivia	29		Nurse	Jenny Sanford
Zach	36	1	Finance	Huma Abedin
Beth	32		Childcare	Jenny Sanford
Hector	34	1	Insurance	Huma Abedin
Kelly	33		Homemaker	Jenny Sanford
Freddy	27		Attorney	Jenny Sanford and Huma Abedin
Gail	24	0	Childcare	Jenny Sanford
John	37	3	Counselor	Huma Abedin
Lynn	31		Teacher	Silda Spitzer
Jim	49	2	Engineering technician	Jenny Sanford
Susan	49		Teacher	Huma Abedin
Robert	52	3	Civil engineer	Huma Abedin
Joyce	52		Teacher	Huma Abedin
Carl	33	1	Doctor	Huma Abedin
Sarah	31		Homemaker	Huma Abedin
Harold	49	2	Software engineer	Huma Abedin
Mila	47		Administrative assistant	Jenny Sanford

*Note: Participants selected aliases for this research project.

Table 8.2   Husbands Only: Would you want your wife to stand next to you—just as Silda Spitzer did—at the Eliot Spitzer press conference?

	Number of Husbands Responding
Yes	2
No	5
Unsure	2
The choice belongs to the wife	2

The wives also expressed a diversity of opinion when asked if they would attend the Eliot Spitzer press conference as the political wife. Four women said they would not attend the event. Two said they would; a third said she would attend the event, although she would stand in the back of the room and not next to her husband. Four wives said they were unsure (table 8.3).

Table 8.3   For Wives Only: Would you attend the Eliot Spitzer press conference as the political wife?

	Number of Wives Responding
Yes	2
No	4
Unsure	4
Would attend but stand in the back, away from public view	1

Of the two husbands who said they'd want their wives to attend the press conference as a supportive and silent spouse in the vein of Silda Spitzer, one wife said she wouldn't attend, and a second wife said she'd attend—but only if she was standing out of view in the back, away from the spotlight. And when you flip the situation around, of the two wives who said they would attend the press conference, one husband said he wouldn't want her there. The second husband said he simply wouldn't ask her since the choice to attend is hers alone. This demonstrates not only the diversity of opinions among wives and husbands but also that when it comes to the Eliot Spitzer press conference, no couple had answers where husband and wife were in synch with what the husband wanted and what the wife was willing to do. When I asked the husbands if they thought their wives would attend the event (distinguishing between *wanting* the wife to attend and asking if she *would* do so when asked) there are only two instances—out of 11 couples—when the husband's answer matched the wife's answer. And in neither case was the wife's answer "Yes." Let's now examine a selection of the responses from the couples about spousal presence at this press conference.

Robert, a 52-year-old civil engineer, said he would want his wife to stand next to him at the Eliot Spitzer press conference. "I would," he said, "assuming that she truly is understanding of my remorse and . . . in my desire to fix the problem and do what I could . . . You would hope that your spouse would never just dump you right away without seeing if there's a way you can fix that." I then asked Robert what his wife might say if he asked her to do this for him. Would she stand up there with him? "I think my wife would," he said.[20]

Joyce, Robert's wife, a 52-year-old teacher, was much less certain about her ability to stand publicly next to a scandal-tarnished husband. She began with an "I don't know," citing the importance of marital vows that center on fidelity, and noting, "I wouldn't want the public to think that

I was supporting my husband having affairs with prostitutes." Joyce felt a conflict roiling inside. On the one hand, she described her husband as her "rock" since "he has been through thick and thin with me in 27 years."[21] During that time, he's advocated for her and supported her through physical and mental health issues, so she wouldn't want to abandon him during his time of need. But the public nature of the press conference gives her pause. After mulling over the potential scenario, she says,

> I would not attend the press conference. Because I feel like that's a very public thing, and the other thing is I feel like this is something that needs to be addressed in private. So I don't know that—I don't think I would address—I don't think I would attend the press conference. I think I would totally want to address this in private.[22]

But Joyce is still unsettled at leaving her husband to face this event without her. The tensions continue to pull at her. The words "for better or worse" nag at her, she said. And even though she feels betrayed by a husband who—in this hypothetical scenario—was sexually unfaithful to her, and whose infidelity was broadcasted widely, she does not want to abandon him publicly, even if she sees the private realm as a more appropriate space for them to work through their issues. Ultimately she settled on being present at the press but out of the limelight, "Maybe in a back corner." She elaborates: "In the case of Spitzer's I would wanna be in the room, but not by his side . . . Because your marriage vows are your marriage vows, and I would wanna give my husband a chance to go through therapy and talk about it."[23] Her condition for attending the press conference—although out of the searing spotlight—is that her husband would attend marriage counseling with her. "I feel that people should always have an opportunity to try and change their behavior," she said.[24]

Moving onto another couple, Carl is a doctor who said he would not want his wife to attend the Spitzer press conference. "You know, I think that if I were going to go with his speech as written I would actually not have my wife at my side. He's asking his constituents to judge him by the same criteria that he would judge others. Nothing about his wife has any effect on the fact that he's resigning from this elected, public position."[25] According to Carl, the political wife in the Spitzer instance is a red herring because he's exiting political life and doesn't need the appearance of a "good wife" to soften the blow of scandal. He elaborates: "If he's truly taking an exit from public office, then I don't think, you know, being in his position I would require or request my wife to be there."[26] That's a good thing, because Carl's wife, Sarah, who works in the home look-ing after their toddler-aged daughter, said she most definitely would not attend a press conference in support of a philandering husband. "I imagine I'd be infuriated with him," she said. "I would want his political career to fail because our marriage had failed. I also would be worried that other people would perceive me as a pushover or not as a strong woman who stood up for herself."[27]

Then there's the couple of Freddy and Gail. He's an attorney and she works in the daycare field. When asked if he'd want his wife present at the press conference, Freddy said, "It would depend on how bad things were with Gail as a result of it."[28] He added, "I only would want her there if I really thought that she was going to be fully there."[29] Therefore, Freddy would welcome her presence if his wife could present herself in a way that wouldn't exacerbate his public standing. Certainly the appearance of a wife who is scowling and grimacing at her scandal-tarnished husband would undercut the purpose of her presence in the first place: to show support and act as a conduit of forgiveness. If the wife's presence does not bring value—after all, she's there to help manage the damage—then she can offer little utility from the perspective of the politician and his handlers.

Gail is uncertain about whether she would attend the press conference. While she and Freddy don't yet have children, Gail sees children as the only reason why she would publicly stand next to her husband. "If there were children and at that point maybe grandchildren involved, I can't say for sure. I mean I might feel that it was important to do that. But I certainly wouldn't enjoy it," she said.[30] But like Joyce, Gail feels a tension that pulls at her. Gail said she'd like to think she'd cut all ties with a phi-landering husband, "Because I think that infidelity is just unforgivable . . . I'd like to think that if I found out that my husband had been unfaithful that I would be filing divorce papers the next morning. But, you know, you hear stories and you read things and people say, 'Oh, there's always two sides.'"[31] Ultimately Gail leaves the possibility open and says she might stand at the podium with her husband even though she would not stay in the marriage afterward. She makes clear, though, that she'd be there "not for his sake" but for their (future) children. She elaborates:

> He's still the children's father, and they deserve to maintain a close relation-ship with him. I wouldn't want to interfere in that unless there were real abuse involved and I didn't feel that they were safe with him. And I think that my presence at that press conference, even though I wouldn't say any-thing . . . would send the message that this is an individual who deserves to be respected in other ways and who deserves the opportunity to rebuild his own life, even if I won't be an intimate part of that going forward.[32]

In each of these three examples, selected as representational interviews from the Spitzer press conference, regardless of whether the
husband said "Yes," "No," or anything in between about wanting his
wife's support, we see husbands talking about their wives in terms ben-
eficial to them. When Robert said he would want his wife present he
said so because, "You would hope that your spouse would never just
dump you right away," indicating that regardless of the hurt the husband
causes, the marital relationship warrants a second chance. Carl, who
didn't want his wife to be present, implied that his wife's presence is not
relevant if he's leaving elected office. And the uncertainty that Freddy
felt about his wife's attendance was based on whether she would be able
to present herself in a way he deemed appropriate. In these instances,
regardless of the husband's answer, the wife's needs are subsumed by those
of the husband.

MARK SANFORD PRESS CONFERENCE

I saw a similar distribution of answers among the husbands in relation
to the Mark Sanford press conference. In every instance except two, the
husbands responded in the same way as they did to the Spitzer scenario
(table 8.4).

With the Sanford press conference, wives were much more likely to
change their opinion from a potential "Yes" or "Unsure" to a "No." Four
of the 11 wives answered differently from the Spitzer press conference and
indicated that if they were a "Yes" or "Unsure" with Spitzer, they were an
"Unsure" or "No," respectively, with Sanford. When I asked the husbands
if they thought their wife would attend the event (again, distinguishing
between *wanting* the wife to attend and speculating whether she would
actually attend when asked), the husband's answer matched the wife's
in 9 of the 11 instances, indicating a reversal from the Spitzer scenario.
That's because most of the husbands guessed their wives would not attend

Table 8.4   For Husbands Only: Would you want your wife to stand next
to you at the Mark Sanford press conference?

	Number of Husbands Responding
Yes	2
No	5
Unsure	2
The choice belongs to the wife	2

this press conference. And they were right. In the two instances where the spousal answers didn't match, the first husband said his wife might attend the event (but the wife said nope!), and another husband said his wife would not attend the press conference (but the wife said she was unsure) (table 8.5). Let's now take a closer look at a representative selection of the responses.

Jim is a 49-year-old engineering technician who is married to 49-year-old Susan, a teacher, with whom they have two teen daughters. We spoke about whether he would want his wife to stand next to him at the Sanford press conference. "I'd want her to be [there] but let's say if she wasn't there I've got nobody to blame but myself,"[33] he said. Jim also said he'd want his wife to attend the event in the Spitzer scenario. In general, he describes a wife's presence as soft comfort. "It's kind of like a security blanket," he said,[34] although acknowledging that he wouldn't deserve that feeling of security. Regardless, it would act as a salve to his scandal wound nonetheless. Yet his wife, Susan, would not be able to offer him any type of security. She said she would not attend the Sanford press conference (not that she would have attended the Spitzer one, for that matter). "For what? He cheated on me," said Susan—putting herself in Jenny Sanford's position as the victimized spouse. "Everybody knows about it. They're wondering what's wrong in our relationship. I don't need everyone knowing my personal business. And I'm not going to stand next to him and smile about it."[35]

Ellis, a 59-year-old manager of a retail store, who is married to Bailee, a homemaker with whom he has two grown children, said he was unsure whether he'd want his wife to attend this press conference. "It would probably make me look less guilty if I had the wife there, you know, like I have support from my family."[36] Regardless, Ellis supported Jenny Sanford's absence from the press conference ("I kind of applaud her," he said) and sees "no excuse for what these guys are doing." He added: "I just don't

Table 8.5 For Wives Only: Would you attend the Mark Sanford press conference as the political wife?

	Number of Wives Responding
Yes	0
No	8
Unsure	2
Would attend but stand in the back, away from public view	1

believe in infidelity, you know, no matter what."[37] His wife, Bailee, is adamant in her refusal to support a husband like Mark Sanford.

> I wouldn't stand by him. He embarrassed her. And he humiliated her. . . .
> He made a fool out of her. Here he's telling everybody he's out in the Appalachians and blah, blah, blah, totally innocent. And then she has to suffer the humiliation of finding out he was *shtupping* some woman in South America? Uh-uh. I wouldn't go.[38]

But regardless of how strongly worded their answers are for the Sanford scenario, both Ellis and Bailee responded in a categorically different way for the Spitzer press conference. Ellis said he wouldn't want his wife to attend that event (while he was unsure for the Sanford event). Meanwhile Bailee said she *would* attend the Spitzer news conference (but wouldn't in Sanford's case). Ellis said he'd feel too much shame to have his wife stand next to him in the Spitzer scenario. "I mean I'd be embarrassed in front of her. I'd be embarrassed in front of the public," he said.[39] But when he watched the Sanford press conference, he changed his answer in that scenario to being unsure about his wife's presence, thereby softening his position, because it would make him look "less guilty" to have a visible support system. When Ellis watched a press conference that had an absent wife, he saw that that the spousal void negatively impacted the politician. Meanwhile, Bailee said she would attend the Spitzer press conference as the political wife because it's about "being the mature one, and not making the situation any worse than it already is . . . Would I stand by him outside of there? Probably not."[40] But she could not act "maturely" in the Sanford instance. "Okay, with Spitzer it was one thing. He solicited a prostitute. It's bad. But he wasn't cheating on his wife, so to speak, with another woman who could be a threat to his marriage."[41]

John is a 37-year-old counselor who is married to married to Lynn, a 31-year-old teacher, and they have two young children. John said he would leave his wife's presence or absence up to her. "I'd want her to have her choice in the matter and you know not subject her anymore to public scrutiny in general."[42] John offered the same answer under the Spitzer scenario, but provided more insight when talking about Spitzer because it was his first time answering the question.

> God forbid this ever happened to us, I would first of all ask her. I wouldn't care what, you know, my political adviser thought . . . I would say, "What do you want?" . . . Maybe Lynn would really feel like I want to be there to

support your mistakes and I want to show that we're strong. Then in that case I would say ok and of course I'd want her there in that case if that was her choice.[43]

John's wife, Lynn, said she probably wouldn't attend the Mark Sanford press conference. "I don't know," she said. "He kinda just sounds like he's going in circles and just talking. Kinda not making sense. Like I feel like you would leave more confused than when you came."[44] But with the Spitzer scenario, Lynn said she would attend it—forced out of a wifely obligation in which her ability to decide for herself would be stripped from her. "I think they would make you go to show you stand behind him and that he is truly sorry for what he's done," she said. "So I think they expect it from the wife—it's just expected."[45]

In the Sanford scenario, we see wives overwhelmingly certain that they would not stand next to their husbands at the scandal press conference. The nature of the scandal, where the politician had a drawn-out love affair with the same woman, and the fact that he intentionally obscured the true nature of his physical whereabouts when he was actually spending time with his mistress, meant no wife interviewed could imagine standing in support of him. Yet the distribution of responses among the husband cohort was the same as the Spitzer event, indicating that the contours of these two scandals did not impact the overall range of answers. Two of the husbands mentioned here—Jim, who said he'd want his wife to be present at the Sanford event, and John, who wanted his wife to make her own decision—would welcome their wife's presence if she wanted to be there. And a third husband, Ellis, said that while he was unsure if he wanted his wife to attend the event, having her stand next to him would make him look "less guilty." In these instances, we learn from the husband's perspective that wife makes right—especially when the husband did wrong.

ANTHONY WEINER PRESS CONFERENCE

With the Anthony Weiner press conference, we see husbands overwhelmingly in favor of a wifely presence at this event. Nine of the 11 husbands answered "Yes" to the question of whether they'd want their wife to attend. One said "No," and one said he'd only want his wife present if she wanted to be there (table 8.6).

The wives, as a group, were also more likely to say they would attend this press conference over the Spitzer or Sanford events, with 7 of the 11

Table 8.6 For Husbands Only: Would you want your wife to stand next to you at the Anthony Weiner press conference?

	Number of Husbands Responding
Yes	9
No	1
The choice belongs to the wife	1

Table 8.7 For Wives Only: Would you attend the Anthony Weiner press conference as the political wife?

	Number of Wives Responding
Yes	7
No	3
Unsure	1

wives saying they would stand next to their husbands just as Huma Abedin did (table 8.7).

When I asked the husbands if they thought their wife would attend the event (distinguishing between *wanting* the wife to attend and *speculating* whether she would) The husbands' answers matched the wives' answers in 7 of the 11 instances. In the four instances where there was a mismatch in answers, two husbands said "Maybe," and the wives said "No"; and one husband said "Yes" while his wife said "Unsure." Let's take a look at how the couples responded to the Anthony Weiner press conference by examining a select portion of the conversations.

Bruce, 30, works for the Department of Justice and is married to Maeghan, 31, a teacher turned homemaker; together they have two young girls. I asked Bruce if he would want his wife to attend this press conference. While he answered "No" to the Spitzer and Sanford events, things were different this time:

> I wouldn't want, again, to put her in the face of the public for my mistakes. But in this situation, it's already been determined that the two are trying to work through their differences and maybe this is the best way for her to just say, "Hey, leave us alone. We're going to try to work through this. I'm going to come out and talk to you and then maybe put it to bed."[46]

Bruce thought his wife would attend the Weiner news conference if asked. And he was right. Maeghan said she could imagine herself standing next to her husband and speaking—just as Huma Abedin did. "You could tell she was very honest and it's probably like the same way that I would probably handle something like that," she said.[47] She elaborated on why she'd remain committed to her marriage in the wake of this scandal:

> Just because if I was in that kind of position I wouldn't want to just like give up on our marriage and our family. We have—we're married for however many years . . . we have children . . . People make mistakes. Nobody's perfect. Things happen. . . . Things can be rocky in marriages. . . . There's temptation like always but I think you know it's human nature and [you] want to work something out with someone that you love and respect and care about—and to hopefully have that relationship come through on the other side and not just give up.[48]

Maeghan said the Weiner press conference represents the one scandal event she'd attend. She offered a "Maybe" for Spitzer and a "No" for Sanford. She found honesty in Huma Abedin's accounting of what the political couple had been through. Silda, she said, was "blank," and she appeared to stand next to her husband "because she has to be there."[49] And with the Sanford press conference, Maeghan said the politician didn't take ownership of the affair or apologize in a meaningful way. But in the Weiner press conference, Maeghan saw "a very supportive wife" and "a husband who's taking responsibility for the actions that he had done in his personal life and you could tell they're like real people."[50]

Hector is a 34-year-old insurance agent married to Kelly, a 33-year-old homemaker. Together, they have a young daughter. Hector said he wouldn't ask his wife to attend the news conference and isn't even really sure if he wants her there. But he then settled on the position that if she wants to attend, then of course she can do that, since "she's probably earned the right to stand there or earned the right to talk, but I don't think I would ask her to do it."[51] He applied the same answer to the previous scandal events.

Kelly said she would not attend the Weiner news conference. At the outset of the interview, she said her father cheated on her mother after almost three decades of marriage and "my mom did everything she could to try to keep her family together even after knowing for months and months and months."[52] Kelly was an adult living independently when she learned of her father's affair, and she sometimes took issue with the length her mother would go to keep a floundering marriage afloat. Kelly's own family experience with infidelity shapes why she wouldn't attend the Weiner press conference. "You know, fool me once, fool me twice," she said, referring to the fact that Weiner had a previous bout with sexting troubles in

2011. "I'd have a very hard time believing that it would change."[53] While Kelly said she felt confident that she would not have attended the Sanford press conference ("I mean. I don't think I would [attend] after [him] being gone for five days, not knowing where he is and finding out that he's with a mistress in Argentina"[54]), she was uncertain about whether she would lend her presence to the Spitzer press conference. While her family experience with marital infidelity shaped her decision *not* to attend the Weiner event, she said she could also imagine not wanting to throw away the work put into a marriage approaching three decades in length.

> He embarrassed your family and now you're going to stand there and support him, but again, there's 25 years of history—as there was with my mom and my dad—that you don't want to just throw away. So I understand her sitting there. I don't know how—it has to be very difficult for her to be doing that.[55]

In the last example, we have Harold, a software engineer who is married to Mila, a 47-year-old administrative assistant, with whom he has two teen children. Harold represents the lone husband out of 11 who said he would not want his wife to attend the Weiner news conference:

> It would not be fair of me to put her through that. I don't believe that the thought to ask her would even cross my mind. From a purely political perspective, I wouldn't want her [there] because her presence would highlight the fact that I'm married and give the people a person with whom to identify and sympathize.[56]

Harold also said he wouldn't want his wife to attend either the Spitzer or Sanford news conferences. "Mila? She would probably be shooting daggers at me with her eyes or something . . . Yeah, she definitely would not be up there with a flat affect."[57] While Harold said Huma Abedin's performance at the news conference reflected positively on her scandal-tarnished husband, Harold added he was surprised that she would publicly make the appeal for Weiner's forgiveness. "I would think that any strong, politically minded woman would not want to go up there and forgive her husband in front of everybody for doing something like this," he said.[58] He later added, reflecting on the Weiner press conference:

> I just wouldn't expect anybody—any wife—to go up there and say anything. First of all, you would think the political advisor would be like, "Whoa! I don't know if we should let the wife up there in front of the cameras and the microphone."[59]

In this instance, Harold implies that the wife's voice is potentially dangerous to the politician and his public image already tarnished by scandal.
A public tongue-lashing wouldn't help his standing. While Huma Abedin's remarks actually bolstered Anthony Weiner—by offering the public
a glimpse into how the political couple privately struggled with the after-
shocks of scandal—Harold views the act of handing a microphone to a
supposedly agitated wife as a clear risk. After all, he said he wouldn't want
his wife to attend the press conferences because his wife would be "shooting daggers" at him, further crucifying an already embattled politician.

Mila, Harold's wife, said she would not attend any of these scandal press
conferences. Of the Spitzer news conference, she said: "It shows a level of
support that I would not authentically be able to give." And of Sanford?
"Never. Never. Never."[60] When asked if she would attend the press conference if she were in Huma Abedin's position, Mila laughs before offering
an unequivocal, "No":

> I'm not attending that press conference for anybody . . . Maybe this is
> immature of me but I think I would be of the opinion, "You made your bed
> now you lie in it. This one's on you—I'm not bailing you out here." I think
> she [Huma Abedin] took the high road and I would not have.[61]

In the Anthony Weiner scandal, we see that 9 of the 11 husbands wanted
their wives to be present, because the political wife with a voice reflected
well on the aggrieved politician. And even seven of the wives said they'd
attend the event after watching Huma Abedin speak in a way that
revealed an authentic and honest position that resonated with their own
views on marriage, commitment, and the possibility of a second chance.

THE RIGHT WIFE?

When faced with the question of which political wife did the right
thing, husbands—as a collective—were clear on one point: not a single
one opted for the prototypical good wife of Silda Spitzer. Instead, nine
husbands found great appeal in the vocal wife of Huma Abedin. Meanwhile, three husbands said that the absent wife of Jenny Sanford resonated with them most. (Note: one husband voted for both Huma Abedin
and Jenny Sanford, while another husband said he couldn't answer the
question. Please see table 8.1.) While no husband opted for Silda Spitzer,
two wives selected her as the political wife who resonated the most with
them. The remaining breakdown for the wives were four votes for Huma
Abedin and five votes for Jenny Sanford.

In a way, Jenny Sanford and Huma Abedin are foils of each other. Jenny spoke out against the husband who cheated on her through press statements, news accounts, and the release of her memoir; she did not attend his tearful press conference and began divorce proceedings against her husband of 21 years in the wake of his sex scandal. And she published *Staying True*, her memoir of their marriage and reflections on the scandal experience in 2010, a year after the scandal broke. In contrast, Huma Abedin was married to Anthony Weiner for only a year when the first round of his Twitter debacle made headlines in 2011. While she was absent from his 2011 press conference where he resigned his congressional seat, she publicly stood in support of him at the press conference in 2013, even as new photos and allegations surfaced—this time when he was running for office with his eyes set on the New York City mayor's office. And while Huma Abedin also shared personal details of the couple's marriage in the wake of the scandal (such as their visits to a marriage counselor and her divulgence that she didn't know if their marriage would work), Abedin did so while standing next to her husband at a press conference in an attempt to show her sticking by him despite his hurtful actions. It's worth drawing these distinctions—in the wake of scandal—between Jenny Sanford and Huma Abedin. After all, they are the two political wives who interview subjects most frequently identified with. Additionally, one political wife appears to embody an independent streak while another encapsulates a hegemonic ideal but with a contemporary veneer of speaking her mind and sharing her experience as a scandalized wife, as it meshes with her husband's political agenda.

It's little wonder that a majority of husbands selected Huma Abedin as their ideal political wife. She exhibited public support to a scandal-tainted husband when he faced searing criticism, mockery, and unyielding media interest of the most unflattering nature. She offered not only the value of her presence to the news conference but also the power of her voice. But what's more interesting is that 4 of the 11 wives selected Huma Abedin as the wife they most identify with—and every wife, with the exception of one, spoke in admiration of Huma Abedin, even if they ultimately identified with a different political wife. In Huma Abedin, we see the complicated embodiment of a hegemonic ideal but also the appearance of a political wife who authentically conveys a genuine and likable sense of self. After all, she lent her support to a husband who sent nudie pics to female college students and porn stars (hegemonic). But she also chastised, albeit lightly, her husband in her remarks—"Anthony has made some horrible mistakes," she said—and conveyed that she stuck with the marriage on her own terms (independent).

Interviews of husbands revealed a thematic thread that showed them hoping and believing that their wives would support them in a scandal crisis, despite the public humiliation that the wives would be forced to endure by nature of these deeply shaming and frenzied events. For instance, Paul, a 29-year-old computer programmer, initially said he wouldn't want his wife to attend the Eliot Spitzer press conference because it would further shame him. But as the interview progressed, and when I asked him if he thought his wife would attend the Spitzer press conference if asked, Paul offered a different perspective. "I have a tiny inkling that she might," he said.[62] (His wife said she would not.) Paul acknowledged the contradiction in his position, that when he watches a political wife at a scandal press conference he doesn't think she should support the politician. "But then when I see my own wife I think, 'Oh she might,'" he said.[63] Paul cited their family as a reason that might compel his wife to stand next to him at the podium. (But, alas, his wife said, "I'm not a prop."[64]) Similarly, Carl, the 33-year-old doctor, said he would not want his wife to attend the Spitzer press conference because he finds the wife's presence irrelevant to the governor's resignation. But what if he asked his wife, Sarah, to attend—would she? "I think it depends on what the family agenda is," replied Carl,[65] indicating that the wife would be on board if it's for a broader family goal. ("Not going to happen," Sarah said.) Bruce, 30, who works for the Department of Justice, also said he wouldn't want his wife to attend the Spitzer event because "I wouldn't want her to be in the public eye when I screw up."[66] But if he asked her to attend, he thinks she would. "She's very selfless," said Bruce, "so I feel that it's more of who she is that she would just do what I asked of her."[67] (His wife said she might attend the Spitzer press conference.) Robert, the 52-year-old civil engineer, said he'd want his wife to give him a shot at a second chance. "At least give me a chance to fix the problem and stand by me,"[68] he said, assuming the relationship was good but hit a sudden rocky patch. He added: "You would hope that your spouse would never just dump you right away without seeing if there's a way you can fix that,"[69] thereby placing the responsibility on the wife to right the ship. Freddy, the attorney, said he'd hope his wife would "You know, swallow one and be able to . . . be there and be supportive. But I know when she—I shouldn't say I know. She certainly knows when she can do that and when she can't,"[70] thereby placing the onus, again, on the wife to be the team player—and not on himself to play by the rules.

Yet other husbands couldn't imagine their wives "swallowing one" or abiding by the "family agenda." Harold, the software engineer, could only envision his wife "shooting daggers at me" if she were to attend a press conference. And he expressed his surprise that a political advisor would "allow" a political wife near a microphone, indicating the dangers of a wife with a voice and the potential torrent she'd unleash at her wayward husband. Ellis, the 59-year-old manager of a retail store, is the lone husband who put himself in the shoes of a political wife. "If I was her," he said, speaking about Silda Spitzer, "I would tell him to go somewhere and get lost and never want to see him again and not support him."[71] Zach, who is 36 and works in finance, said if his wife was allowed near the microphone, as Huma Abedin was, she would speak more pointedly, offering "backhand" remarks, "You know, making me feel guilty."[72] Let's now take a closer look at how interview participants described each of the political wives in order to further understand the appeal of Huma Abedin's vocal presence in support of her husband.

SILDA SPITZER AS UNKNOWABLE

In a digital age where everything seems knowable, whether it's the ability to secure information via Google or scroll through people's whereabouts and read their opinions and updates on social media platforms, Silda Spitzer represents the unknowable political wife. She attended her husband's press conference but did not speak. She released no memoir nor granted any post-scandal interviews. She offered no access into the private sanctuary of her mind and life, an anomaly in a world increasingly defined by personal brands and the public's demand for voyeuristic content. Instead, Silda Spitzer maintained a firm grasp on her life, keeping its narrative on lockdown. Where the divulgence of private information has become the norm, as the boundary between public and private has disintegrated, Silda Spitzer represents an anomaly simply because she gives the impression of a private person. Perhaps this explains why not a single husband selected Silda Spitzer as the political wife that they'd seek in a scandal moment. A political wife who is not knowable cannot be likable. But two wives found resonance in her. "She was a class act," said Bailee, the 59-year-old homemaker. "She really was."[73] (Bailee's comment mimics what *New York Times* columnist Maureen Dowd wrote in 2009, as she chastised Jenny Sanford's vocal opposition to her husband's scandal, in comparison to Silda Spitzer's "dignified . . . silence."[74]) Lynn, the 31-year-old teacher, also picked Silda Spitzer as the political wife with whom she most identifies, but she was not enthusiastic in her selection. "I don't know," she said. "I think people give up too easily and just get divorced. It takes work to be married. It's not always happy all the time."[75] When I asked Lynn why she selected Silda Spitzer and not Huma Abedin, Lynn felt Huma's remarks were "forced" at Anthony Weiner's press conference. "Maybe he's . . . telling her what to say?" she wondered.[76] Lynn's comment indicates that a wife's articulated viewpoint, as she stands next to a scandal-tarnished husband, is part of scandal's enforced gender and spousal roles.

As a cohort, the interviewed women overwhelmingly described Silda Spitzer as the "supposed to/expected to wife." In these references, fulfilling one's wifely "obligations" in a supposed to/expected manner is not a laudatory practice. Just because she is supposed to and expected to perform the role of a public, silent, supportive wife does not mean she *should*. Even Silda Spitzer's two supporters—Bailee and Lynn—noted her compulsory attendance. Her appearance, said Bailee, is "forced. Like she was there because she had to [be]. Obligatory."[77] And Lynn said, "I think she feels that he embarrassed her, but she has to do it."[78] Paul, the 29-year-old computer programmer, said Silda Spitzer did not seem to be a willing participant in the press event. "I would think it was at least partially motivated by politics—how it would look to the press, rather than completely just her wanting to stand by him . . . for her own reasons."[79] His wife, Olivia, a nurse, said this political wife "looks like she's trying to be there just for the sake of being there, without expressing too much of her own personal feelings."[80] Harold, the software engineer, said Silda Spitzer's appearance seemed contrived. "It looked like she had been coached to stand there next to him and what to do because it seemed weird . . . her mannerisms just weren't natural."[81] Harold's wife, Mila, the 47-year-old administrative assistant, felt similarly. "I wonder how hard she had to work or what coaching she had to have" to stand up there, Mila wondered. She later added: "I'm sure she could have refused. I mean she doesn't have to get out of her car. I'm sure she could have been adamant, but I'm sure she was instructed to stand next to him. I bet you it wasn't her idea."[82]

Maeghan, the 31-year-old homemaker, also described Silda Spitzer as the "supposed to" wife. "It just looks like she's standing there just because she has . . . to be there."[83] Gail, 24, who works in childcare, echoed that view. "I think she feels like she has to be there," she said.[84] And Susan, a 49-year-old teacher, agreed. "Her body language and her facial expressions show she didn't want to be there. But there was some reason she showed up."[85]

As the wife who fulfills what's expected of her, by doing what she's supposed to do even if the reason why is not articulated to the public, Silda Spitzer exhibits a lack of self-efficacy and authority that unnerved many participants.

JENNY SANFORD

Because Jenny Sanford was absent from the press conference, and therefore not visible, husbands and wives could not judge her appearance—only her decision. "I guess I would probably be like Sanford's wife and not be there," said Olivia, the nurse.[86] For Kelly, the 31-year-old home-maker, Jenny Sanford's absence was "more honest." She elaborates: "This is just my opinion, but I would think that more people would not stand by than would stand by and so for me that feels more real."[87] Mila, the administrative assistant also felt Jenny Sanford's absence to be believable within the context of the lurid scandal. "I don't know how you can be supportive, knowing that he [Mark Sanford] allowed her to have that experience. How could she stand by that? I think that's asking too much of any human," she said.[88] Mila's husband, Harold, sees Jenny Sanford as confident. "Maybe she has her own independent means, but she obviously does not have low self-esteem and is not gonna stand for something like this. It doesn't matter who he is. She's not attached to him just because he's a governor," he said.[89] Freddy, the 27-year-old attorney, also tied the issue to self-esteem. "For a woman to be . . . cheated on and then go back and smile for the cameras as if nothing ever happened—she doesn't really value herself that much," he said.[90] Of Jenny Sanford's absence and imme-diate divorce, Freddy said: "Good for her." Joyce, the 52-year-old teacher, sees Jenny Sanford's absence as "a cut and dry kind of thing."[91] She puts herself in Jenny Sanford's position and imagines what she must have said to Mark Sanford: "Like, 'I can't believe you did this. What does this say about you? There's no way I'm standing [there]. What does this say about our marriage, vows, and about family values?'"[92]

While 5 out of the 11 wives identified with Jenny Sanford as the politi-cal wife to emulate during a scandal, and three of the husbands said her absence resonated with them, they did not glorify her absence. They did not speak of her as the political wife who broke the mold. Her absence did not invoke enthusiastic responses categorized by relief and admiration. Instead, the popular political wife award goes to Huma Abedin. Even though she received one less vote than Jenny Sanford among the wives, interview participants gushed with praise because here was a political wife who was likable, believable, and seemingly a regular woman, an irony that will be explored later in the chapter.

HUMA ABEDIN

In every instance where a female participant said she most identified with Jenny Sanford, that participant also had a positive outlook toward Huma Abedin. However, if a participant identified with Silda Spitzer, she did not express a positive orientation toward Huma Abedin. This is note-worthy, because the media frequently questioned Huma Abedin's agency and presence in support of her husband, with headlines like, "Is Huma Abe-din Doing the Right Thing?"; "Anthony Weiner and Huma Abedin Give

Most Awkward Sext-Splanatory Press Conference in Human History"; and "The Public Humiliation of Huma Abedin."[93] But interview participants saw Huma Abedin's presence in more personal and positive terms.

Huma Abedin was believable because she was read as authentically herself. "I don't get the sense she's trying to project something," said Sarah, the 31-year-old homemaker.[94] "That's a regular person buying a regular dress," said Mila, a 47-year-old married administrative assistant, referencing to the political wife's sartorial presentation.[95] Susan, the 49-year-old teacher, echoed Huma Abedin's everyday appeal: "Oh, that's the one I could be friends with—or someone I know. She looks like a regular woman, which I think makes her more relatable," she said.[96] Overall, participants found Huma Abedin to be believable because they read her appearance and demeanor as relatable and open. Rather than being untouchable like Silda Spitzer, whose highly manicured presence also conveyed a sense of unease with her attendance and therefore removed from her sense of self, Huma Abedin gave the impression that she was, as Mila described, "human," that she was "a real person who was scared and honest and nervous."[97] Jim, the 49-year-old engineering technician said Huma Abedin took "repossession" of the press conference. "I give her a lot of credit for basically telling people that this is between us—it's not between other people."[98] Maeghan, the 31-year-old homemaker, said Anthony Weiner and Huma Abedin gave the impression of being "real people." I asked her to elaborate. "I feel like what she's saying they went through is what normal people—not in the spotlight—would probably do in this situation." She added: "You could tell she genuinely . . . [was] being honest and she's there and she was present in that press conference. Whereas the first one—Silda? She was just . . . standing there."[99] Harold, the software engineer, described Huma Abedin's mannerisms as "very natural." He added:

> I was watching her while he was talking, and she actually seemed more natural than he did . . . You know, you could see that flash of anger, but then she also smiled. She was just very genuine the whole time, and she was very forceful in her statements. I mean she just said, "Hey, this is my decision. We went through therapy." Just very credible.[100]

And Carl, the 33-year-old doctor, also said that Huma Abedin's reference to therapy made her believable. He said that

> it kind of also verifies, you know, some of the things that I would think, which was this was an extremely [trying] time in their marriage, that

they had a difficult time with it. It required therapy. All these things are believable and she seems to be reiterating that and explaining her thought process.[101]

With Huma Abedin, we see husbands and wives relating to this political wife because she exudes an air of authentic approachability, contrasting with media coverage of her.

THE CURIOUS CASE OF THE "REGULAR" HUMA ABEDIN

While interview participants might have lauded Anthony Weiner's wife for her relatable impressions, there's little in Huma Abedin's biography that shows her as "regular." Her biography is easily accessible online, so it won't be recounted here, but a key element for consideration is her career as top aide to Hillary Rodham Clinton, one of the most powerful political figures in the United States and, by extension, globally. Additionally, as the (now-estranged) wife of a former U.S. congressman, whose wedding was officiated by Bill Clinton, Abedin lives a high-profile life and works closely with power players throughout the world. Indeed, a photograph search of Huma Abedin using the "AP Images" database shows Huma Abedin working with top leaders, including President Barack Obama. Therefore, the fact that Abedin came across as "relatable" and "regular" is worth unpacking, because she is not a "regular" woman. She is a member of the power elite who moves in high-cultured and powered spheres.

If Abedin came across as believable in support of her scandal-tainted husband and in her motivation to attend his press conference and speak at it, and if she conveyed a sense of approachability, it is because of something both surface (her style) and deeper (the conveyance of a secure self-identity). It is the combination of (a) breaking the mold of what a political wife is expected to look like, by wearing a less buttoned-up outfit, along with her humbled style of speech delivery; and (b) comfort with (her)self at the press conference, which allowed Abedin to be read as a believable and regular figure in contrast to Silda Spitzer's tight presence.

STYLE

Huma Abedin appeared unlike Silda Spitzer in both her style and in the way she revealed herself to her audience by exercising her voice. Let us first revisit the style of Silda Spitzer.

Participants noted that Silda Spitzer "appears like a political wife" and also noted that Silda Spitzer "doesn't want to be there." In contrast, participants also noted that Huma Abedin appears "alive" and that her manner of dress is "alternative, funky, and folksy." As the "expected to, supposed to" wife, Silda Spitzer fulfills her role by delivering what is expected of her in terms of her attendance and her polished style. Sarah, the 31-year-old homemaker, says "Eliot Spitzer's wife appears to me like another politician." She goes on:

> Silda looks very much like Hillary Clinton, although looking at their faces they don't look anything alike, but the hair and the presentation, wearing an expensive suit and Hermes scarf . . . You can't see any skin. She's definitely trying to project a masculine power presentation while maintaining that she's like—she's not conservative, but she's very conservatively dressed.[102]

Indeed, the style, or "the way in which we do something,"[103] of Huma Abedin and Silda Spitzer stands in stark contrast to one another. Silda Spitzer even looks like a politician, since she so deeply embodies those who inhabit the political world. (The irony is that Huma Abedin is directly employed by that political world but did not dress the part at the press conference.) Whether worn by a man or a woman, "The suit helps to create an illusion of a hard, or at least a firm and proper, body that is autonomous, in control, rational and masculine."[104] Therefore, for participant Sarah, it is Silda Spitzer's *style* that is reminiscent of Hillary Clinton, the pinnacle of a powerful female figure, which plants Silda Spitzer firmly into the field of high-level politics and maneuvering. Yet while Silda Spitzer exudes, "power, wealth, but also strength," according to Sarah, her power suit cannot mask an impression that she "doesn't want to be there."[105] It is as if Silda Spitzer is entrapped by the privileged position of wealth, politics, and power that does not seem to "contaminate" Huma Abedin, a woman who maneuvers through those privileged elements every day as part of her paid work. But Huma Abedin is frequently described as "alive, lively," as well as "alternative, funky, folksy," not bound by the "control, rational and masculine" uniform of a suit that binds Silda Spitzer. Huma Abedin does not wear the power suit but instead opts for a contemporary dress and cardigan ensemble, featuring bright green and abstract shapes, adorned in dangling earrings (in contrast to Silda Spitzer's pearl earrings) and wearing bright red lipstick. Her hair is pulled back from her face in a way that appears casual and not professionally styled. While "It's never an easy decision for women in exposed positions to choose a feminine style when presenting themselves in public,"[106] in this case it worked well for Huma Abedin. Participants described her outfit as something she—or they—could wear to the office. Her dress did not embody the stiff masculine power of Silda Spitzer's suit. It was relatable because it was outside the moneyed spheres of the power suit adorned with a carefully draped scarf and styled hair; she was accessible because it was not styled into polished perfection. It was "a little bit disheveled," according to participant Sarah, making her "more authentic." Huma Abedin's appearance as a mom shone through. Huma Abedin wore the clothes. For Silda Spitzer, the clothes wore her; they placed her in a demographic of power, privilege and influence but to which she had to pay a high price by adhering to what was expected of her rather than acting out of self-agency. Silda Spitzer was present, even as participants noted that she appeared as if she didn't want to be there, but in a polished, politically adorned style that was controlled, and that seemed to undermine an emotional connection to her husband and audience. The fact that she was so polished under such traumatic circumstances was suspect in terms of the authenticity of her marriage, making her less relatable and believable, and more a part of the strategic maneuvering of the political realm she embodied:

> **Sarah:** She just looks very pulled together. And this is right after her incident, right? . . .
> **Interviewer:** Mm-hmmm. . . .
> **Sarah:** This [Anthony Weiner's press conference] is years later [after the initial sexting scandal] and she's still kind of disheveled and uncomfortable with the setting whereas Silda, two days later, is able to obviously put some thought into her outfit and her hair.
> **Interviewer:** So what are you implying?
> **Sarah:** That maybe she wasn't that broken up about what went down, that maybe their marriage really was more about a strategy or joining their powers, whether it's financial or otherwise. I don't know, I guess I'm just less sympathetic to that woman. I don't know exactly why.

The combination of Silda Spitzer's sartorial choice, along with her silent presence, and the impression that she would rather be elsewhere, impressed upon participants that "the surface may be substance."[107] Silda Spitzer's holistic style, her way of doing something that extends beyond fashion but encompasses presence, imparts meaning—like a language—that is interpreted by an audience of receivers. Intuitively, it makes sense that style, like a language, "creates systems of categories for social perception."[108] In doing so, "style creates tensions between social allegiance and individuality . . . The social organization of style is never value free. Style's aesthetic organizes such value-laden dimensions of the social as gender and sexual identity, class, time, and space."[109] While one can reasonably assume that Silda Spitzer and Huma Abedin belong to the same social class, the styled appearances of the two women conveyed different "value-laden" impressions about their persona.

THE AUTHENTICITY OF A WIFE WITH A VOICE

It was not only Huma Abedin's sartorial style that made her more believable and relatable to most participants. It was also the manner in which she defended her husband that made her presence sympathetic to them. Participants read her as having worked through her issues and therefore established a rapport of togetherness with her scandal-suffering husband. By telling her audience that she and her husband attended therapy, she used her voice to give access to her experience. However, by speaking in defense of her husband and by directly echoing his remarks that immediately preceded hers, one could also argue that Huma Abedin was indeed "standing by her man" by publicly defending him. Yet participants found her remarks believable, in opposition to Silda Spitzer's silent stoicism.

Huma Abedin did not appear to betray her sense of self by attending the press conference and by speaking in support of her husband because there was intentionality in her presence. Huma Abedin did not convey, according to participants, that she'd rather be somewhere (or anywhere!) else—as Silda Spitzer did. Therefore, while Huma Abedin stood in solidarity with her scandal-suffering husband, most participants did not read Abedin's support as "standing by her man," the reference to female passivity and loyalty in the wake of male sexual betrayal cemented in the 1968 Tammy Wynette song.[110] Rather, participant support for Huma was strong because they saw her spousal support as the result of having worked through her issues in therapy. They saw her spousal support as indicative of her *strength*, of committing to the taxing emotional work to repair a relationship following an intimate and public betrayal. In this way, Huma Abedin is not the silent passive wife that Silda Spitzer appeared publicly to be. She is not the hegemonic poster-wife who embodies the subordinate position within the marital dyad. Rather, Huma Abedin offered her audience information about herself in the midst of scandal and constructed herself as a wife in charge of the marriage, who made a decision about *her* future. She says: "It was not an easy choice in any way. But I made the decision that it was worth staying in this marriage. That was a decision I made for me, for our son and for our family. I didn't know how it would work out. But I did know that I wanted to give it a try." Therefore, Huma

Abedin assumes the masculine role as the household's decision-marker, where the stability of the family hangs in the balance until the wife calls the shots as chief-decider. Huma Abedin, while working her way through a disruptive scandal that destroyed her husband's political career, did not display "existential anxiety."[111]

According to sociologist Anthony Giddens, an individual with a normal sense of identity "has a feeling of biographical continuity which she is able to grasp reflexively and, to a greater or less degree, communicate to other people."[112] The self is embodied, and Huma Abedin, through quiet smiles and an unsteady voice, offers visual and physical evidence to back her claim that "I'm very nervous," a sentiment one would reasonably expect her to feel as she address a frenzied media crowd, knowing the press conference would lead national news. Therefore, Huma Abedin's embodied self, while nervous but stable, fulfills for her audience the reasonable expectation that although she is not in her element (Abedin admits that she had never spoken at a press conference before), she can exert a strong presence that does not betray (her)self. Meanwhile, Silda Spitzer displays control over her physical body during a time of frenzied spectacle where not even a single hair appears out of place. Yet despite her efforts at a polished surface presentation, she gives the impression that her highly stylized construction is too perfect during a moment of frenetic national attention to be believable and authentic; and that, in times of crisis, physical perfection is associated with masking suppressed anger. For participants, a lovely, manicured appearance, in the wake of spousal infidelity—when your family's private business is split open for the nation to dissect—does not make a political wife believable. Believability can be found in imperfection, nervousness, and a self-styled outfit and hairdo.

"Seeing comes before words," writes John Berger in *Ways of Seeing*.[113] But we don't look at people, objects—or art, Berger's focus—without the context of our social positions as providing the subtext for interpretation and message decoding.[114] A man's presence is dependent on "power which he embodies,"[115] while a woman's presence is too often dependent on "her gestures, voice, opinions, expressions, clothes, chosen surroundings, taste—indeed there is nothing she can do which does not contribute to her presence."[116] These elements make up the individual female's image, which is continuously placed under surveillance by the woman herself. "She is almost continually accompanied by her own image of herself."[117]

Interviews with everyday couples demonstrated a clear pattern in the way they "read" and interpreted the presence of Silda Spitzer and Huma Abedin at their respective husband's press conferences. Everyday couples upheld the cultural view of Silda Spitzer as *The Good Wife*, who stood silent in her effort to support a husband whose private actions brought public shame. In contrast, Huma Abedin was read in a counterhegemonic manner: even though she stood and spoke in support of her husband, she gave the impression of doing so on her own terms and voicing an authentic sense of self that also took aim at her husband's lewd behavior. But ultimately she stood with him, fulfilling her role within the scandal script, albeit with her own independent twist.

Through these interviews, it is possible to crack open the "ideological seams"[118] that complicate the cultural image of an apparently meek, betrayed wife "standing by her man." Instead, this work has demonstrated that presence is not always read as unquestioning support. Presence can also be read as strength and as an opportunity for a wife to voice her experience. Presence can hold a spouse accountable. By listening to these political wives and everyday women, it is possible to see the "intersection between two different patriarchal practices"[119]: the practice of a wife standing with her husband-politician at a sex-scandal press conference and the practice of talking about, critiquing, and dissecting that wife's decision to do so. Ultimately, we see a visible seam—it certainly is not seamless. Even though I have asked married couples to place these political wives under their gaze, we have revealed a gentler and more complex narrative of "standing by one's man." When examining the couples' responses as collective, Huma Abedin received the most "votes" as the political wife that they could relate to, with four wives identifying with her and eight husbands selecting Huma Abedin as the wife who did right. Jenny Sanford received a total of eight votes, with five from wives and three from husbands. Silda Spitzer only received two votes from wives and none from husbands.[120] The breakdown of wifely identification (or which political wife these everyday couples ally themselves with) is noteworthy. A majority of husbands allied with Huma Abedin because she gave the impression of authentically lending her voice in support of her scandal-tainted husband. Additionally, 4 of the 11 everyday wives said they identified with her because she was not only likable and believable but she was honest: she revealed that the couple went to therapy together and that she was working on the marriage on her own terms. Yet it is not a coincidence that even more women said they identified with Jenny Sanford, with five everyday women casting their support to the absent wife, while three husbands allied with Jenny Sanford. After all, Jenny Sanford was the wife who became the new "role model" for a scandalized spouse.[121] She acted in her own best interest and would not let her presence be exploited by a philandering husband. Only three of the everyday husbands connected with Jenny Sanford over the other political wives, perhaps indicating—in these cases —respect for a woman's autonomy while also exhibiting scandal fatigue of the reoccurring scandal script that mandates a wife's presence at her husband's press conference.

What is most striking is that not a single husband selected Silda Spitzer—the iconic "Good Wife"—as the wife who speaks to them. While Silda Spitzer was present but cool, her thoughts were unknowable and ultimately created an awkward dynamic that may have further shamed the husband because she was not able to voice her experience; she was merely evidence of his misdeed as exhibited in the somber expression on her face. Two wives, however, did select Silda Spitzer as the wife who did the right thing.

The presence/absence of the political wife can either support or under-cut the position of the husband-politician. "The decorous woman who always knows her place, both in public and in relation to her husband, is what undergirds the masculinist regime," writes rhetoric scholar Melissa Deem.[122] Therefore, it is no surprise that fewer husbands supported the absent wife than they did the wife who was present and vocal. But the silent *and* present wife—the traditional wifely figure within scandal scripts—received no support from the interviewed husbands, indicating that even if the political wife "always knows her place," thereby sup-porting a chauvinistic system, she secured no support among everyday husbands who find her silence unsettling and unrealistic within the con-straints of an authentic marriage. "[T]he logic of scandal seems to take on specific characteristics in relation to feminism in the public sphere," adds Deem.[123] While it is the husband-politician caught in a sexually transgressing moment, media and public attention quickly shifts to his wife—who was not directly engaged in the scandalous activity—but she becomes implicated nonetheless. Her presence or absence as a supportive or outspoken character within the scandal script raises questions connect-ing to the public presentation of feminism. If she supports a husband who sexually "betrayed" her, causing public humiliation, can she be a feminist? And if she is absent from a scandal news conference is she automatically cast as a feminist and therefore in opposition to her husband?

This study found that a political wife who carefully walks the line between asserting her own voice and independence of thought, within the constraints of supporting a scandal-scraped husband, is viewed most positively among these married couples. Five years after the Spitzer press conference in 2008, Huma Abedin is the contemporary good wife, because she is not read as traditionally dressed and silent. She is independ-ent of her husband but ultimately supportive of him and believes that he deserves a second (or third, as it may be) chance. She is, therefore, a subversively hegemonic wife who supports her spouse but first chastises him publicly as she voices her reasons for, effectively, "standing by him."

Future political wives who find their husbands ensnared in scandal might want to consider the reactions of these interview participants, of everyday couples whose reading of Huma Abedin complicated the notion of "standing by one's man." In an era that blurs publicness and privacy, the scandal-infected political wife embodies a liminal state.[124] She is a public figure who is not elected by the public. Her husband's private behavior brings her symbolic presence into the spotlight even though she did not have the extramarital affair—her husband did. She represents a figure of public interest often because the public wonders what she is thinking, feeling, and saying behind the scenes, because her public presentation of self—like in the case of Silda Spitzer—often does not reveal an authentic persona. In contrast, everyday women found Huma Abedin relatable because of the way she personalized her public status by offering a glimpse into her experience through her remarks at her husband's sex-scandal press conference. By emanating a quietly confident sense of self and intentionality, by offering her voice to share her experience with an audience, by wearing an outfit considered "folksy" as opposed to buttoned up, participants saw Huma Abedin as a believable, likable, and relatable woman in crisis whose actions were brave. In this instance, media construction of Huma Abedin[125] as a wimpy, humiliated, passive wife[126] conflicted with participants' more supportive reading of her as a woman who authentically preserved (her)self in the face of media frenzy.

CHAPTER 9

Concluding Thoughts: Scandal and Gender in the 21st Century

In the decade since I've been researching political sex scandals, one question persists at lectures, public talks, family BBQs, and dinner parties: *Why do they do it?* The "they" refers to politicians, and the "it" refers not so much to illicit, incriminating, cringe-worthy sex but to something more abstract. In this case the "it" is the act of risking it all for pleasure or lust-fueled pursuit, without considering—or unscrupulously dismissing—"its" consequences.

In these professional and social settings I often lacked a succinct answer to that question of *Why do they do it?* After all, I wasn't a psychologist but a simple media scholar. So I typically quipped: "That answer is above my pay grade."

However, it remains the million-dollar question, and one that I'm grateful for, because media outlets, pundits, journalists, and the rest of us in casual conversation spend unfathomable amounts of mental energy trying to figure it out whenever news of the latest political sex scandal reaches our brain cavity. This leaves researchers like myself with seemingly endless data for analysis and excavation.

Yet that pesky question persists. *Why do they do it?*

While this book focuses on what happens after "they" do "it"—girded by media and cultural systems hungry for titillating frenzies to dissect, and the implications of the frenzy for the political field in the United States—it's worth reflecting on an answer in general terms. I will not play armchair psychologist because that will take us down a rabbit's hole of unproductive speculation. Rather, I will simply argue that the answer to that question is knowable but not understandable. We actually know *why they do it*. We can select from any personality and/or behavioral issue, perhaps rooted in childhood trauma or midlife circumstance, to explain why certain politicians head down a scandalous path:

- Recklessness
- Compulsion (sexual or otherwise)
- Power-grabber
- Boredom
- Narcissism
- Poor executive function
- Need for attention
- Risk-taker
- Carelessness
- Apathy
- Just because

Yet even when we *know* potential and likely answers to the pressing question of *Why do they do it*, it is still difficult to fully *understand* them. That's because the question assumes rational behavior and a powerful ability of people to self-regulate and self-correct detrimental habits.

"These kinds of decisions are not made intellectually, but rather emotionally. And we all know (or have known), some very wise, yet emotionally challenged individuals who can function at a very high level intellectually—but not so emotionally, especially when under stress," said Robert Weiss, MSW, a leading sex-addiction clinician and author.[1] "Such people—in the moment—are not thinking 'big picture,' [like] making decisions with their career, family and public life in mind. They are instead making highly impulsive, emotionally based decisions, which can have far-reaching negative consequences in their lives."

Weiss added that if you're looking for the common denominator of those caught in political sex scandals, it's the effects of a potent mixture involving "power, narcissism, the need to be seen as special, important, [and those] lacking stable self-esteem," he said. It's the dynamic encapsulated by the view that "I'm so wanted and desired that people are electing me to influence their lives."

Yet the egoism embedded in that statement, and the effects of that potent mixture to lead one toward scandal, may itself be gendered, as political science Professor Alison Dagnes of Shippensburg noted in chapter 1: when a politician emerges victorious after a grueling campaign, a male politician may consider himself Superman. The spoils of war are his to conquer. But for a female politician, the doors are now open to her, thanks to her new grasp on power. This is a reflection of how far she's come. Therefore, the male and female's approach to the perks of power may indeed be rooted in their struggles to reach the apex. In chapter 2 we learned through numbers what we already knew to be true anecdotally: that men overwhelming dominate the sex-scandal landscape. But the chapter also revealed a less obvious truth: that nearly all of the women caught in scandal are Republicans and that scandal is an equal-opportunity career destroyer in instances when men and women get caught in its web at the start of their careers. Chapter 3 showed us how political cartoonists depict scandal-tarnished (male) politicians as harmless, goofy idiots who are ignorant to their demise. While the artistic renderings are hardly flattering, they also don't represent the politicians as menacing and predatory or as politicos whose behavior is harmful to the political system or the office environment in which they work. In chapter 4 we took a close examination of two young women at the center of prominent scandals belonging to former New York governor Eliot Spitzer and former New York congressman Anthony Weiner. Through an analysis of tabloid news coverage and photographic displays, it became clear that the outspoken "other woman" was represented as someone prostituting herself for fame and attention, while the "other woman" who actually worked as a prostitute was desirable because she chose to limit media exposure, post-scandal.

In chapter 5 we saw a similar dynamic for two political wives, where Jenny Sanford, representing the wife with a voice who condemned her husband's affair, was castigated as too gruff and unfeminine by the media. Meanwhile the silent wife—Silda Spitzer, who was present at her husband's press conference—was ultimately described as elegant and dignified. In chapter 6, interviews with New York State lawmakers whose colleagues in the state assembly had witnessed firsthand the impacts of sex scandals on a legislative body, revealed the continuum of gendered power among assembly members and interns. Chapter 7 showcased a public viewpoint describing scandal as an indication for corruption in other aspects of political life. And chapter 8 indicated that we should rethink what it means to "stand by your man," with interview participants expressing surprising support for a political wife who not only attends her husband's scandal press conference but also speaks in support of him at the event.

The goal of this book was to complicate the popularly recurring political sex-scandal "script" as outlined in the introduction. It's true that from the outside we see sameness: male politicians getting caught in sexual acts that disrupt their reputations and careers as "people of character." But my hope is that by digging deeper into these morality tales we've begun to see difference among the elements of this script that include not only the mostly male politicians but also the political wives, the "other women," the frenzied media coverage, and the politicians themselves. By dissecting scandal we can see it not as a monolith but as a complicated system bolstered by issues surrounding gender, power, morality, privacy, and public expectations of elected officials' private lives, and civic consequences.

I wrote this book a decade and a half into the start of a new century. And already we can see a shifting scandal climate, which chapter 2 began to delineate. It is notable that the median year for political sex-scandal occurrences is 2007, with the first contemporary scandal in 1942. This means that today's scandals are occurring at faster rates now than in previous decades. What is popularly referred to as "the digital age" has disrupted power systems once again and has made what was once unknowable— such as images, text exchanges, and audio recordings of illicit events—not only knowable but also "witness-able" and sharable. The digital age has certainly upended the public's knowledge and consumption of scandal, which my research partner, Gina Masullo Chen, and I explore in the book *Scandal in a Digital Age*.[2] Yet it doesn't seem as if politicians have become savvy to the technological advances of mobile devices that so easily—too easily—allow their transgressive behavior to become public. But again I'm making the assumption these politicians are even capable of controlling the behavior that lands them in hot water—and the blinding prime-time glare—in the first place. Considering the game-changing nature of digital tools on social practices, I offer the following predictions for political sex scandals moving forward:

1. I predict more instances of scandal evidence in digital form at the center of future political sex scandals. Therefore, illicit and intimate texts, photos, audio, and video involving the scandal-tarnished politician will form the core of new scandals. In other words, we'll see more scandals à la Anthony Weiner, where bulging shots of his nether regions accompanied news accounts, and the images themselves became the center of the story. We will see less scandals of the Eliot Spitzer variety—which is an old-fashioned scandal even though it occurred in 2008. After all, in the Spitzer instance we only knew of his sexual encounters with prostitutes through news reports, but no digital evidence allowed us to hear or see these intimate interactions. What remains to be seen is how women politicians may or may not be caught up in scandals that are digitally centric. After all, of the nine scandals involving women politicians, as explored in chapter 2, none involved digital evidence leaked to the news media. Similarly,

of the seven scandals involving selfie-sexting politicians—with the first instance noted in 2011—all involved men.

2. I predict increased attempts by political operatives to smear opponents (or for politicians to smear each other) by leaking scandal or insinuating it. In this way scandal, or manufactured scandal, will serve as a political weapon. Statistics bear out what people intuitively sense: scandal has career- and reputation-debilitating effects on those caught in its web. Therefore, what better way to derail a political career than to just hint at impropriety. We saw this unfold in Roch-

POLITICAL KRYPTONITE
BY GENDER

While women politicians have not (yet) gotten caught in the tech-rich minefield of sexting and selfie scandals, we do not yet know—due to the infrequency of female political sex scandals overall—what may make them particularly vulnerable to scandal in the future. (Courtesy of Hinda Mandell)

ester, New York. C. Stephen Eckel, a Democrat, was a county-level legislator up for reelection in 2011. He had been serving in that position since 2005. Eckel also was a fine-art photographer who had a personal website featuring a portfolio of his photographic work. Included in his online portfolio were nude photographs that the artist took of himself—a type of so-called fine-art nude selfies—interspersed with his other photographic work. (Eckel earned a Master's of Fine Arts degree in 2001.) During the 2011 campaign "A GOP activist on the Monroe County Republican Committee alerted the TV station WHAM [an ABC affiliate news channel] to the Web page and the nude pics of Eckel," according to a New York Post article written about the scandal.[3] With the specter of a nude-photo scandal raised, Eckel couldn't overcome the narrative that he was a perverted politician ill-equipped to handle the responsibilities of public office—even though he was the incumbent. "How do you trust someone who posts naked pictures of himself on the Internet," asked Eckel's opponent, Tony Micciche, recategorizing (and repurposing) fine-art nude photographs as illicit selfies.[4] It's worth noting the timeline of the Eckel "scandal." It occurred in November 2011—nine months after the married New York congressman Chris Lee resigned after sending topless photos of himself to a woman (using his congressional e-mail address) whom he connected with via Craigslist. The manufactured Eckel scandal also occurred five months after the married Congressman Anthony Weiner resigned for tweeting photos of his erect penis. Clearly, the narrative of selfie-crazed politicians, who can barely remain clothed, fed into the downfall of Eckel. Days before Eckel lost reelection to Micciche, he told the *New York Post*, "They have to resort to these lowdown, slimy tricks . . . This is just a low attack on me to put my stuff from an artistic portfolio to be used to smear me. My integrity as a photographer and as an artist is strong and powerful, and my integrity as a county legislator is strong and powerful."[5] Micciche remains in office at the time of writing. In the Eckel instance a manufactured smear campaign used scandal to usher an incumbent out of office.

There is also the bizarre instance of a Michigan legislator who concocted a fake scandal to cover up an actual scandal. In 2015 the married-to-a-woman-with-four-kids Legislator Todd Courser sent an e-mail from a made-up account (signed with a fake name) accusing Courser (i.e., himself) of having sex with another man. The real-but-fake e-mail was meant to distract from the fact that Courser was actually having sex with a woman, a married-to-a-man-with-three-kids fellow legislator, Cindy Gamrat, within the Michigan House of Representatives.[6] (The "logic" is beyond reason so don't attempt to understand his motives.) The convoluted and partially manufactured scandal resulted in the resignation of Courser and the expulsion of Gamrat from the Michigan House one month after Courser sent that notorious e-mail. While both politicians sought reelection in November 2015—they both lost. At the time of writing in 2016 they both face felony charges of misconduct for using public money to cover up their affair.[7] With this scandal, we see both an attempted self-smear campaign that also has elements of digital scandal, since the e-mail Courser sent was published in news accounts. Since digital tools and their digital traces are seamlessly woven into our everyday interactions, I predict that the abundance of online content that politicians (not unlike the rest of us) leave behind will act as fodder for future scandal—as politicians misuse digital tools—and political opponents use these digital traces to manufacture scandal.

3. I predict we'll see more woman engaged in scandal—but not necessarily at the national level. The continued rise in populism[8] may increasingly draw women to run for political office. Yet the risk is that those new to politics may be unvetted by the political elite. We have already seen Tea Party politicians (such as Todd Courser, Cindy Gamrat, and upstate New York's Gia Arnold) who've emerged from a political atmosphere that jabs at the establishment, get caught in sex scandals. As more people express frustration with a political system that they feel does not speak for them or work for their interests, I predict that people whom we consider to be unusual political candidates—for lack of experience in the fields of politics, business, law, and nonprofit—will run for local office. Additionally, the crude incivility and "screw-you" bluntness of Donald J. Trump's 2016 presidential campaign may encourage others with antiauthoritarian attitudes, unpolished ideas, and prickly demeanors to run for office. It remains to be seen how many of these candidates may be women. But the numbers in chapter 2 indicate that of the nine political sex scandals involving women politicians, they've all taken place within the last decade, even as women have made marginal gains at the national level[9] and whose presence in statewide elected office has decreased between 2004 and 2015.[10]

After spending eight years researching, pondering, and writing about political sex scandals in an academic setting, and almost two years devoted to writing this book, I've arrived at another pivotal question that needs answering: *What purpose do these sex scandals serve in our political ecosystem?* (In the introduction to this book I answered why it's important to study these events. Reminder: scandal, when viewed as a social institution, reveals norms surrounding gender and morality.) But what pokes at me now is trying to understand the role these events play in our political system. *What is their point?* Embedded in that question, again, is that pesky attempt at rationality—trying to make sense of events that, by default, are sensational and driven by emotion and impulse rather than logic. But let us attempt to be rational for a moment. If we approach the political system in the United States as an ecosystem that's driven by a community of interacting biological organisms, we must consider the purpose of the political sex scandal within this environment, since these events occur at regular-enough intervals—even if they are not daily, weekly, or monthly events. They warrant attention, and the media system (a different but interacting ecosystem) awards significant attention when a big-enough scandal comes along. There is also the fact that in most instances—as established in chapter 2—a majority of politicians caught in sex scandals face political failure. This has the potential to shift—although not upend—this ecosystem. Add to this pot a bubbling, low-grade sense of mistrust that the public already nurtures and that these events further stoke, and it becomes clear that sex scandals leave their mark on the political ecosphere. The fact that they have an impact is something we can intuitively grasp. But in biological systems all elements have a purpose and play their part from a Darwinian sense. So what would Charles Darwin say about the purpose of political sex scandals, considering that scandals are a persistent part of political culture and that politicians do not appear to be "smartening" (or adapting in an evolutionary sense) to the contemporary dangers of taking the risk that can result in scandal?[11] In asking this question I am focusing on the issue of behavior within sex scandal—not the physical body—as the evolutionary element that needs attention.

One could answer that the purpose of these events is to serve as cautionary morality tales. But cautionary tales for whom? *The public* who consumes them? *The politicians* considering a romp? We can rule out *the public* because they are not at risk for political failure by reading and talking about the antics of oversexed politicians. We can also rule out *the politicians* because risk-embracing and compulsion-driven politicos are not deterred by the sex-shenanigans of their peers. Remember, politicians caught in scandal aren't thinking logically—nor are they giving serious weight to the ruinous consequences of their actions—as a rule. To prove the carelessness of scandal-embarking politicians and to show that many scandal-embarking politicians don't heed the teachable moments of the scandal peers who came before them, consider the phenomenon where *Politician A* resigns in sex-scandal disgrace. An immediate successor, *Politician B*, is elected to office and *Politician B* then has his/her own sex scandal. If we view the purpose of political sex scandals as cautionary tales then this actual phenomenon wouldn't exist because *Politician B* would be on excellent behavior considering the humiliating and devastating fate of *Politician A*. But that is not what happened in the following instances I've identified:

1. In 1989, news reports detailed the groping by Illinois representative Gus Savage of a Peace Corps worker in Zaire. Savage was ousted in the subsequent primary elections and succeeded by Mel Reynolds,

who resigned from Congress in 1995 after he was convicted of statutory rape.

2. In 1999, Louisiana senator Robert Livingston was outed by *Hustler* magazine for having an extramarital affair. Livingston resigned and was succeeded by David Vitter, who had his own scandal when news broke of his affair with prostitutes in 2007.

3. Florida representative Mark Foley resigned in 2006 when news broke that he had sent sexually explicit pager messages to male interns. His congressional replacement, Tim Mahoney, resigned in disgrace in 2008 when he admitted to an extramarital affair with a former staffer to whom he paid hush money.

4. In 2009, then South Carolina governor Mark Sanford (currently a congressman from that state) admitted to an affair with an Argentinean woman. The governor who succeeded Sanford, Nikki Haley, had to fight public rumors reported in the news in 2011 that she had extramarital affairs with a blogger and a lobbyist, which she has vehemently denied.

5. New York State assemblywoman Angela Wozniak was sanctioned by the state's ethics committee for retaliating against her chief of staff, with whom she was having an extramarital affair. Wozniak campaigned in 2014 on a platform of integrity and ethics following the disgraced resignation of Assemblyman Dennis Gabryszak. He sent lewd video to his staff members. Within six months of assuming elected office in 2015 Wozniak began her own extramarital affair.

Therefore, I think we can safely assert that it does not make sense to view scandals' purpose as cautionary tales. After all, politicians do scandalous things even when their immediate predecessors resigned in scandal disgrace. Perhaps, then, sex scandals are indicative of natural selection within the political ecosphere. The competitive nature of the field, the grueling media attention lobbed onto those who act out sexually, and the withering public opinion that results when a politician is caught in scandal can result in the ouster of politicians who are liabilities due to their sexual compulsion, bad behavior, and poor choices. After all, we now know from chapter 2 that nearly three-quarters of male politicians caught in scandal at any point in their career have political failure; that chances of political failure increase the shorter their political resume and decrease if they've spent more than two years in political office. This might indicate that if politicians build political capital and grow roots in their district and in the nation's capital, they might be better equipped to weather the sex-scandal storm.

We also know from chapter 7 that there is a vocal strain of Americans who see illicit and ill-conceived private behavior as indicative of potentially corrupt public behavior. Therefore, from this perspective scandal-blemished politicians are unworthy of holding office, and they need to get the boot. The natural-selection theory for political sex scandals is validated in instances when disgraced politicians get caught in *another* round of tawdry activity, or related behavior of ill repute, *after* the initial scandal caused them to buckle at the knees. In these cases trouble continues to find these scandal-tarnished politicians, post-scandal. Therefore, according to natural selection theory they should be ousted from the political ecosphere. For instance, there's now the classic case of Anthony Weiner. Apparently he didn't get a big enough dose of humiliation in 2011 with his first round of nudie sex-tweets. After his resignation that year he kept on carrying on with women well into 2016 (at the time of writing). He was not evolutionarily capable of adapting his bad behavior once caught red-handed the first time around. Natural selection would take care of him. Again. Weiner would be booted from politics, again, and remains so at the time of writing.

There is also the example of former New York governor Eliot Spitzer who resigned in 2008 after admitting to have multiple affairs with prostitutes. Fast forward to 2016, and now divorced from his wife who stood next to him silently at his iconic press conference, Spitzer is under federal investigation for allegedly choking his girlfriend in the New York Plaza Hotel.[12] He also remains estranged from the political field.

There is also the example of New York State Senate candidate Gia Arnold, who halted her campaign in 2014 after announcing her extra-marital affair. In 2016, and no longer with her husband, Arnold was arrested with her boyfriend, "after a small arsenal [of guns and an assault weapon] was found in her vehicle when she was pulled over in Niagara Falls."[13] She is also voted out of the political arena at the time of writing. And let us consider the example of former Florida lieutenant governor Jennifer Carroll, who was accused of engaging in oral sex with her aide in 2012, which she vehemently denied. The following year Carroll resigned her position at the urging of the state's governor due to her connection to a "massive criminal probe against the operators of dozens of gambling outlets in the state."[14] The sex scandal may have been unconnected to the gambling scandal but an underlying theme of corruption connects Carroll's involvement in both incidents. She is no longer involved in politics.

Along this vein, let us also consider the case of former Nevada governor Jim Gibbons, who weathered (barely) a sexual assault case brought by a waitress during his gubernatorial campaign in 2006, only to be named "as one of the nation's worst governors in 2011 by Citizens for Responsibility and Ethics in Washington."[15] These aforementioned instances represent only a handful examples of politicians whose sex scandals act as preludes to other corruption charges and alleged illegal activities post-scandal. (For even more examples, look into the various rounds of scandal belonging to former Ohio Attorney General Marc Dann, former Detroit mayor Kwame Kilpatrick, and for international examples there's the former director of the International Monetary Fund, Dominique Strauss-Kahn, and former prime minister of Italy, Silvio Berlusconi.)

In today's political ecosphere we now know that a majority of politicians caught in scandal face career failure. But that leaves a minority who continue in their positions, and even some of those reach political-icon status post-scandal. Two such examples include now deceased Massachusetts senator Ted Kennedy and the retired Massachusetts congressman Barney Frank. It is beyond the scope of this chapter to explore the dynastic family that may have contributed to the circumstances that allowed Kennedy to flourish politically after he crashed the car, intoxicated, which also killed his young passenger in 1969; as it is also beyond the capabilities and space constraints to explore why Frank had a successful career after it was revealed—in 1985 while he was still "in the closet" as a gay man—that he had on his payroll, and with whom he lived, a man working as a prostitute. Therefore, scandal did not snuff out their careers when they occurred decades ago. Yet one wonders if they would have had that same "luck" if their respective scandals occurred more recently in the digital age. The point is that the combination of a more forgiving and less jaded public, a less intrusive, round-the-clock media system, and the politicians' own already-established professional networks that held them in high esteem, allowed Kennedy and Frank to continue in their positions as public servants and accomplish important work related to ethics reform, education, health care reform, financial reform, civil rights, and LGBT and women's rights throughout their storied, multi-decade careers. Kennedy became known as the "Lion of the Senate,"[16] and Frank was also regarded as one of the most powerful lawmakers in Washington.[17] These two examples show that one can get caught in scandal but possess the political wherewithal to subsequently engage in impactful political work. But in recent years this appears to be less likely the case as media systems hound the offending politicians to the point of hijacking the news and political systems; as visual evidence of their misdeeds is increasingly a part of the scandal process; as we face shifting notions of the public/private divide; and as issues of "character" and "trustworthiness" impact the public's view of a politician's capability to govern. All of these elements contribute to scandal's powerful place within the political ecosphere today. As a result, a majority of scandal-suffering politicians can't make the grade, evolutionarily speaking.

Yet there are always anomalies, abnormalities, and curiosities in the scientific world, and that's why it's worth reflecting for a moment on how a Donald J. Trump presidency might affect the occurrence and nature of contemporary political sex scandals. Timing here is important because I completed this book's manuscript two months prior to the 2016 presidential election that saw Trump defeat Hillary Clinton. And the copyedited manuscript was returned to me one month after Trump was elected (but lost the popular vote "by [a] greater margin than any US president"[18]). No doubt, the question of whether a Trump presidency might impact the nature of political sex scandals is certainly a reasonable one since a *New York Times* headline called him "Groper in Chief;"[19] since he has a history of judging women based on their appearance and physical attributes;[20] since women have accused him of sexual assault[21] and sexual harassment;[22] since he also has a track record of making derogatory and sexually explicit comments to and about women;[23] and, perhaps most notoriously, since he boasted in a private audio recording that was leaked one month before the 2016 presidential election that he touches women without their consent and that his "star" status allows him to do this: "Grab 'em by the pussy," he said. "You can do anything."[24] The accusations against Trump, and his comments and behavior that have entered the public record, seem to belie a finding of this book: those without political experience, and who encounter scandal as political newbies, are more likely to face political failure than established politicians. So why was Trump, who never before held elected office, elected to the highest office in the land? Of course the contours of the 2016 presidential election are far outside the bounds of this book, but I'd argue the following as it relates to scandal: Trump never positioned himself as a standard political candidate decked in moral armor. Instead, he boasted about his outsider credentials. His crassness was an attribute to his supporters because it was read as authentic (in his maleness, and in his refusal to play nice for the sake of superficial niceness). Beyond his experience as a businessman and the name behind an international brand, Trump exceled in the pop-culture domain, a reality TV celebrity who commodified his image and lifestyle. His gruff, say-what-you-really-think quality no doubt appealed to a portion of the electorate frustrated with what they saw as a crippling political correctness to emerge from our culture. It remains to be seen how the mantle of presidential responsibility may alter Trump's previous pattern of behavior toward women, and his Teflon exterior may weaken as he adjusts to the role of president of the United States (where certain behaviors are expected of the person who assumes that position and where an unpolished candidate becomes, no doubt, the most influential person in the world). So who knows—we might yet still see a sex scandal topple or derail a Trump White House. It wouldn't be the first time that such an event would overtake the American presidency.

Approaching political sex scandals from an ecosphere perspective helps us make sense as to why these events continue to unfold in the first place. Our advanced media system covers these events with glee. It's been decades since journalists have considered politicians' amorous pursuits as off-limits for publication. In this contemporary political ecosphere the news media has obliterated a public-private divide, even as politicians ask the public to respect their privacy in moments of sex-scandal hysteria. After all, it may be a Herculean task for scandal-tarnished politicians to reclaim the reins of the sex-scandal narrative once the media has sanctioned its dogged pursuit of the story. Just ask former New York congressman Anthony Weiner, as quoted in the 2016 documentary *Weiner*, which chronicles his attempted political comeback in 2013. "Everything is being engulfed by this thing," he says. "Maybe that's kinda what happens."

From a cynical perspective one can point to the *utter frivolity* of political sex scandals as nonstories that become dominating stories in a larger political ecosystem when more pressing issues relating to gun control, health care, education, racism, and wars abroad require the immediate attention of the political class. But as scandals demonstrate time and again, bad habits and bad behavior can hijack the political ecosphere for an extended period, until the complex biological system rights itself—at least for the time being.

APPENDIX A

Scandal-Defining Variables for Scandal Compilation

1. Did the politician have/solicit sex with/from male prostitutes?
2. Did the politician have sex with female prostitutes?
3. Did the politician have extramarital sexual relations with a man?
4. Did the politician have extramarital sexual relations with a woman?
5. Did the politician attempt to solicit sex from undercover authorities?
6. Were Nazis involved?
7. Did the affair produce children?
8. Did the politician have an affair with a female stripper?
9. Did alcohol play a role in the scandalous events?
10. Did the politician break the law?
11. Was the politician charged with a crime?
12. Did the politician spend time in jail/prison?
13. Did the politician engage in sexual activity with his female staff subordinates?
14. Did the politician engage in sexual activity with his male staff subordinates?
15. Did the politician engage in sexual activity with his male intern?
16. Did the politician engage in sexual activity with his female intern?
17. Was the scandal linked to murder?
18. Did the politician philander with a lobbyist?
19. Did sexual activity involve underage people?
20. Was evidence of his affair presented in media coverage?
21. Initially did the politician publicly deny sexual impropriety by addressing the media?
22. Was the politician accused of sexual harassment?
23. Did the politician have relations with a model/beauty figure?
24. Did the scandal involve child pornography?

25. Was the politician caught in real time by police when engaged in scandalous activity?
26. Was the scandalized politician critical of Clinton's behavior (and then subsequently caught in his own sex scandal)?
27. Did the politician hold a press conference/TV interview to address the scandal?
28. Did sex acts involve coercion?
29. Was there sexting?
30. Was the politician accused of physical abuse?
31. Did the politician or his associates make payments as hush/settlement money to his mistress?
32. Was the politician accused of sex abuse/assault?
33. Was the politician accused of satanic rituals?
34. Was the politician antigay, or did he vote against gay rights/issues and then caught in a gay scandal?
35. Did the politician expose himself?
36. Did the politician rape someone?
37. Did the politician molest someone within his charge (daughter, stepdaughter)?
38. Sentenced to house arrest?
39. Required to register as sex offender?
40. Was the politician accused by someone else as engaging in sexual activity that the politician denies?
41. Did the politician admit to using meth?
42. Did the scandal involve a sex tape of the politician?
43. Did the scandal/affair result in marriage?
44. Did the politician have an affair with a colleague?

APPENDIX B

Guiding Questions for Textual Analysis of Printed Text

1. What are the descriptive phrases that describe political wives in news coverage of them?
2. In what context are these women written about?
3. Who speaks for these women in the articles?
4. Who speaks about these women in these articles?
5. In which ways are their voices represented?
6. As theorist Charmaz asked, "How is language used"?[1]
7. "What, if any, unintended information and meanings might you see in the text"?[2]

APPENDIX C

Interview Protocol for Married Couples

For wives: after watching each of the press conferences:

1. What were you thinking/feeling as you watched this?
2. Would you attend this press conference if your husband was up there?
3. Why/why not?
4. If your husband wanted you there, but you were hesitant, would you attempt to negotiate something for your attendance—so you could get something from it? (Perhaps monetarily or otherwise?)
5. Which wife do you most identify with?
6. Why?
7. Did anything you say today surprise you?

For husbands: after watching each of the press conferences:

1. What were you thinking/feeling as you watched this?
2. Would you want your wife to attend this press conference if you were a politician caught in a scandal?
3. Why/why not?
4. If you were to ask your wife to attend, what would she say?
5. Which wife resonates with you most? Why?
6. Did anything you say today surprise you?

Notes

SERIES FOREWORD

1. Barbara Risman, "Gender as a Social Structure: Theory Wrestling with Activism," *Gender & Society* 2004, 18: 429–450.
2. See, e.g., Leslie McCall, "The Complexity of Intersectionality," *Signs* 2005, 30: 1771–1800.

CHAPTER 1

1. Denise Jewell Gee, "Wozniak Shattered the Wrong Glass Ceiling," *Buffalo (NY) News*, March 20, 2016, http://www.buffalonews.com/columns/denise-jewell-gee/wozniak-shattered-the-wrong-glass-ceiling-20160320.
2. Tom Precious, "Angela Wozniak Faces Range of Sanctions after Affair with Staffer," *Buffalo News*, March 9, 2016, http://www.buffalonews.com/city-region/albany-politics/angela-wozniak-faces-range-of-sanctions-after-affair-with-staffer-20160309.
3. Jill Perkins, "Wozniak Releases Video Response to Sexual Harassment Sanctions," *Buffalo News*, March 10, 2016, http://www.wkbw.com/news/wozniak-responds-to-sexual-harassment-sanctions.
4. "Assemblywoman Angela Wozniak's First Day in Albany," January 6, 2015, https://youtu.be/dvXLXrYqohs.
5. Because I found so few examples of philandering women politicians, I expanded the search to include female aides who cheated on their husbands.
6. Hunter Walker and Steve Huff, "David Petraeus Allegedly Had an Affair with His Biographer, Paula Broadwell," *New York Observer*, November 9, 2012.
7. Paul Kane and Howard Kurtz, "Husband of Ex-Mistress Sought Cash, Ensign Says," *Washington Post*, June 20, 2009, A01.
8. Josh Richman and Kristen J. Bender, "California State Treasurer Bill Lockyer Seeks Divorce from Former Supervisor Nadia Lockyer," *Contra Costa (CA) Times*, July 17, 2012.

9. Lara Brown and Jeff Gulati, "Spending More Time with My Family: Scandals and Premature Departures from the House," in *Scandal!: An Interdisciplinary Approach to the Consequences, Outcomes, and Significance of Political Scandals*, ed. Alison Dagnes and Mark Sachleben (New York: Bloomsbury, 2014), 51–77.

10. Alison Dagnes and Mark Sachleben, eds., *Scandal!: An Interdisciplinary Approach to the Consequences, Outcomes, and Significance of Political Scandals* (New York: Bloomsbury, 2014).

11. Adam Goldman and Alan Rappeport, "Emails in Anthony Weiner Inquiry Jolt Hillary Clinton's Campaign," *New York Times*, October 28, 2016, http://www.nytimes.com/2016/10/29/us/politics/fbi-hillary-clinton-email.html?_r=0.

12. Peter L. Berger and Thomas Luckmann, *The Social Construction of Reality* (New York: Anchor Books, 1966).

13. Joshua Gamson, "Normal Sins: Sex Scandal Narratives as Institutional Morality Tales," in *Public Affairs: Politics in the Age of Sex Scandals*, ed. Paul Apostolidis and Juliet A. Williams (Durham, NC: Duke University Press, 2004), 40.

14. Ibid.

15. Monica Anderson, "Sanford, Weiner and Spitzer: Trying to Overcome the Headlines from Their Scandals," *Pew Research Center*, July 10, 2013, http://www.pewresearch.org/fact-tank/2013/07/10/sanford-weiner-and-spitzer-trying-to-overcome-the-headlines-from-their-scandals/.

16. Apostolidis and Williams, *Public Affairs*.

17. John B. Thompson, *Political Scandal: Power and Visibility in the Media Age* (Cambridge: Blackwell, 2000), 13.

18. Apostolidis and Williams, *Public Affairs*; Mark D. West, *Secrets, Sex, and Spectacle: The Rules of Scandal in Japan and the United States* (Chicago: The University of Chicago Press, 2006).

19. Candace West and Don H. Zimmerman, "Doing Gender," *Gender & Society* 1, no. 3 (1987): 125–151.

20. Ibid., 142.

21. Ibid.; Jan E. Stets and Stacy A. Hammons, "Gender, Control, and Marital Commitment," *Journal of Family Issues* 23, no. 1 (2002).

22. West and Zimmerman, "Doing Gender," 142.

23. Ibid.

24. Dorwin Cartwright, *Studies in Social Power*, ed. Dorwin Cartwright (Ann Arbor, MI: Research Center for Group Dynamics Institute for Social Research, 1959).

25. Ibid., 184.

26. Ibid., 186.

27. Ibid.

28. Katherine E. Smith, "Problematising Power Relations in 'Elite' Interviews," *Geoforum* 37, no. 4 (2006): 643–653.

29. Ibid., 645.

30. Michael Woods, "Rethinking Elites: Networks, Space, and Local Politics," *Environment and planning A* 30, no. 12 (1998): 2106.

31. "Women in U.S. Congress 2015," *Center for American Women and Politics, Rutgers University*, http://www.cawp.rutgers.edu/women-us-congress-2015.

32. "Women's History Matters," *Montanawomenshistory.org*, http://montana womenshistory.org/suffrage/.

33. "Women in Congress," *History, Art & Archives, United States House of Representatives*, accessed August 22, 2016, http://history.house.gov/Exhibition -and-Publications/WIC/Women-in-Congress/.

34. Amanda Marcotte, "Congress Won't Be 50 Percent Women Until 2121. What Is the Holdup?," *Slate*, June 19, 2014, http://www.slate.com/blogs/xx_factor /2014/06/19/congress_won_t_be_half_women_until_2121_more_than_100 _years_to_go_says_new.html.

35. Christopher Ingraham, "How Republican and Democratic Sex Scandals Differ," *Washington Post*, April 10, 2014, http://www.washingtonpost.com/blogs /wonkblog/wp/2014/04/10/how-republican-and-democratic-sex-scandals-differ/.

36. John H. Summers, "What Happened to Sex Scandals? Politics and Peccadilloes, Jefferson to Kennedy," *Journal of American History* 87, no. 3 (2000): 825–854.

37. The selfie-sexting politicians include Congressman Chris Lee of New York, Republican, who resigned in 2011 after sending a topless photo of himself to women from his congressional e-mail address; Congressman Anthony Weiner of New York, Democrat, who resigned in 2011 after sending numerous photos, including an erect bulge of his penis in underwear, to women via Twitter (his sexting saga continued again in 2013 and 2016); Joe Stagni, a Republican New Orleans councilman of Louisiana, who apologized in 2011 when he sent photos to an administration employee of himself in his undies; Louis N. Magazzu, a New Jersey Democrat in 2011, who resigned from local elected office after texting nude photos of himself to a woman he had never met; Randy Boehning, a Republican state legislator from North Dakota, who voted against LGBT legislation, sent illicit photos of himself to other men on Grindr (he apologized); John Diehl, a Republican House speaker from Missouri, who ultimately resigned after exchanging sexy texts and photos with an intern; and Democrat Justin Moed, an Indiana legislator, who sent nude photos and gifts—signing his communication as "Bitch Boy"—to Sydney Leathers, the same woman with whom Anthony Weiner sexted in 2013 during his second round of scandal (he apologized).

38. Hinda Mandell, "From Hot to Not: Political Failure and Resilience When Illicit Selfies Go Viral" (Kern Conference presentation, Rochester Institute of Technology, Rochester, NY, April 16, 2016).

39. "Will Folks, SC Blogger: I Had Affair with Nikki Haley, Republican Can-didate for Governor," *Huffington Post*, May 24, 2010, http://www.huffingtonpost .com/2010/05/24/will-folks-sc-blogger-i-h_n_586990.html.

40. Nikki Haley, *Can't Is Not an Option: My American Story* (New York: Penguin, 2012), 159.

41. Michael Peltier, "Jennifer Carroll Sex Scandal: Florida Lieutenant Governor Accused of Misconduct by Former Aide Carletha Cole," *Huffington Post*, July

12, 2012, http://www.huffingtonpost.com/2012/07/12/lt-governor-jennifer-carroll
-lesbian-sex-scandal-florida_n_1668318.html.

42. Christine Jordan Sexton and Lizette Alvarez, "Florida's Lieutenant Governor
Resigns Amid Inquiry into Sweepstakes Firm," *New York Times*, March 13, 2013,
http://www.nytimes.com/2013/03/14/us/lt-gov-jennifer-carroll-of-florida-resigns
.html?_r=1.

43. Jennifer L. Lawless and Richard L. Fox, "Girls Just Wanna Not Run: The
Gender Gap in Young Americans' Political Ambition," School of Public Affairs,
American University, 2013, https://www.american.edu/spa/wpi/upload/Girls-Just
-Wanna-Not-Run_Policy-Report.pdf.

44. Ibid., 4.

45. Jennifer L. Lawless and Richard L. Fox, "Why Don't Women Run for
Office?," Brown University Policy Report (Providence, RI: Taubman Center for
Public Policy, 2004).

46. Jennifer L. Lawless and Richard Fox, "Why Are Women Still Not Running
for Office?," *Issues in Governance Studies* 16 (2008), https://www.brookings.edu
/wp-content/uploads/2016/06/05_women_lawless_fox.pdf.

CHAPTER 2

1. John H. Summers, "What Happened to Sex Scandals? Politics and Peccadilloes, Jefferson to Kennedy," *Journal of American History* 87, no. 3 (2000): 826.

2. Ibid., 827.

3. Ibid., 829.

4. Ibid.

5. Ibid., 835.

6. Ibid., 842.

7. Scott Basinger, Lara Brown, Douglas B. Harris, and Girish J. Gulati,
"Preface: Counting and Classifying Congressional Scandals," in *Scandal!: An
Interdisciplinary Approach to the Consequences, Outcomes, and Significance of Political Scandals*, ed. Alison Dagnes and Mark Sachleben (New York: Bloomsbury,
2014), 3–28.

8. I extend a heartfelt thank you to Gina Masullo Chen, PhD, assistant professor in the School of Journalism at The University of Texas at Austin, for her
statistical analysis that made this chapter possible.

9. For this reason, President John F. Kennedy was excluded from this list because
while he was known as a philanderer there was not a single event, marked as a
scandal, to be covered by the press. As noted previously, we assume that scandalous behavior occurs with regular frequency but it only becomes a "scandal" when
the public learns about it through news coverage.

10. List found here: http://en.wikipedia.org/wiki/List_of_federal_political
_sex_scandals_in_the_United_States.

11. List found here: http://en.wikipedia.org/wiki/List_of_state_and_local_political
_sex_scandals_in_the_United_States.

12. Charles Arthur, "The History of Smartphones: Timeline," *The Guardian*, January 24, 2012, https://www.theguardian.com/technology/2012/jan/24/smartphones-timeline.

13. Simon Hall, "The 11 Moments That Defined BlackBerry's Rise and Fall," *TechRadar.com*, September 23, 2013, http://www.techradar.com/us/news/phone-and-communications/mobile-phones/the-10-moments-that-defined-blackberry-s-rise-and-fall-1175428.

14. "Number of Active Users at Facebook Over the Years," *Yahoo! Finance*, October 23, 2012, http://finance.yahoo.com/news/number-active-users-facebook-over-years-214600186--finance.html.

15. "Stats," accessed June 3, 2016, http://newsroom.fb.com/company-info/.

16. John Weinberg, "The Great Recession and Its Aftermath," *FederalReserve History.org*, http://www.federalreservehistory.org/Period/Essay/15.

17. Mike Collins, "The Big Bank Bail Out," *Forbes.com*, July 14, 2015, http://www.forbes.com/sites/mikecollins/2015/07/14/the-big-bank-bailout/#40e20a7f3723.

CHAPTER 3

1. Janis L. Edwards, "Running in the Shadows in Campaign 2000: Candidate Metaphors in Editorial Cartoons," *American Behavioral Scientist* 44, no. 12 (2001): 2149.

2. Charlotte Templin, "Hillary Clinton as Threat to Gender Norms: Cartoon Images of the First Lady," *Journal of Communication Inquiry* 23, no. 1 (1999): 20.

3. Ibid.

4. Joan L. Conners, "Barack versus Hillary: Race, Gender, and Political Cartoon Imagery of the 2008 Presidential Primaries," *American Behavioral Scientist* 54, no. 3 (2010): 299.

5. Juana I. Marín-Arrese, "Cognition and Culture in Political Cartoons," *Intercultural Pragmatics* 5, no. 1 (2008): 29.

6. Janis L. Edwards, "Drawing Politics in Pink and Blue," *PS: Political Science & Politics* 40, no. 2 (2007): 249.

7. Ibid., 251.

8. Martin J. Medhurst and Michael A. DeSousa, "Political Cartoons as Rhetorical Form: A Taxonomy of Graphic Discourse," *Communications Monographs* 48, no. 3 (1981): 198.

9. Ibid., 219.

10. Diana E. Popa, "Multimodal Metaphors in Political Entertainment," *Review of Cognitive Linguistics* 11, no. 2 (2013): 304.

11. Ibid., 303.

12. Ibid.

13. Candace West and Don H. Zimmerman, "Doing Gender," *Gender & Society* 1, no. 2 (1987): 125–151.

14. Ibid., 129.

15. Edwards, "Running in the Shadows," 2140–2151.

16. Conners, "Barack versus Hillary," 302.

17. Bob Englehart, "Eliot Spitzer," illustration, *Hartford Courant*, March 11, 2008, from *Cagle.com*.

18. John Darkow, "John Edwards Two Americas," illustration, *Columbia Daily Tribune*, August 11, 2008, from *Cagle.com*.

19. Taylor Jones, "Weinerwear," illustration, *Politicalcartoons.com*, June 2, 2011.

20. John Cole, "Weiner Resigns," illustration, *Scranton Times-Tribune*, June 17, 2011, from *Cagle.com*.

21. TMZ Staff, "Congressman Pic Raises Questions about Hacking," TMZ *.com*, June 6, 2011, http://www.tmz.com/2011/06/06/congressman-anthony-weiner-pictures-naked-underwear-bulge-shirtless-chest-pecs-twitter-hacked-weinergate/.

22. Daryl Cagle, "Anthony Weiner Forever," illustration, *CagleCartoons.com*, July 24, 2013.

23. Daryl Cagle, "Weiner—Jerk," illustration, *CagleCartoons.com*, June 2, 2011.

24. John Cole, "Weiner Roasted," illustration, *Scranton Times-Tribune*, June 8, 2011.

25. Gary McCoy, "Acceptable to Democrats," illustration, *CagleCartoons.com*, October 6, 2006.

26. Eliana Dockterman, "Clinton: I Never Denied Smoking Pot," *Time.com*, December 3, 2013, http://swampland.time.com/2013/12/03/clinton-i-never-denied-smoking-pot/.

27. John Cole, "Edwards Affair," illustration, *Scranton Times-Tribune*, August 8, 2008.

28. Lisa Myers and Michael Austin, "John Edwards Admits He Fathered Rielle Hunter's Child," *ABC News*, January 21, 2010, http://abcnews.go.com/GMA/john-edwards-admits-fathered-rielle-hunter-child-affair/story?id=9620812.

29. Gary McCoy, "Expert Deviant Bill," illustration, *Cagle.com*, October 6, 2006.

30. Rick McKee, "Clinton Gives Cain a Pass," illustration, *Augusta (GA) Chronicle*, November 1, 2011.

31. Michael A. DeSousa and Martin J. Medhurst, "Political Cartoons and American Culture: Significant Symbols of Campaign 1980," *Studies in Visual Communication* 8, no. 1 (1982): 369.

32. Ibid.

33. Pew Research Center Journalism & Media Staff, "Top Newsmakers," *Pew Research Center*, December 21, 2011, http://www.journalism.org/2011/12/21/top-newsmakers/.

34. Ibid.

35. "Two Explosive Scandals Top the News," *Pew Research Center*, November 13, 2011, http://www.journalism.org/2011/11/13/pej-news-coverage-index-november-713-2011/.

36. Ibid.

37. "Economy, Weiner Top Public's News Interests," *Pew Research Center*, June 22, 2011, http://www.pewresearch.org/2011/06/22/economy-weiner-top-publics-news-interests/.

38. Katharine Q. Seelye, "Edwards Admits to Affair in 2006," *New York Times*, August 8, 2008, http://www.nytimes.com/2008/08/09/us/politics/09edwards.html ?pagewanted=all.

39. In the second round of Anthony Weiner's sexting scandal in 2013 when he was running for mayor of New York City, he did not halt his campaign. But he did lose in the primaries.

40. John McArdle, "Craig Arrested, Pleads Guilty Following Incident in Airport Restroom," *Roll Call*, August 27, 2007, http://www.rollcall.com/news/-19763 -1.html.

41. "Transcript of Police Interview of Sen. Larry Craig," *CNN.com*, August 3, 2007, http://www.cnn.com/2007/POLITICS/08/30/craig.transcript/index.html ?iref=newsearch.

42. "Transcript: Sen. Larry Craig," *Fox News*, August 28, 2007, http://www .foxnews.com/story/2007/08/28/transcript-sen-larry-craig.html.

43. Daryl Cagle, "Craig Tap Dance," illustration, *CagleCartoons.com*, September 5, 2007; RJ Matson, "Senator Craig Has Happy Feet," illustration, *CagleCartoons .com*, September 6, 2007; Christo Komarnitski, "The Inconvenient Craig," illustration, October 18, 2007.

44. RJ Matson, "Spitzer Spitzered," illustration, *New York Observer*, March 13, 2008.

45. Pat Bagley, "Cain Unable to Explain," illustration, *Salt Lake Tribune*, November 1, 2011; John Cole, "Cain Harassment Cases," illustration, *Scranton Times-Tribune*, November 2, 2011; Larry Wright, "Vote Cain," illustration, *CagleCartoons.com*, November 2, 2011; Adam Zyglis, "Hermit Cain," illustration, *Buffalo (NY) News*, November 3, 2011; RJ Matson, "Herman Cain," illustration, *CagleCartoons.com*, November 3, 2011; Taylor Jones, "Herman Cain Explains," illustration, *Politicalcartoon.com*, November 4, 2011.

46. Taylor Jones, "Herman Cain Complains," illustration, *Politicalcartoons.com*, November 10, 2011.

47. In Gary McCoy's November 14, 2011, cartoon, "Cain's Press Coverage," we see two TV anchors delivering the news. They have donned blackface, and a box that says "Black shoe polish" by their desk confirms as much. These two anchors represent all of "Mainstream media news," according to a placard on their desk. Their white eyes bulge from their faces, and each has a shock crop of black hair. The female anchor also wears a bone as a hair accessory in her bun. The cartoon clearly depicts media coverage of the Cain scandal as racist but this cartoon depiction is puzzling. That's because when someone dons blackface— historically—it is to act out in a crude, lewd manner that a person's whiteness (or non-blackness) would not typically permit. (Brittney Cooper, "The First Rule of Blackface: It's Not Hard to Understand, Everyone," *Salon*, October 29, 2013, http://www.salon.com/2013/10/29/the_first_rule_of_blackface_its_not_hard _to_understand_everyone/.) But the newscasters' behavior was not unusual other than their appearance. Therefore the blackface depiction seems misplaced. It may certainly well be that mainstream media depiction of Cain was racist—but

I can't say without conducting an analysis investigating that (which I did not do) or reviewing analysis of such coverage (which I could not find).

48. John Darkow, "Weiner Twitter," illustration, *Columbia Daily Tribune*, June 7, 2011; Randall Enos, "Weiner Seeks Help," illustration, *CagleCartoons.com*, June 14, 2011; RJ Matson, "Anthony Weiner Announces Candidacy," illustration, *CagleCartoons.com*, May 24, 2013; Christopher Wevant, "Big Dog," illustration, *The Hill*, July 24, 2013. Steve Sack, "Big Weenie," illustration, *Minneapolis Star Tribune*, July 25, 2013.

49. Christopher Weyant, "Big Dog," illustration, *The Hill*, July 24, 2013.

50. Christo Komarnitski, "New York State Gov. Eliot Spitzer," illustration, *Cagle.com*, March 11, 2008.

51. Pat Bagley, "Spitzer Zipper," illustration, *Salt Lake Tribune*, March 11, 2008.

52. Nate Beeler, "Eliot Spitzer the Crusader," illustration, *Columbus (OH) Dispatch*, March 11, 2008.

53. Pat Bagley, "Sen. Craig's Long Goodbye," illustration, *Salt Lake Tribune*, October 8, 2007.

54. RJ Matson, "Herman Cain," illustration, *CagleCartoons.com*, November 3, 2011; RJ Matson, "Herman Cain," illustration, *CagleCartoons.com*, December 7, 2011.

55. Adam Zyglis, "Massa Reasons for Resigning," illustration, *Buffalo News*, March 11, 2007.

56. Taylor Jones, "Weinerwear," illustration, *Politicalcartoons.com*, June 2, 2011; RJ Matson, "Weiner Mobile Gate," illustration, *Roll Call*, June 2, 2011; Daryl Cagle, "Weiner—Jerk," illustration, *CagleCartoons.com*, June 2, 2011; John Darkow, "Weiner Twitter," illustration, *Columbia Daily Tribune*, June 7, 2011; RJ Matson, "Clear History," illustration, *Roll Call*, June 7, 2011; Randall Enos, "Weiner Resigns," illustration, *Cagle.com*, June 16, 2011.

57. John Cole, "The Hyperloon," illustration, *Scranton Times-Tribune*, August 15, 2013.

58. RJ Matson, "More Indecent Exposure," illustration, *Roll Call*, June 17, 2011.

59. Gary McCoy, "ObamaCare Texting," illustration, *CagleCartoons.com*, July 31, 2013.

60. John Darkow, "Take a Hike," illustration, *Columbia Daily Tribune*, June 29, 2009.

61. RJ Matson, "What I Did on My Summer Vacation," illustration, *New York Observer*, September 5, 2007.

62. Adam Zyglis, "Eliot Spitzer Calls Prostitute," illustration, *Buffalo News*, March 10, 2008; Bob Englehart, "Eliot Spitzer," illustration, *Hartford Courant*, March 11, 2008; John Cole, "Spitzer Resigns," illustration, *Scranton Times-Tribune*, March 12, 2008; Adam Zyglis, "NY State Spitzer Passing the Torch," illustration, *Buffalo News*, March 14, 2008.

63. Gary McCoy, "John Edwards' Trash," illustration, *CagleCartoons.com*, August 9, 2008.

64. RJ Matson, "Don't Cry for Governor Sanford," illustration, *Roll Call*, June 24, 2009.

65. Mike Keefe, "Cain Allegations," illustration, *CagleCartoons.com*, November 3, 2011.

66. Nate Beeler, "Weiner Check-Up," illustration, *Columbus Dispatch*, June 2, 2011; Randall Enos, "Weiner Apologizes," illustration, *CagleCartoons.com*, June 6, 2011.

67. Gary McCoy, "Acceptable to Democrats," illustration, *CagleCartoons.com*, October 6, 2006.

68. Daryl Cagle, "Vitter and Craig," illustration, *CagleCartoons.com*, September 4, 2007.

69. Christo Komarnitski, "Spot the Difference," illustration, *CagleCartoons.com*, September 26, 2007.

70. John Cole, "Spitzer and Prostitutes," illustration, *Scranton Times-Tribune*, March 10, 2008.

71. Daryl Cagle, "Republicans and Adultery," illustration, *CagleCartoons.com*, June 25, 2009.

72. Nate Beeler, "Souder Affair," illustration, *Columbus Dispatch*, May 18, 2010.

73. Christo Komarnitski, "Go Hillary!," illustration, *PoliticalCartoons.com*, March 12, 2008.

74. Daryl Cagle, "Spitzer Resigns Shadow," illustration, *CagleCartoons.com*, March 12, 2008.

75. Taylor Jones, "John and Elizabeth Edwards," illustration, *Politicalcartoons.com*, January 21, 2010.

76. David Fitzsimmons, "Cain Pain," illustration, *Arizona Star*, November 29, 2011.

77. RJ Matson, "Governor Sanford's Personal Odyssey," illustration, *CagleCartoons.com*, June 24, 2009.

78. Sean Delonas, "Anthony and Huma Weiner," illustration, *CagleCartoons.com*, July 24, 2013.

79. Andrea Drusch, "How Close Are Huma Abedin and Hillary Clinton?," *Politico*, July 30, 2013, http://www.politico.com/gallery/2013/07/how-close-are-huma-abedin-and-hillary-clinton-001048?slide=0.

80. Taylor Jones, "Huma Consults Hillary," illustration, *Politicalcartoons.com*, July 24, 2013.

81. Adam Goldman and Alan Rappeport, "Emails in Anthony Weiner Inquiry Jolt Hillary Clinton's Campaign," *New York Times*, October 28, 2016, http://www.nytimes.com/2016/10/29/us/politics/fbi-hillary-clinton-email.html?_r=0.

82. Edwards, "Drawing Politics," 251.

83. Ibid., 250.

CHAPTER 4

1. S. Elizabeth Bird, *For Enquiring Minds: A Cultural Study of Supermarket Tabloids* (Knoxville: University of Tennessee Press, 1992), 2.

2. Serge F. Kovaleski and Ian Urbina, "For an Aspiring Singer, a Harsher Spotlight," *New York Times*, March 13, 2008, http://www.nytimes.com/2008/03/13/nyregion/12cnd-kristen.html?_r=0.

3. "The Daily News Is a Top 10 Paper in the U.S.," *NYDailyNews.com*, http://multimedia.nydailynews.com/mediakit/Circulation2014.pdf.

4. Rich Shapiro, Annie Karni, and Jennifer Fermino, "Damsel of 'Danger' Gal Loves Fame Pol Started Affair with a 'Poke,'" *New York Daily News*, July 25, 2013, 4.

5. Carl Campanile, "Meet Carlos Danger: He's Carlos the Jerkel!," *New York Post*, July 24, 2013, 4.

6. Ibid.

7. Ibid.

8. Ibid.

9. Andrea Peyser, "Boo-ho! Don't Shed Any Tears for this Busty Brat," *New York Post*, March 14, 2008, 10.

10. Kovaleski and Urbina, "For an Aspiring Singer, a Harsher Spotlight."

11. Dave Goldiner, "Spitzer Scandal Call Girl Thanks Fans on MySpace Page," *New York Daily News*, June 24, 2008, http://www.nydailynews.com/entertainment/gossip/spitzer-scandal-call-girl-ashley-dupre-thanks-fans-myspace-page-article-1.297218.

12. Mallory Simon, "Dupré's MySpace Page Evolves with Scandal," *CNN.com*, March 14, 2008, http://www.cnn.com/2008/US/03/13/ashley.myspace/index.html?eref=yahoo.

13. "Twitter Usage Statistics," *InternetLiveStats.com*, http://www.internetlivestats.com/twitter-statistics/.

14. Carl Campanile, "Carlos for Mayor Sext Maniac's Limps XXXcuse Weiner Blames Rocky Marriage," *New York Post*, July 25, 2013, 4.

15. Beth DeFalco and Jeane MacIntosh, "Carlos for Mayor: Weiner's Dirty Baker's Dozen," *New York Post*, July 26, 2013, 4.

16. Post Sports Desk, "Hondo: Go with Gonzo!," *New York Post*, July 31, 2013, 42.

17. DeFalco and MacIntosh, "Carlos for Mayor."

18. Lorena Mongelli and Jeane MacIntosh, "Huma Gets Coldcocked!," *New York Post*, July 27, 2013, 4.

19. Sean Evans and Larry McShane, "She Came to N.Y. Looking for Record Deal, Instead She Got Hooker Ring Offer," *New York Daily News*, March 14, 2008, http://www.nydailynews.com/news/n-y-record-deal-hooker-ring-offer-article-1.285687.

20. Joshua Gamson, "Jessica Hahn, Media Whore: Sex Scandals and Female Publicity," *Critical Studies in Media Communication* 18, no. 2 (2001).

21. Ibid., 158.

22. Ibid., 171.

23. David K. Li and Beth DeFalco, "Yo, Tony, Have We Got a Porn Video for You!," *New York Post*, August, 6, 2013.

24. Gamson, "Jessica Hahn," 162.

25. Matthew Nestel, Jennifer Fermino, and Samuel Goldsmith, "'Good Girl' Planned Catholic Nups," *New York Post*, March 16, 2008, 8.

26. Lukas I. Alpert and Samuel Goldsmith, "Eliot's Gal a Shared Asset," *New York Post*, March 16, 2008, 9.

27. Ibid.

28. Ibid.

29. Peyser, "Boo-ho!"

30. Sean Evans and Larry McShane, "She Was Sexiest & Hottest Girl I Had," *New York Post*, March 14, 2008, 2.

31. Ibid.

32. Peyser, "Boo-ho!"

33. "'Kristen' Steps Out at Hot Club," *New York Post*, May 3, 2008, 10.

34. Ibid.

35. Ibid.

36. "Hooker Hits the Scene," *New York Post*, March 24, 2008, 11.

37. Kati Cornell and Samuel Goldsmith, "Songs Have a Catchy Hook," *New York Post*, March 15, 2008, 7.

38. Ibid.

39. Ibid.

40. Ibid.

41. Ibid.

42. Stephanie Gaskell and Richard Huff, "Gazillion Dollar Baby!," *New York Post*, March 14, 2008, 5.

43. Cornell and Goldsmith, "Songs Have a Catchy Hook."

44. Christopher Napolitano, "Ashley Dupré," *Playboy*, May 2010, cover story.

45. Ashley Dupré, "Ask Ashley," *New York Post*, December 13, 2009, http://nypost.com/2009/12/13/ask-ashley/.

46. Carl Campanile, "Meet Carlos Danger."

47. Ibid.

48. Ibid.

49. Rich Shapiro and Jennifer Fermino, "Woman who Sexted Anthony Weiner Said She Loved Him but Is 'Disgusted by Him' Now," *New York Daily News*, July 26, 2013, http://www.nydailynews.com/news/national/weiner-sexting -pal-tells-relationship-article-1.1409147.

50. "Spinning Sydney," *New York Post*, July 29, 2013, 12.

51. Tara Palmeri and Josh Saul, "Fight for the Future: Weiner 'Flips' Out in Defeat," *New York Post*, September 11, 2013, 4.

52. Shapiro et al., "Damsel of 'Danger.'"

53. Ibid.

54. Lorena Mongelli and Jeane MacIntosh, "Huma Gets Coldcocked! Weiner's Sex Partner Says Wife in It for Power & Fame," *New York Post*, July 27, 2013, 4.

55. Nancy Dillon, "Weiner Just [Luv's] Weiner," *New York Daily News*, August 4, 2013, 8.

56. Nancy Dillon, "S-HIV-ERS! Weiner Porn Pal at Exposure Risk," *New York Daily News*, August 23, 2013, 3.

57. Jeane MacIntosh, "Leathers a Bathing 'Booty,'" *New York Post*, July 29, 2013, 5.

58. Ibid.

59. Ibid.

60. "Leathers Models Leather Pants," *New York Post*, August 1, 2013, 7.

61. Ibid.

62. Ibid.

63. Ibid.

64. Li and DeFalco, "Yo, Tony."

65. Ibid.

66. "Worn-out Leathers," *New York Post*, August 15, 2013, 16.

67. Ibid.

68. Ibid.

69. Li and DeFalco, "Yo, Tony."

70. "Worn-out Leathers."

71. Nancy Dillon, "Sext Pal Tells of His Giant-Sized Ego," *New York Daily News*, August 4, 2013, 8.

72. Kyle Smith, "Hard to Get XXX-Cited," *New York Post*, August 22, 2013, 9.

73. See Nancy Dillon and Jennifer Fermino, "His Star Is Porn," *New York Daily News*, July 31, 2013, 4–5; Beth DeFalco, "Sex Gal Says Jerky Pol Would Call 5 Times a Day," *New York Post*, July 31, 2013, 7; Nancy Dillon, Irving DeJohn, Mara Gay, and Larry McShane, "Jerky Weiner Flips Bird in Defeat," *New York Daily News*, September 11, 2013, 12–13; Dillon, "Sext Pal."

74. See Lorena Mongelli and Jeane MacIntosh, "Huma Gets Coldcocked," *New York Post*, July 27, 2013, 4–5; Jeane MacIntosh and Laura Italiano, "Vixen Gets Leg Up on Loser," *New York Post*, July 26, 2013, 7.

75. "Fight for the Future 'Right' on Schedule," *New York Post*, September 12, 2013, 7.

76. See Lukas I. Alpert and Samuel Goldsmith, "Shared Asset," *New York Post*, March 16, 2008, 9; "Ka-ching! Spitzer's 'Score' Girl Is Already Raking in the Dough," *New York Post*, March 15, 2008, 6–7; Ben Widdicombe and Sean Evans, "A Dupré Deal May Be Tricky," *New York Post*, April 28, 2008, 18.

77. "Special Edition: The Spitzer Resignation," *New York Post*, March 13, 2008, 1.

78. Colleen Long, "Call Girl's Lawyer Lashes Out at Media," *Victoria Advocate*, March 16, 2008, https://news.google.com/newspapers?nid=861&dat=20080316&id=Q5I_AAAAIBAJ&sjid=6FUMAAAAIBAJ&pg=1430,3288064&hl=en.

79. Evans and McShane, "Hottest Girl."

80. Raakhee Mirchandani, "The 50 Most Powerful Women in NYC," *New York Post*, June 1, 2008, 12.

81. "Even THIS Creep Thinks Weiner's a Bad Husband!," *New York Daily News*, July 27, 2013, 1.

82. Huma Abedin announced her separation from Anthony Weiner in August 2016, following a third round of illicit sexts.

83. "POT, MEET KETTLE," *New York Post*, July 30, 2013, 1.

84. Jennifer Bain and Michael Gartland, "Campaign Chief Quits as Scandal Grows," *New York Post*, July 28, 2013, 4.

85. P. David Marshall, *Celebrity and Power: Fame in Contemporary Culture* (Minneapolis: University of Minnesota Press, 1997).

86. Ibid., 219.

87. Ashley Dupré, "Ask Ashley," *New York Post*, December 13, 2009, http://nypost.com/2009/12/13/ask-ashley/.

88. Marianne Garvey, Brian Niemietz, Lachlan Cartwright, and Molly Friedman, "Ashley Dupré, the One-Time Escort Who Helped Sock it to Former Gov. Eliot Spitzer, Marries Construction Honcho in Paris," *New York Daily News*, October 26, 2013, http://www.nydailynews.com/entertainment/gossip/confidential/ashley-dupre-marries-construction-honcho-paris-article-1.1497765.

89. Barbara Ross, Brian Niemietz, and Dareh Gregorian, "Exclusive: Eliot Spitzer and Longtime Wife Silda Wall File Divorce Papers," *New York Daily News*, January 16, 2014, http://www.nydailynews.com/news/politics/eliot-spitzer-wife-silda-file-divorce-papers-article-1.1580897.

90. Christopher Napolitano, "Ashley Dupré," *Playboy*. May 2010, n.p.

91. Ibid.

92. John T. Ward, "Ashley Dupré Sets Up Shop and Moves On," *Redbankgreen.com*, May 15, 2012, http://www.redbankgreen.com/2012/05/ashley-dupre-sets-up-shop-and-moves-on/.

93. Instagram post, Femme by Ashley, August 5, 2015, https://www.instagram.com/p/6A92nZRxKV/.

94. @sydneyelainexo Twitter page, https://twitter.com/sydneyelainexo?lang=en.

95. Social media descriptions for the mistresses were current at the time of writing, and I acknowledge that some items—such as their Twitter bios—may change by the time of publication and beyond.

96. Will Higgins, "Sydney Leathers, from Sexting to Studying," *USA Today*, September 17, 2014, http://www.usatoday.com/story/news/politics/2014/09/17/sydney-leathers-from-sexting-to-studying/15757323/.

97. Diane Falzone, "Sydney Leathers: Justin Moed's Texts 'a Million Times More Shocking' than Anthony Weiner's," *Foxnews.com*, March 18, 2015, http://www.foxnews.com/entertainment/2015/03/18/sydney-leathers-just-moed-sexts-million-times-more-shocking-than-anthony-weiner/.

98. Gamson, "Jessica Hahn," 171.

99. Ibid., 170.

100. Ibid.

CHAPTER 5

1. Paul Apostolidis and Juliet J. Williams, eds., *Public Affairs: Politics in the Age of Sex Scandals* (Durham, NC: Duke University Press, 2004).

2. Andrei Markovits and Mark Silverstein, *The Politics of Scandal: Power and Process in Liberal Democracies* (New York: Holmes & Meier, 1988), vii.

3. Calvin G. Mackenzie and Michael Hafken, *Scandal Proof: Do Ethics Laws Make Government Ethical?* (Washington, DC: Brookings Institution Press, 2002); Theodore J. Lowi, "Power and Corruption: Political Competition and the Scandal Market," in *Public Affairs: Politics in the Age of Sex Scandals*, ed. Paul Apostolidis and Juliet A. Williams (Durham, NC: Duke University Press, 2004), 69–98.

4. Apostolidis and Williams, *Public Affairs*.

5. Ibid.

6. Ibid., 40.

7. Michael Grynbaum, "Spitzers Say They Are Set to Divorce," *New York Times*, A23, December 25, 2013.

8. Candace West and Don H. Zimmerman, "Doing Gender," *Gender & Society* 1, no. 2 (1987): 125–151.

9. Susan Maushart, *Wifework: What Marriage Really Means for Women* (New York: Bloomsbury, 2001).

10. See, for instance: Lewis L. Gould, ed., *American First Ladies: Their Lives and Their Legacy* (New York: Garland, 1996); Dorothy Schneider and Carl J. Schneider, *First Ladies: A Biographical Dictionary* (New York: Facts On File, 2010); Betty Caroli, *First Ladies: From Martha Washington to Michelle Obama* (New York: Oxford University Press, 2010).

11. Libby Copeland and Monica Hesse, "Silda Spitzer, Profile of an Accomplished Woman," *Washington Post*, C1, March 13, 2008.

12. Apostolidis and Williams, *Public Affairs*.

13. Hinda Mandell, "'Stand by Your Man' Revisited: Political Wives and Scandal," in *Media Depictions of Brides, Wives, and Mothers*, ed. Alena A. Ruggerio (Lanham, MD: Lexington Books, 2012), 143–154.

14. Ibid.

15. Mark D. West, *Secrets, Sex, and Spectacle: The Rules of Scandal in Japan and the United States* (Chicago: The University of Chicago Press, 2006).

16. Ibid.; John B. Thompson, *The Media and Modernity: A Social Theory of the Media* (Redwood City, CA: Stanford University Press, 1995); Apostolidis and Williams, *Public Affairs*.

17. Thompson, *The Media and Modernity*.

18. Elizabeth S. Bird, *The Audience in Everyday Life: Living in a Media World* (New York: Routledge, 2003).

19. West, *Secrets, Sex*.

20. Bird, *The Audience*.

21. Mandell, "'Stand by Your Man.'"

22. Ann Swidler, *Talk of Love: How Culture Matters* (Chicago: University of Chicago Press, 2001); Robert O. Blood, *Marriage* (New York: Free Press, 1978); Robert O. Blood and Donald M. Wolfe, *Husbands and Wives: The Dynamics of Married Living* (New York: Free Press, 1960); J. Richard Udry, *The Social Context of Marriage* (Philadelphia: Lippincott, 1971).

23. Udry, *The Social Context of Marriage*.

24. Ibid., 20.

25. Mandell, "'Stand by Your Man.'"

26. Swidler, *Talk of Love*; Blood, *Marriage*; Blood and Wolfe, *Husbands and Wives*; Udry, *The Social Context of Marriage*; Miriam M. Johnson, *Strong Mothers, Weak Wives: The Search for Gender Equality* (Berkeley: University of California Press, 1988).

27. Sally Foreman and Rudi Dallos, "Inequalities of Power and Sexual Problems," *Journal of Family Therapy* 14 (1992): 349–369.

28. Foreman and Dallos, "Inequalities of Power"; West and Zimmerman, "Doing Difference"; Maushart, *Wifework*; Johnson, *Strong Mothers*; Kathleen Hall Jamieson, *Beyond the Double Bind: Women and Leadership* (New York: Oxford University Press, 1995).

29. Joshua Gamson, Mark West, personal communication, April 21, 2010.

30. Apostolidis and Williams, *Public Affairs*.

31. David Crary, "More Women in Political Spotlight But Gap Remains," *Associated Press*, August 25, 2010; Jennifer Lawless, "Why More Women Don't Hold Office," *AFLCIO.com*, September 1, 2010.

32. Lane Wallace, "The Sex Difference in Sex Scandals," *TheAtlantic.com*, May 19, 2011, http://www.theatlantic.com/national/archive/2011/05/the-sex -difference-in-sex-scandals/239155/.

33. Joe Garofoli, "Why Do Political Wives Stand By Their Men?," *San Francisco Chronicle*, March 12, 2008.

34. Mike Celizic, "Why Wives Stand by Scandal-Stained Husbands," *Today*, March 11, 2008, http://today.msnbc.msn.com/id/23572178.

35. Anushay Hossain, "Today's Politician's Wife Is No Longer Standing by Her Man," *Huffington Post*, December 1, 2009.

36. Rachael Larimore, "Is There Such a Thing as the Perfect Political Wife?," *Slate*, January 22, 2010.

37. Betty Houchin Winfield and Barbara Friedman, "Gender Politics: New Coverage of the Candidates' Wives in Campaign 2000," *Journalism & Mass Communications Quarterly* 80, no. 3 (2003): 548–566; J. Swan, "Newspaper Coverage of Cindy McCain and Michelle Obama in the 2008 Presidential Election," *Media Report to Women* 38, no. 2 (Spring 2010): 6–20.

38. Asa Kroon Lundell and Mats Ekström, "The Complex Visual Gendering of Political Women in the Press," *Journalism Studies* 9, no. 6 (2008): 891.

39. Betty Houchin Winfield, "The Making of an Image: Hillary Rodham Clinton and American Journalists," *Political Communication* 14, no. 2 (1997): 241–253.

40. Winfield, "The Making of an Image," 241.

41. Winfield and Friedman, "Gender Politics."

42. Ibid., 558.

43. Swan, "Newspaper Coverage."

44. Ibid.

45. Ibid.

46. Lori Montalbano-Phelps, "Performing Politics: Media Aesthetics for Women in Political Campaigns," in *Women and the Media: Diverse Perspective*,

ed. Theresa Carilli and Jane Campbell (Toronto: University Press of America, 2005), 184–198; Diana B. Carlin and Kelly L. Winfrey, "Have You Come a Long Way, Baby? Hillary Clinton, Sarah Palin, and Sexism in 2008 Campaign Coverage," *Communication Studies* 60, no. 4 (2009): 326–343.

47. Carlin and Winfrey, "Have You Come"; James Devitt, "Framing Gender on the Campaign Trail: Female Gubernatorial Candidates and the Press," *Journalism & Mass Communication Quarterly* 79, no. 2 (2002): 445–463.

48. Lundell and Ekström, "The Complex Visual Gendering."

49. Jamieson, *Beyond the Double Bind*; Carlin and Winfrey, "Have You Come"; Lawless, "Why More Women."

50. Jamieson, *Beyond the Double Bind*.

51. Ibid., 23.

52. Ibid., 22.

53. Ibid.

54. Melissa Deem, "Scandal, Heteronormative Culture, and the Disciplining of Feminism," *Review and Criticism* 16, no. 1 (2009): 88.

55. Carlin and Winfrey, "Have You Come."

56. Ibid., 330.

57. Devitt, "Framing Gender"; Lesa Hatley Major and Renita Coleman, "The Intersection of Race and Gender in Election Coverage: What Happens When the Candidates Don't Fit the Stereotypes?," *Howard Journal of Communications* 19 (2008): 315–333.

58. Devitt, "Framing Gender."

59. Ibid.

60. Hanna Papanek, "Men, Women, and Work: Reflections on the Two-Person Career," *American Journal of Sociology* 78, no. 4 (1973): 852–872.

61. Ibid., 853.

62. John B. Thompson, *Political Scandal: Power and Visibility in the Media Age* (Malden, MA: Blackwell, 2000).

63. Papanek, "Men, Women, and Work."

64. Ibid., 862.

65. Peter L. Berger and Thomas Luckmann, *The Social Construction of Reality: A Treatise in the Sociology of Knowledge* (Garden City, NY: Anchor Books, 1967).

66. Todd Gitlin, *The Whole World Is Watching: Mass Media in the Making and Unmaking of the New Left* (Berkeley: University of California Press, 2003); Stuart Hall, "The Whites of Their Eyes: Racist Ideologies and the Media," in *Gender, Race, and Class in Media*, ed. Gail Dines and Jean M. Humez (Thousand Oaks, CA: Sage, 1995), 18–22; Antonio Gramsci, "(i) History of the Subaltern Classes; (ii) The Concept of 'Ideology'; (iii) Cultural Themes: Ideological Material," in *Media and Cultural Studies*, ed. Meenakshi Gigi Durham and Douglas M. Kellner (Malden, MA: Blackwell, 2006), 13–17.

67. Andrew Kohut, Carroll Doherty, Michael Dimock, and Scott Keeter, "Ideological News Sources: Who Watches and Why," *Pew Research Center*, September 12, 2010, http://www.people-press.org/files/legacy-pdf/652.pdf.

68. "Top news sites," *Alexa.com*, n.d., http://www.alexa.com/topsites/category/Top/News.

69. Kathy Charmaz, *Constructing Grounded Theory: A Practical Guide through Qualitative Analysis* (Thousand Oaks, CA: Sage, 2006), 46.

70. Ibid.

71. Alan McKee, *Textual Analysis: A Beginner's Guide* (Thousand Oaks, CA: Sage, 2003).

72. Barney G. Glaser, *The Grounded Theory Perspective: Conceptualization Contrasted with Description* (Mill Valley, CA: Sociology Press, 2001), 191.

73. McKee, *Textual Analysis*.

74. Ibid.

75. Andy Barr, "Sanford on Vacation, This Time with Wife," *Politico*, July 15, 2009, http://www.politico.com/news/stories/0709/24975.html; Monica Davey, "In Storm, Governor's Wife Is Hurt but Unbowed," *New York Times*, A1, June 27, 2009; Philip Rucker, "In S.C., the Governor's Wife Is 'the Hero in the Story,'" *Washington Post*, June 29, 2009, http://www.washingtonpost.com/wpdyn/content/article/2009/06/28/AR2009062802436.html; Philip Rucker, "Hiking the High Road," *Washington Post*, C1; A3, December 12, 2009.

76. "5 Key Factors," *State* (Columbia, SC), 10, December 20, 2009; Roddie Burris, John O'Connor, and Gina Smith, "How Sanford Avoided Impeachment," *State*, 1, December 20, 2009; John O'Connor, "Why Tide Against Sanford Ebbed," *State*, 1, July 12, 2009; Shaila Dewan, "Sanford's Wife Moves Family Out of Governor's Mansion," *New York Times*, A9, August 8, 2009.

77. Stuart Hall, "Encoding/Decoding," in *Media and Cultural Studies*, ed. Meenakshi Gigi Durham and Douglas M. Kellner (Malden, MA: Blackwell, 2006), 163–173.

78. Stuart Hall, "The Whites of Their Eyes: Racist Ideologies and the Media," in *Gender, Race, and Class in Media*, ed. Gail Dines and Jean M. Humez (Thousand Oaks, CA: Sage, 1995), 18–22.

79. Barthes, "Operation Margarine."

80. Emma Rosenblum, "Scenes from a Marriage," *New York Magazine*, September 13, 2009, http://nymag.com/arts/tv/profiles/58990/.

81. Berger and Thomas Luckmann, *The Social Construction of Reality*.

82. Deem, "Scandal, Heteronormative Culture."

83. Monica Hesse, "In One Man's Fall, Bruises for All," *Washington Post*, C1, March 15, 2008.

84. Ibid.

85. Jan Hoffman, "Public Infidelity, Private Debate: Not My Husband (Right?)," *New York Times*, March 16, 2008, Style, 1.

86. Ibid.

87. Gina Masullo Chen, Hinda Mandell, and John M. Martin, "Political-Sex Scandal News Stories and Personal Fear of Betrayal: An Online Experiment," manuscript submitted for publication, 2016.

88. Hoffman, "Public Infidelity."

89. S. Morris, "Keep Wives Out of Public Confessionals," *Times Union* (Albany, NY), A7, March 15, 2008.

90. Kristi Gustafson, "First Comes Love and Now Forgiveness?," *Times Union*, G16, March 16, 2008.

91. Ruth Marcus, "Spitzer's Tragic Flaw," *Washington Post*, A19, March 12, 2008; Leslie Kaufman, "Political Wife's Hard Line Strikes Chord," *New York Times*, A12, June 27, 2009; Roger Cohen, "Affairs of the Hearth," *Washington Post*, A17, February 9, 2010; Lisa Bloom, "Elin Woods' Absence Speaks Volume," *CNN.com*, February 22, 2010, http://www.cnn.com/2010/OPINION/02/19/bloom.woods.elin/.

92. Ruth Marcus, "Jenny Sanford, Role Model," *Washington Post*, A21, July 1, 2009.

93. Ibid.

94. Leslie Kaufman, "Political Wife's Hard Line Strikes Chord," *New York Times*, A12, June 27, 2009.

95. Robin Givhan, "In Hubby's Time of Trouble She Can't Be Bothered," *Washington Post*, E1, July 5, 2009; Marcus, "Jenny Sanford, Role Model"; Rucker, "In S.C., the Governor's Wife"; Davey, "In Storm, Governor's Wife"; Seanna Adcox, "Jenny Sanford Breaks Pattern of Betrayed," *State*, 9, June 26, 2009; Cohen, "Affairs of the Hearth"; Jessica Ravitz, "Silent No More, Wives Go Public about Their Husbands' Affairs," *CNN.com*, February 4, 2010, http://www.cnn.com/2010/LIVING/02/04/famous.wives.infidelity/.

96. Marcus, "Jenny Sanford, Role Model"; Robin Givhan, "In Hubby's Time of Trouble She Can't Be Bothered"; Philip Rucker and Manuel Roig-Franzia, "S.C. Gov. Sanford Admits to Affair," *Washington Post*, A1, June 25, 2009.

97. Kaufman, "Political Wife's Hard Line"; Adcox, "Jenny Sanford Breaks Pattern."

98. Kaufman, "Political Wife's Hard Line."

99. Ibid.

100. Marcus, "Jenny Sanford, Role Model."

101. Cohen, "Affairs of the Hearth."

102. Ibid.

103. Ibid.

104. Davey, "In Storm, Governor's Wife."

105. Ibid.

106. Givhan, "In Hubby's Time of Trouble She Can't Be Bothered."

107. Ibid.

108. Marcus, "Jenny Sanford, Role Model."

109. Rucker, "In S.C."

110. Rucker, "Hiking the High Road."

111. Adcox, "Jenny Sanford Breaks Pattern of Betrayed."

112. Maureen Dowd, "Rules of the Wronged," *New York Times*, June 30, 2009, A33.

113. J. Herlong, "Staying True . . . To What?," *State*, 7, February 8, 2010.

114. Dowd, "Rules of the Wronged."

115. Bird, *The Audience.*

116. Berger and Luckmann, *The Social Construction of Reality.*

117. Thompson, *The Media and Modernity*; Lull and Hinerman, *Media Scandals*; Bird, *The Audience*; Apostolidis and Williams, *Public Affairs.*

118. Bird, *The Audience.*

119. Thompson, *The Media and Modernity.*

120. Chen et al., "Vicariously Rejected"; Bird, *The Audience.*

121. Berger and Luckmann, *The Social Construction of Reality.*

122. Papanek, "Men, Women, and Work."

123. Deem, "Scandal, Heteronormative Culture."

124. Ibid., 88.

125. Ibid.

126. Elizabeth Kolbert, "The Tyranny of High Expectations," in *30 Ways of Looking at Hillary*, ed. Susan Morrison (New York: HarperCollins, 2008), 11.

127. Deem, "Scandal, Heteronormative Culture."

128. Carlin and Winfrey, "Have You Come"; Lawless, "Why More Women Don't Hold Office"; Deem, "Scandal, Heteronormative Culture"; Kolbert, "The Tyranny."

129. Adrianna Kezar, "Transformational Elite Interviews: Principles and Problems," *Qualitative Inquiry* 9, no. 3 (2003): 395–415.

CHAPTER 6

1. Chris Churchill, "Albany Needs Political Corruption Museum," *Times Union* (Albany, NY), August 1, 2013, http://www.timesunion.com/local/article/Albany-needs-political-corruption-museum-4699630.php.

2. Interview with assemblyman, July 2, 2015.

3. "A Decade of Albany Sex Scandals," *Buffalo (NY) News*, December 20, 2013, http://www.buffalonews.com/city-region/albany-politics/a-decade-of-albany-sex-scandals-20131220.

4. Anne M. O'Leary-Kelly, Paul Tiedt, and Lynn Bowes Sperry, "Answering Accountability Questions in Sexual Harassment: Insights Regarding Harassers, Targets, and Observers," *Human Resource Management Review* 14, no. 1 (2004): 85–106.

5. Joan Acker, "Hierarchies, Jobs, Bodies: A Theory of Gendered Organizations," *Gender & Society* 4, no. 2 (1990): 139.

6. Ari Adut, *On Scandal: Moral Disturbances in Society, Politics, and Art* (Cambridge: Cambridge University Press, 2008).

7. CBS News, "New York Assembly Pays 205K to Firm for Sexual Harassment Reform, Probes," *CBS New York*, February 25, 2014, http://newyork.cbslocal.com/2014/02/25/new-york-assembly-pays-205k-to-firm-for-sexual-harassment-reform-probes/.

8. Kenneth Lovett, "Exclusive: Hotline Launched for State Government Staffers to Report Sexual Harassment and Other Complaints," *New York Daily News*,

June 23, 2014, sec. A, http://www.nydailynews.com/new-york/harass-hotline
-set-state-government-workers-article-1.1839917.

9. Denise Jewell Gee, "Wozniak Shattered the Wrong Glass Ceiling," *Buffalo News*, March 20, 2016, http://www.buffalonews.com/columns/denise-jewell-gee
/wozniak-shattered-the-wrong-glass-ceiling-20160320.

10. Adut, *On Scandal*.

11. Ibid., 22.

12. Danny Hakim, "Lawmaker Is Censured over Sexual Harassment," *New York Times*, August 24, 2012, http://www.nytimes.com/2012/08/25/nyregion/assemblyman
-vito-lopez-censured-for-sexual-harassment.html.

13. Danny Hakim, "Lopez Declines to Testify on Allegations That He Sexually Harassed Aides," *New York Times*, sec. A, January 24, 2013.

14. Thomas Kaplan and Jesse McKinley, "State Legislator Facing Expulsion Says He'll Resign," *New York Times*, May 18, 2013, http://www.nytimes
.com/2013/05/18/nyregion/vito-lopez-facing-possible-expulsion-says-hell-resign
.html?_r=0.

15. Danny Hakim and Thomas Kaplan, "Lopez Is Said to Be Fined over Sexual Abuse," *New York Times*, June 4, 2013, http://www.nytimes.com/2013/06/05
/nyregion/vito-lopez-said-to-face-330000-fine-for-sexual-abuse.html.

16. Danny Hakim, "Assembly Lawyer to Step Down over Failure to Investigate Sex Harassment Claims," *New York Times*, sec. B, July 23, 2013, http://www
.nytimes.com/2013/07/24/nyregion/assembly-speaker-removing-lawyer-citing
-ignored-claims-of-sexual-harassment.html.

17. Ibid.

18. James M. Odato, "New Sex Case Ends Career of Silver Aide," *Times Union*, July 25, 2013, http://www.timesunion.com/news/article/New-sex-case-ends-career
-of-Silver-aide-4683854.php.

19. Jill Colvin, "Micah Kellner Punished after Assembly Investigates Harassment Allegations," *Observer*, December 30, 2013, http://observer.com/2013/12
/micah-kellner-punished-after-assembly-investigates-harassment-allegations/.

20. Kenneth Lovett, "Micah Kellner Raises Possibility of Suing over Harassment Sanctions," *New York Daily News*, December 2, 2014, sec. B, http://www
.nydailynews.com/blogs/dailypolitics/micah-kellner-hints-lawsuit-assembly
-blog-entry-1.2030253.

21. Thomas Kaplan, "Assemblyman to Resign over Harassment Claims," *New York Times*, January 12, 2014.

22. HuffPost New York, "Here's Assemblyman Dennis Gabryszak Pretending to Get Oral Sex in Video Allegedly Sent to Staffers," *HuffPost New York*, January 15, 2014, http://www.huffingtonpost.com/2014/01/15/dennis-gabryszak_n_4602918
.html.

23. Center for American Women and Politics, "Women in State Legislatures 2014," Eagleton Institute of Politics, Rutgers University, 2014, http://www.cawp
.rutgers.edu/sites/default/files/resources/stleg2014.pdf.

24. When I raised New York's ranking with an interview subject, she said, "The . . . number of women in a legislature is far more closely correlated with how much legislators are paid. So where it's $2,000 a year, [it's] loaded with women." New York State legislators are paid $79,500 annually plus a per diem. In Colorado, they are paid $30,000 plus a per diem (National Conference of State Legislators, 2014).

25. Goldstein, "Getting in the Door."

26. Peabody et al., "Interviewing Political Elites"; Aberbach and Rockman, "Conducting and Coding"; Goldstein, "Getting in the Door."

27. McDowell, "Elites in the City of London"; Harvey, "Strategies for Conducting."

28. Hinda Mandell, "She Legislates, He Scandalizes: Reenvisioning the Impact of Political Sex Scandals on Assemblywomen in New York," *Journal of Feminist Scholarship* 9 (Fall 2015): 30.

29. "State Fact Sheet—New York," Eagleton Institute of Politics, Rutgers University, http://www.cawp.rutgers.edu/state_fact_sheets/ny.

30. The term "assembly member" is commonly truncated to "member" by both assembly members and their staff.

31. D. Jean Clandinin, "Narrative Inquiry: A Methodology for Studying Lived Experience," *Research Studies in Music Education* 27, no. 1 (2006): 44–54.

32. F. Michael Connelly and Jean D. Clandinin, "Narrative Inquiry," in *Handbook of Contemporary Methods in Education Research*, ed. J. L. Green, G. Camilli, and P. Elmore, 3rd ed. (Mahwah, NJ: Erlbaum, 2006), 477.

33. Clandinin, "Narrative Inquiry," 51.

34. Ibid., 41.

35. Joanne Martin, "Deconstructing Organizational Taboos: The Suppression of Gender Conflict in Organizations," *Organization Science* 1, no. 4 (1990): 339–359.

36. Ibid., 355.

37. Ibid., 340.

38. Ibid.

39. Ibid., 342.

40. The Associated Press, "Sex Scandals Highlight Dearth of Women in Politics," June 19, 2011, http://www.mlive.com/news/usworld/index.ssf/2011/06/sex_scandals_highlight_dearth.html.

41. Interview with assemblywoman, June 9, 2015.

42. Interview with assemblywoman, July 8, 2015.

43. Interview with assemblywoman, August 20, 2015.

44. Interview with assemblywoman, July 8, 2015.

45. Interview with assemblywoman, June 8, 2015.

46. Interview with assemblywoman, May 2014.

47. Interview with assemblywoman, May 2014.

48. Interview with assemblywoman, August 2014.

49. Interview with assemblywoman, May 2014.

50. Interview with assemblywoman, June 8, 2015.

51. Interview with assemblyman, June 9, 2015.

52. Interview with assemblyman, July 2, 2015.

53. Interview with assemblyman, June 4, 2015.

54. Interview with assemblyman, July 2, 2015.

55. Interview with assemblyman, August 19, 2015.

56. Interview with assemblyman, July 9, 2015.

57. Interview with assemblyman, June 9, 2015.

58. Interview with assemblyman, June 11, 2015.

59. Interview with assemblyman, June 9, 2015.

60. Martin, "Deconstructing Organizational Taboos," 355.

61. Ibid.

62. Ibid.

63. Ibid., 350.

64. Ibid., 355.

65. Jack Levin and Arnold Arluke, "An Exploratory Analysis of Sex Differences in Gossip," *Sex Roles* 12, no. 3-4 (1985): 281–286.

66. "The New York State Assembly Policy Prohibiting Harassment, Discrimination, and Retaliation," issued August 16, 1984, 6; reissued May 5, 2015, public record.

67. "Men Against Abuse Now," Stanford University, http://web.stanford.edu/group/maan/cgi-bin/?page_id=297.

68. Catherine Burr, "False Allegations of Sexual Harassment: Misunderstandings and Realities," *Academic Matters*, October-November 2011, http://www.academicmatters.ca/2011/10/false-allegations-of-sexual-harassment-misunderstandings-and-realities/.

69. I did not clarify whether the women who drag the assemblyman into the bathroom are staff or assemblywomen.

70. Katherine E. Smith, "Problematising Power Relations in 'Elite' Interviews," *Geoforum* 37, no. 4 (2006): 643–653.

71. Ibid., 2106.

CHAPTER 7

1. The gendered pronoun is used intentionally since the cultural script nearly always finds a male politician caught in sexual scandal, and his spouse is most always, in these instances, a woman.

2. Joan Walsh, "Why David Vitter Matters," *Salon*, July 16, 2007, http://www.salon.com/2007/07/16/vitter_10/.

3. Tim Mahoney's predecessor in office, former Florida congressman Mark Foley, resigned in disgrace in 2006 after sending sexually explicit text messages to congressional pages.

4. Catherine Rampell, "U.S. Women on the Rise as Family Breadwinner," *New York Times*, May 29, 2013, http://www.nytimes.com/2013/05/30/business /economy/women-as-family-breadwinner-on-the-rise-study-says.html?_r=0.

5. Videos of the three press conferences shown to respondents can be accessed here: Eliot Spitzer (March 2008), http://www.youtube.com/watch ?v=3TIOP5-8_-o; Mark Sanford (June 2009), http://www.youtube.com/watch ?v=uLUTvOo5vR8; Anthony Weiner (July 2013), http://www.youtube.com /watch?v=mCzdpkokwCQ.

6. Hinda Mandell, "Political Wives, Scandal, and the Double Bind: Press Construction of Silda Spitzer and Jenny Sanford Through a Gendered Lens," *Women's Studies in Communication* 38, no. 1 (1998): 57–77.

7. Myra MacPherson, *Power Lovers: An Intimate Look at Politicians and Their Marriages* (New York: Putnam and Thompson, 1975); John B. Thompson, *The Media and Modernity: A Social Theory of the Media* (Redwood City, CA: Stanford University Press, 1995); John B. Thompson, *Political Scandal: Power and Visibility in the Media Age* (London: Polity, 2000).

8. MacPherson, *Power Lovers.*

9. Elizabeth Edwards, the late and former wife of presidential candidate John Edwards, reportedly knew that her husband was carrying on an affair with his campaign videographer, Rielle Hunter, which ultimately produced a child born in 2008. Elizabeth learned of the affair in 2006, during his 2008 presidential campaign, when her breast cancer was in remission. After Elizabeth Edwards found out—but before the affair became public—John Edwards continued to campaign for the presidency. When Elizabeth Edwards learned that her husband continued his sexual relationship with Rielle Hunter in 2007, her breast cancer now returning as stage IV, she became enraged. News reports cite staffers describing a scene where Elizabeth Edwards "'collapsed in a ball' in an airport parking lot" where she tore off her shirt and bra, her husband standing nearby. This startling image, far from any podium at a press conference, stands in stark contrast to the scripted, contained imagery of political wives who stand next to husbands at their public scandal announcements. Information according to: "John Edwards Fast Facts," *CNN.com*, May 24, 2015, http://www.cnn.com/2013/06/14/us/john -edwards-fast-facts/; James Hill and Beth Loyd, "John Edwards' Wife Tore off Her Shirt and Collapsed Over His Affair," *ABC News*, May 2, 2012, http://abcnews .go.com/US/john-edwards-wife-tore-off-shirt-collapsed-affair/story?id=16259328.

10. P. David Marshall, *Celebrity and Power: Fame in Contemporary Culture* (Minneapolis: University of Minnesota Press, 1997).

11. Susan Maushart, *Wifework: What Marriage Really Means for Women* (New York: Bloomsbury, 2001).

12. Ibid., 4.

13. Hinda Mandell, "'Stand by Your Man' Revisited: Political Wives and Scandal," in *Media Depictions of Women as Brides, Wives, and Mothers*, ed. Alena A. Ruggerio (Lanham, MD: Lexington Books, 2012), 143–154.

14. Christine Delphy, *Close to Home: A Materialist Analysis of Women's Oppression* (London: Hutchinson, 1984).

15. Ibid., 59.

16. Ibid., 60.

17. Janet Finch, *Married to the Job: Wives' Incorporation in Men's Work* (Boston: Allen and Unwin, 1983).

18. Hanna Papanek, "Men, Women, and Work: Reflections on the Two-Person Career," *American Journal of Sociology* 78, no. 4 (1973): 852–872.

19. Tammy Wynette, "Stand by Your Man," http://www.azlyrics.com/lyrics /tammywynette/standbyyourman.html.

20. Interview with a New York State assemblywoman, granted anonymity, July 8, 2015.

21. Kelly Norris Martin and Hinda Mandell, "Faces of Political Sex Scandal: Investigating Pathways to Penance, Remedy and Resolution through Iconic Scandal," *Visual Communication Quarterly* 21, no. 4 (2014): 236–247.

22. David Saltonstall, "South Carolina Gov. Mark Sanford: Mistress Is 'Soul Mate,' But I Want to Fall Back in Love with Wife," *New York Daily News*, June 30, 2009, http://www.nydailynews.com/news/politics/south-carolina-gov-mark -sanford-mistress-soul-mate-fall-back-love-wife-article-1.379260.

23. "Mark Sanford's Press Briefing," *New York Times*, June 24, 2009, http:// www.nytimes.com/2009/06/24/us/24text-sanford.html?pagewanted=all.

24. Ruth Marcus, "Jenny Sanford, Role Model," *Washington Post*, July 2, 2009.

25. Mandell, "Political Wives, Scandal, and the Double Bind."

26. Chris Cillizza, "Anthony Weiner: Can't Say with 'Certitude' Lewd Image Isn't Me," *Washington Post*, http://www.washingtonpost.com/blogs/the-fix/post /anthony-weiner-cant-say-with-certitude-lewd-image-isnt-me/2011/06/01 /AGoCGgGH_blog.html.

27. Thompson, *Political Scandal*, 245.

28. Ibid., 95.

29. Thompson, *The Media and Modernity*.

30. Thompson, *Political Scandal*, 40.

31. Ibid.

32. Ibid., 112.

33. Ibid., 41.

34. Richard Sennett, *The Fall of Public Man* (New York: W. W. Norton, 1977), 25.

35. Ibid.

36. Ibid., 26.

37. Ibid., 24.

38. Ibid., 283.

39. Ibid., 27.

40. Joshua Meyrowitz, *No Sense of Place: The Impact of Electronic Media on Social Behavior* (New York: Oxford University Press, 1985), 311.

41. Ibid.

42. Christopher Meyers, "Justifying Journalistic Harms: Right to Know vs. Interest in Knowing," *Journal of Mass Media Ethics* 8, no. 3 (1993).

43. Adam J. Berinsky, Gregory A. Huber, and Gabriel S. Lenz, "Using Mechanical Turk as a Subject Recruitment Tool for Experimental Research," June 20, 2011, 1–2, http://web.mit.edu/berinsky/www/files/MT.pdf.

44. Barney G. Glaser and Anselm L. Strauss, "The Constant Comparative Method of Qualitative Analysis," *Social Problems* 12, no. 4 (1965): 436–445.

45. To maintain the authenticity of the respondents' comments, they are presented "as is," which includes—in some instances, misspellings or other grammatical inconsistences.

46. Thompson, *Political Scandal*, 103.

47. Ibid., 105.

48. Ibid., 112.

49. Ibid., 112–113.

50. Ibid., 126.

51. Jean Seaton, "Public, Private and the Media," *Political Quarterly* 74, no. 2 (2003): 175.

52. Bartosz W. Wojdynski and Daniel Riffe, "What Kind of Media, and When? Public Opinion about Press Coverage of Politicians' Private Lives," *Journal of Mass Media Ethics* 26, no. 3 (2011): 214.

53. Thompson, *The Media and Modernity*, 133–134; and Meyrowitz, *No Sense of Place*, 322.

54. P. David Marshall, *Celebrity and Power: Fame in Contemporary Culture* (Minneapolis: University of Minnesota Press, 1997), 218.

55. Ibid.

56. Ibid., 219.

57. Ibid., 218–219.

58. Ibid., 204.

CHAPTER 8

1. Gloria Anzaldúa, *Borderlands: La Frontera* (San Francisco: Aunt Lute Books, 1999), 91.

2. Hinda Mandell, "Political Wives and Scandal: Reading Agency in Silence at Press Conferences," *Catalan Journal of Communication and Cultural Studies* 4, no. 2 (2012): 203–220.

3. Janice Radway, "Identifying Ideological Seams: Mass Culture, Analytical Method, and Political Practice," *Communication* 9, no. 1 (1986): 93–123.

4. Ibid., 96.

5. Ibid., 108.

6. Ibid., 110.

7. Mike Celizic, "Why Wives Stand by Scandal-Stained Husbands," *Today*, March 11, 2008, http://today.msnbc.msn.com/id/23572178; Frank Cerabino, "Not Cool to Use Your Jilted Wife as an Apology Prop," *Palm Beach (FL) Post*,

October 15, 2008; Kathleen Deveny, "Scorned: A User's Manual," *Newsweek*, June 25, 2009; Joe Garofoli, "Why Do Political Wives Stand by Their Men?," *San Francisco Chronicle*, March 12, 2008, http://articles.sfgate.com/2008-03-12 /news/17165937_1_silda-wall-spitzer-political-theater-state-employee; Jennifer Gish and Kristi Gustafson, "Stand by Her Man? Capital Region Responds," *Times Union* (Albany, NY), March 12, 2008.

8. The following are examples of wives who did not attend their husband's press conference: Darlene Ensign in 2009, wife of former Nevada senator John Ensign; Jenny Sanford, now ex-wife of former South Carolina governor Mark Sanford in 2009; Huma Abedin, wife of former New York congressman Anthony Weiner in 2011.

9. Hinda Mandell, "'Stand by Your Man' Revisited: Political Wives and Scandal," in *Media Depictions of Women as Brides, Wives, and Mothers*, ed. Alena A. Ruggerio (Lanham, MD: Lexington Books, 2012), 143–154.

10. John B. Thompson, *The Media and Modernity: A Social Theory of the Media* (Redwood City, CA: Stanford University Press, 1995).

11. Ibid.

12. Paul Grondahl, "A Woman Betrayed with a Future to Ponder," *Times Union*, March 13, 2008; Kristi Gustafson, "First Comes Love and Now Forgiveness?," *Times Union*, March 16, 2008. Please see Mandell, "'Stand by Your Man,'" for an analysis of news coverage.

13. Ruth Marcus, "Jenny Sanford, Role Model," *Washington Post*, July 1, 2009.

14. Jenny Sanford, *Staying True* (New York: Ballantine Books, 2010).

15. "Transcript of Weiner's Statement Confessing to Twitter Photo, Past Relationships," *NBCNewYork.com*, June 7, 2011, accessed September 13, 2015, http:// www.nbcnewyork.com/news/local/Weiner-Admits-Confesses-Photo-Twitter -Relationships-123268493.html.

16. "Naughty" might appear to be a salty word choice for a recruitment flyer, but I was motivated to capture the attention of potential participants and to accurately portray the nature of the research, which deals with sexual indiscretions.

17. Shulamit Reinharz and Lynn Davidman, *Feminist Methods in Social Research* (New York: Oxford University Press, 1992), 41.

18. Steinar Kvale, *InterViews: An Introduction to Qualitative Research Interviewing* (Thousand Oaks, CA: Sage, 1996).

19. Hennie Boeije, "A Purposeful Approach to the Constant Comparative Method in the Analysis of Qualitative Interviews," *Quality and Quantity* 36, no. 4 (2002): 391–409.

20. Interview with Robert, April 8, 2015.

21. Interview with Joyce, July 6, 2014.

22. Ibid.

23. Ibid.

24. Ibid.

25. Interview with Carl, May 27, 2015.

26. Ibid.

27. Interview with Sarah, May 30, 2014.

28. Interview with Freddy, May 12, 2015.
29. Ibid.
30. Interview with Gail, July 1, 2014.
31. Ibid.
32. Gail, e-mail message to author, September 1, 2015.
33. Interview with Jim, March 20, 2015.
34. Ibid.
35. Interview with Susan, July 27, 2014.
36. Interview with Ellis, March 16, 2015.
37. Ibid.
38. Interview with Bailee, July 29, 2014.
39. Interview with Ellis, March 16, 2015.
40. Interview with Bailee, July 29, 2014.
41. Ibid.
42. Interview with John, March 22, 2015.
43. Ibid.
44. Interview with Lynn, June 27, 2014.
45. Ibid.
46. Interview with Bruce, April 13, 2015.
47. Interview with Maeghan, April 8, 2015.
48. Ibid.
49. Ibid.
50. Ibid.
51. Interview with Hector, May 30, 2015.
52. Interview with Kelly, May 30, 2015.
53. Ibid.
54. Ibid.
55. Ibid.
56. Harold, e-mail message to author, August 27, 2015.
57. Interview with Harold, March 17, 2015.
58. Ibid.
59. Ibid.
60. Interview with Mila, June 23, 2014.
61. Ibid.
62. Interview with Paul, March 14, 2015.
63. Ibid.
64. Interview with Olivia, June 24, 2014.
65. Interview with Carl, May 27, 2015.
66. Interview with Bruce, April 13, 2015.
67. Ibid.
68. Interview with Robert, April 8, 2015.
69. Ibid.
70. Interview with Freddy, May 12, 2015.
71. Interview with Ellis, March 16, 2015.
72. Interview with Zach, March 17, 2015.

73. Interview with Bailee, July 29, 2014.

74. Maureen Dowd, "Rules of the Wronged," *New York Times*, June 30, 2009, A33.

75. Interview with Lynn, June 27, 2014.

76. Ibid.

77. Interview with Bailee, July 29, 2014.

78. Interview with Lynn, June 27, 2014.

79. Interview with Paul, March 14, 2015.

80. Interview with Olivia, June 24, 2014.

81. Interview with Harold, March 17, 2015.

82. Interview with Mila, June 23, 2014.

83. Interview with Maeghan, April 8, 2015.

84. Interview with Gail, July 1, 2014.

85. Interview with Susan, July 27, 2014.

86. Interview with Olivia, June 24, 2014.

87. Interview with Kelly, May 30, 2015.

88. Interview with Mila, June 23, 2014.

89. Interview with Harold, March 17, 2015.

90. Interview with Freddy, May 12, 2015.

91. Interview with Joyce, July 6, 2014.

92. Ibid.

93. Susan Adams, "Is Huma Abedin Doing the Right Thing?," *Forbes.com*, July 25, 2013, http://www.forbes.com/sites/susanadams/2013/07/25/is-huma-abedin-doing-the-right-thing/; Juli Weiner, "Anthony Weiner and Huma Abedin Give Most Awkward Sext-Splanatory Press Conference in Human History," *VanityFair.com*, July 23, 2013, http://www.vanityfair.com/online/daily/2013/07/anthony-weiner-and-huma-abedin-give-most-awkward-sext-splanatory-press-conference-in-human-history; Lisa Bloom, "The Public Humiliation of Huma Abedin," *CNN.com*, July 25, 2013, http://www.cnn.com/2013/07/24/opinion/bloom-huma-political-wives/index.html.

94. Interview with Sarah, May 30, 2014.

95. Interview with Mila, June 23, 2014.

96. Interview with Susan, July 27, 2014.

97. Interview with Mila, June 23, 2014.

98. Interview with Jim, March 20, 2015.

99. Interview with Maeghan, April 8, 2015.

100. Interview with Harold, March 17, 2015.

101. Interview with Carl, May 27, 2015.

102. Interview with Sarah, May 30, 2014.

103. Barry Brummet, *A Rhetoric of Style* (Carbondale: Southern Illinois University Press, 2008), 5.

104. Eva Flicker, "Fashionable (Dis-)order in Politics: Gender, Power and the Dilemma of the Suit," *International Journal of Media and Cultural Politics* 9, no. 2 (2013): 207.

105. Interview with Sarah, May 30, 2014.

106. Flicker, "Fashionable (Dis-)order," 213.

107. Brummett, *A Rhetoric of Style*, 12.

108. Ibid., 43.

109. Ibid.

110. Mandell, "'Stand by Your Man.'"

111. Anthony Giddens, *Modernity and Self-Identity: Self and Society in the Late Modern Age* (Cambridge: Polity Press, 1991), 53.

112. Giddens, *Modernity and Self-Identity*, 54.

113. John Berger, *Ways of Seeing* (New York: Penguin, 1972), 7.

114. Stuart Hall, "Encoding/Decoding," in *Media and Cultural Studies*, ed. Meenakshi Gigi Durham and Douglas M. Kellner (Malden, MA: Blackwell, 2006), 163–173.

115. Berger, *Ways of Seeing*, 45.

116. Ibid.

117. Ibid., 46.

118. Janice Radway, "Identifying Ideological Seams: Mass Culture, Analytical Method, and Political Practice," *Communication* 9, no. 1 (1986): 93–123.

119. Ibid., 114.

120. One husband said he couldn't answer which wife he felt did the right thing, and a second husband voted for both Huma Abedin and Jenny Sanford.

121. Marcus, "Jenny Sanford, Role Model."

122. Melissa Deem, "Scandal, Heteronormative Culture, and the Disciplining of Feminism," *Critical Studies in Mass Communication* 16, no. 1 (1999): 88.

123. Ibid., 86.

124. Stephen Coleman and Karen Ross, *The Media and the Public: "Them" and "Us" in Media Discourse* (Malden, MA: Wiley, 2010).

125. Lisa Bloom, "The Public Humiliation of Huma Abedin," *CNN.com*, July 25, 2013, http://www.cnn.com/2013/07/24/opinion/bloom-huma-political-wives/index.html.

126. Susan Adams, "Is Huma Abedin Doing the Right Thing?," *Forbes.com*, July 25, 2013, http://www.forbes.com/sites/susanadams/2013/07/25/is-huma-abedin-doing-the-right-thing/.

CHAPTER 9

1. Robert Weiss's work can be found at http://www.robertweissmsw.com.

2. Hinda Mandell and Gina Masullo Chen, eds., *Scandal in a Digital Age* (New York: Palgrave Macmillan, 2016).

3. Tim Perone, "Pol's, Uh, Art Bared," *New York Post*, November 6, 2011, http://nypost.com/2011/11/06/pols-uh-art-bared/.

4. Ibid.

5. Ibid.

6. Jonathan Oosting, "Michigan Political Points: Todd Courser Sex Scandal Email Cracks Up Jimmy Fallon," *MLive.com*, August 15, 2015, http://www.mlive.com/lansing-news/index.ssf/2015/08/michigan_political_points_todd.html.

7. Chad Livengood, "Ex-State Reps. Courser, Gamrat, Face Felony Charges," *DetroitNews.com*, February 27, 2016, http://www.detroitnews.com/story/news/politics/2016/02/26/courser-gamrat/80986942/.

8. Pippa Norris, "It's Not Just Trump. Authoritarian Populism Is Rising across the West. Here's Why," *WashingtonPost.com*, March 11, 2016, https://www.washingtonpost.com/news/monkey-cage/wp/2016/03/11/its-not-just-trump-authoritarian-populism-is-rising-across-the-west-heres-why/.

9. Steven Hill, "Why Does the US Still Have So Few Women in Office?," *Nation*, March 7, 2014, https://www.thenation.com/article/why-does-us-still-have-so-few-women-office/.

10. "Trends in Women's Political Participation," Status of Women in the States, http://statusofwomendata.org/explore-the-data/political-participation/political-participation-full-section/#pptrends.

11. We know from chapter 2 that many politicians don't appear to be "smartening" to the risk of political sex scandals contemporarily because from 1942 to 2016, the median year for scandal—with half of the scandals occurring before the date and half after it—is 2007. This means that in our contemporary world there's been a lot more scandal in the past decade than in the previous decades before it.

12. William K. Rashbaum and James Barron, "Police Investigating Claim Eliot Spitzer Choked Woman in Plaza Hotel," *New York Times*, February 15, 2016, http://www.nytimes.com/2016/02/16/nyregion/eliot-spitzers-lawyer-says-woman-retracted-claim-he-choked-her.html.

13. WKBW staff, "One-Time Candidate for NYS Senate Arrested Over Assault Weapon," *WKBW.com*, February 12, 2016, http://www.wkbw.com/news/police-blotter/one-time-candidate-for-nys-senate-arrested-over-assault-weapon.

14. Adam Weinstein, "Florida Lt. Governor's Bizarre Resignation Raises Questions about Gambling, Guns, Graft," *Mother Jones*, March 14, 2013, http://www.motherjones.com/politics/2013/03/florida-jennifer-carroll-gambling-scott-republicans.

15. Ed Vogel, "Gibbons Named on List of Worst Governors," *Las Vegas Review-Journal*, April 21, 2010, http://www.reviewjournal.com/news/gibbons-named-list-worst-governors.

16. Susan Page, "When Washington Worked, and a Lion Roared," *USA Today*, November 10, 2015, http://www.usatoday.com/story/life/books/2015/11/10/lion-of-the-senate-when-ted-kennedy-rallied-the-democrats-in-a-gop-congress/75453980/.

17. Matthew Huisman, "Frank, Kennedy, Kerry Ranked Among Most Powerful Members of Congress," *South Coast Today*, March 9, 2008, http://www.southcoasttoday.com/article/20080309/NEWS/803090304.

18. Ben Kentish, "Donald Trump Lost Popular Vote by Greater Margin Than Any US President," *Independent*, December 12, 2016, http://www.independent.co .uk/news/world/americas/us-elections/donald-trump-lost-popular-vote-hillary -clinton-us-election-president-history-a7470116.html.

19. Nicholas Kristof, "Donald Trump, Groper in Chief," *New York Times*, October 7, 2016, http://www.nytimes.com/2016/10/09/opinion/sunday/donald-trump -groper-in-chief.html?_r=0.

20. Ilene Prusher, "Opinion: Trump Judges Women by Their Bodies. Do You?" *CNN.com*, November 5, 2016, http://www.cnn.com/2016/11/04/opinions/trumps -1-to-10-scale-is-nothing-new-for-women-prusher/.

21. Danielle Kurtzleben, "1 More Woman Accuses Trump of Inappropriate Sexual Conduct. Here's the Full List," *NPR.org*, October 20, 2016, http://www.npr .org/2016/10/13/497799354/a-list-of-donald-trumps-accusers-of-inappropriate -sexual-conduct.

22. Max Blau, "These Women Have Accused Trump of Sexual Harassment," *CNN.com*, October 24, 2016, http://www.cnn.com/2016/10/14/politics/trump -women-accusers/.

23. Claire Cohen, "Donald Trump Sexism Tracker: Every Offensive Comment in One Place," *Telegraph*, November 9, 2016, http://www.telegraph.co.uk/women /politics/donald-trump-sexism-tracker-every-offensive-comment-in-one-place/.

24. "Transcript: Donald Trump Taped Comments about Women," *New York Times*, October 8, 2016, http://www.nytimes.com/2016/10/08/us/donald-trump-tape -transcript.html.

APPENDIX B

1. Kathy Charmaz, *Constructing Grounded Theory: A Practical Guide through Qualitative Analysis* (Thousand Oaks, CA: Sage, 2006), 40.

2. Ibid.

Index

Taft, William, 18
Tea Party, 31, 195
Television/TV, 9, 19, 50, 65, 74, 100, 140, 138–139, 157, 159–160, 193, 200, 215n47
Textual analysis, 79, 83, 86, 88
TheDirty.com, 60, 66
Thomas, Clarence, 10
Thompson, John B., 5, 138–139, 153, 159
Trust, 138, 149, 155, 194; distrust, 78; mistrust, 2, 4, 22, 138; trusted, 10, 15, 149, 150; trustworthiness, 139, 153, 199
Twitter, 52, 59–61, 73–75, 78, 93, 107, 137, 161, 175, 211n37

USA Today, 74, 82, 86–87

Variable, 5, 20, 39
Victorian Era, 140–141, 154
Vitter, David, 9, 40, 49, 53, 77, 131, 197; D.C. Madam, 9; "diaper play," 9
Vivid Entertainment, 68
Voice, 74, 95, 112, 115, 122, 174–175, 181, 184–188, 191; voiceless, 89
Voyeurism, 140
Voyeuristic, 148, 177

Wallace, Lane, 82
Washington, George, 8
Washington Post, 3, 6, 86–87, 90, 92–95
Watergate, 10, 18, 78, 133
Weiner, Anthony, 4, 9, 15–16, 26, 41–43, 47–52, 57–63, 66–71, 78, 107, 132, 137, 141, 151, 160–162,
170–175, 177, 179–183, 191–192, 194, 198, 201, 211n37; tweeting, 9, 26, 49, 70, 74, 132, 194, 198. See also Twitter
Weiss, Robert, 190, 237n1
West, Candace, 38
Wife, 165–178, 181, 184, 187, 191, 198; absent, 169, 174, 186, 187; agitated, 174; attendance, 167; betrayed, 186; hegemonic poster-wife, 184; needs, 167; obligation, 170, 178; present, 167–170, 176, 187; right, 174; scandalized, 175; "scowling and grimacing," 166; silent passive, 184, 191; subversively hegemonic, 188; supportive, 167, 178; "supposed to/expected to" wife, 178, 182; "very supportive wife," 172; vocal, 174; wifely, 98, 132–133, 144, 170, 178, 186–187; "wimpy, humiliated, passive," 188. See also "Good wife," The Good Wife, Political wife
Wifeness, 80–81, 89–90, 95, 97, 134
Wifework, 134–135
Wilson, Woodrow, 10, 18
Winfield, Betty Houchin, 83
Wozniak, Angela, 1–2, 33, 101, 197; apology, 1; ethics committee, 197; freshman state legislator, 1; political failure, 1; "wrong glass ceiling," 1
Wynette, Tammy, 135, 144, 184

YouTube, 141, 162

Zimmerman, Don H., 38

About the Author

Hinda Mandell, PhD, is an assistant professor in the School of Communication at Rochester Institute of Technology. She is coeditor of the book *Scandal in a Digital Age* (with Gina Masullo Chen). A frequent blogger for the *Huffington Post* and NPR outlets, Mandell's essays on topics ranging from politics to gender and parenting have appeared in *Politico*, the *Boston Herald*, the *Chicago Tribune*, *USA Today*, and the *Los Angeles Times*. She is a former correspondent for the *Boston Globe*. Her academic writing has been published in *Women's Studies in Communication*, *Explorations in Media Ecology*, and *Visual Communication Quarterly*, among other outlets. Her website is omghinda.com. Follow her on Twitter: @hindamandell.

www.ingramcontent.com/pod-product-compliance
Lightning Source LLC
Chambersburg PA
CBHW050416280326
41932CB00013BA/1884

9798765130018